Post-traumatic Attachments to the Eerily Moving Image

This book explores how traumatic experiences of impingement and neglect – in childhood and adulthood, and at both the family and the state level – may create a desire in us to be parented by certain kinds of screen media that we unconsciously believe are "watching over" us when nothing else seems to be.

Andrew Asibong explores how viewers make psychical use of eerily moving images, observed in film and television and later taken into an already traumatised mind, in order to facilitate some form of reparation for a stolen experience of caregiving. It explores the possibility of a media-based "working through" of both the general traumas of early environmental failure and the particular traumas of viewers racialised as Black, eventually asking how politicised film groups in the age of Black Lives Matter might heal from a troubled past and prepare for an uncertain future through the spontaneous discussion – in the here and now – of enlivening images of potentially deadly vulnerability.

Post-traumatic Attachments to the Eerily Moving Image: Something to Watch Over Me will be of great interest to academics and students of film, media and television studies, trauma studies and psychoanalysis, culture, race and ethnicity.

Andrew Asibong, PhD, is a psychotherapist and film theorist. He is a member of the Tavistock Society of Psychotherapists and a registrant of the British Psychoanalytic Council.

Psychoanalysis and Popular Culture Series
Series Editors: Caroline Bainbridge and Candida Yates
Consulting Editor: Brett Kahr

This series builds on the work done since 2009 by the Media and the Inner World research network. It aims to consider the relationship between psychoanalysis and popular culture as a lived experience that is ever more emotionalised in the contemporary age. In contrast to many scholarly applications of psychoanalysis, works in this series set out to explore the creative tensions of thinking about cultural experience and its processes whilst also paying attention to observations from both the clinical and scholarly fields. The series provides space for a dialogue between these different groups with a view to evoking new perspectives on the values and pitfalls of a psychoanalytic approach to ideas of selfhood, society, politics, and popular culture. In particular, the series strives to develop a psycho-cultural approach by foregrounding the usefulness of a post-Freudian, object relations perspective for examining the importance of emotional relationships and experience. We nevertheless welcome proposals from all fields of psychoanalytic enquiry. The series is edited by Caroline Bainbridge and Candida Yates, with Brett Kahr as the Consulting Editor.
Other titles in the Psychoanalysis and Popular Culture Series:

What Holds Us Together: Popular Culture and Social Cohesion
by Barry Richards

The Culture-Breast in Psychoanalysis: Cultural Experiences and the Clinic
by Noreen Giffney

Post-traumatic Attachments to the Eerily Moving Image: Something to Watch Over Me
by Andrew Asibong

Fantasy, Online Misogyny and the Manosphere: Male Bodies of Dis/Inhibition
by Jacob Johanssen

For more information about this series, please visit: https://www.routledge.com/The-Psychoanalysis-and-Popular-Culture-Series/book-series/KARNPSYPOP

"Drawing on an encyclopaedic knowledge of cinema and television, as well as a nuanced understanding of clinical psychodynamic practice, and a generous openness to insights gleaned from his own personal experience, Andrew Asibong offers us a brilliant analysis of the psychic function of the moving image in relation to both defence and repair in the face of post-traumatic experience. Arguing that we may turn to particular moving images when in serious psychic danger in order to attempt a 'cure', or at least to survive, Asibong draws us into a journey that links the visual realm of film and the complex terrain of fantasy in clinical psychoanalysis, in order to help us understand film-watching as itself a form of reparative fantasy. For children whose caregivers may have been unable to reflect their inner world, not just because of their own unworked through traumas but because of the racist and unequal worlds they find themselves in, film may 'watch over' us, providing the child with a landscape which, in all its fantastical potentiality, may enable new links, new psychic connections to internal figures to be made. Innovative, moving, scholarly, and brilliantly argued, this is a truly original contribution to our understanding of the power of the moving image to shape and repair our inner worlds."
– *Lisa Baraitser, Professor of Psychosocial Theory, Birkbeck, University of London*

"This is an extraordinary book, taking us into the experiences of individuals who are saved from traumatic childhoods by films and television that seem to "watch over" them like a parental therapist. Tracking through his own biography and working with the reactions of a small community of viewers responding to the television series *Six Feet Under*, Asibong ends with one of the most powerful evocations of solidarity and hope in the face of racialised violence that I have ever read. This is a profoundly moving and life-enhancing work."
– *Stephen Frosh, Professor of Psychology, Birkbeck, University of London*

"In this illuminating and deeply moving work, Asibong takes us on an intimate journey into the intrapsychic world of the traumatized self. Weaving his own dreams and memories with an impressive range of theoretical vantage points, he offers us a unique view of the ways that cultural experience may offer revelation, solace, and transformation. Exploring the intersection of film, television, and psychotherapy, *Post-traumatic Attachments to the Eerily Moving Image* helps us envision a world attentive to its own hurt and disorder."
– *Jed Sekoff, PhD, Training Analyst, Psychoanalytic Institute of Northern California*

"In *Post-traumatic Attachments to the Eerily Moving Image*, Andrew Asibong presents readers with a brilliant meditation on our emotional attachments to moving images, generously informed by his work as a film theorist, activist and psychotherapist. Drawing on an impressive range of psychotherapeutic approaches and moving images while formulating a new psychosocially-informed methodology, Asibong skilfully explores the ways in which films and television shows provide psychic care for people who have experienced environmental deprivation and trauma. Asibong considers, in an astute and affecting way, how repeated engagements with moving images can facilitate individuals re-connecting with parts of themselves that were previously inaccessible to them on account of developmental trauma. The book also offers readers a meticulously theorised discussion of how films and television series provide sites for group reflection and solidarity in societal contexts underpinned by crisis and racialised violence. This scholarly and reflective book is an indispensable resource for anyone wishing to understand how moving images can function as objects for emotional connection and survival, while also operating as conduits for psychic growth."

– *Noreen Giffney, Psychoanalytic Psychotherapist, and Lecturer in Counselling, Ulster University, Belfast, Northern Ireland*

Post-traumatic Attachments to the Eerily Moving Image

Something to Watch Over Me

Andrew Asibong

LONDON AND NEW YORK

First published 2022
by Routledge
2 Park Square, Milton Park, Abingdon, Oxon OX14 4RN

and by Routledge
605 Third Avenue, New York, NY 10158

Routledge is an imprint of the Taylor & Francis Group, an informa business

© 2022 Andrew Asibong

The right of Andrew Asibong to be identified as author of this work has been asserted by him in accordance with sections 77 and 78 of the Copyright, Designs and Patents Act 1988.

All rights reserved. No part of this book may be reprinted or reproduced or utilised in any form or by any electronic, mechanical, or other means, now known or hereafter invented, including photocopying and recording, or in any information storage or retrieval system, without permission in writing from the publishers.

Trademark notice: Product or corporate names may be trademarks or registered trademarks, and are used only for identification and explanation without intent to infringe.

British Library Cataloguing-in-Publication Data
A catalogue record for this book is available from the British Library

Library of Congress Cataloging-in-Publication Data
A catalog record has been requested for this book

ISBN: 978-1-032-02787-6 (hbk)
ISBN: 978-1-032-02788-3 (pbk)
ISBN: 978-1-003-18517-8 (ebk)

DOI: 10.4324/9781003185178

Typeset in Times New Roman
by KnowledgeWorks Global Ltd.

The film-lover is an orphan. This orphan chooses to be kidnapped by a rather odd stranger, who thoughtfully guides him or her towards an understanding of the world.

Serge Daney
Itinéraire d'un ciné-fils (A Film-Son's Travel Plan), p. 31

Contents

Acknowledgments   x
Series preface   xi
About the book   xiii
About the author   xiv

Introduction: Something to watch over me   1

1   It's a hard world for little things: Post-traumatic attachments to the eerily moving image: a theoretical framework   10

2   I just wanted to tell you that everything's going to be all right: My life in the bush of film-ghosts: an autoethnographic analysis   47

3   May I be alive when I die!: Psycho-televisual regeneration six feet under: an audience study   83

4   In this here place, we flesh: Racialised vulnerability and collective dreaming: film groups in the time of #BlackLivesMatter   126

References   163
Index   174

Acknowledgments

I couldn't have finished this book without the emotional generosity, curiosity, and love of my partner, Duje; the writing-companionship and solidarity of my friend, Eleanor; the intelligence and integrity of my friend, Hywel; and the numinous, exhilarating visions of my friend, Hannah. My capacity to create has been enriched so much by the constancy and aliveness of these four people, and by the kinship and wisdom offered to me during the creative process by Giorgia, Silke, kitt, Moses, Betsy, Jane, June, Mick, and Nigel. I dedicate this book to the friends, comrades, clients, patients, fellow travellers, therapists (especially F.), students, supervisees, supervisors (especially J.), colleagues, Fruitvale Film Club community (especially Matthew), and *Six Feet Under* research project community who have taught me so much about watching, seeing, feeling watched over, and feeling seen.

"Sarah O'Connor's house in Topanga" in Chapter 3 is by an anonymous participant in the *Six Feet Under* audience study conducted for this book. Reproduced by kind permission of the artist.

All other illustrations (including cover image) © Hannah Eaton, 2021.

Series preface

The application of psychoanalytic ideas and theories to culture has a long tradition and this is especially the case with cultural artefacts that might be considered "classical" in some way. For Sigmund Freud, the works of William Shakespeare and Johann Wolfgang von Goethe were as instrumental as those of culturally renowned poets and philosophers of classical civilisation in helping to formulate the key ideas underpinning psychoanalysis as a psychological method. In the academic fields of the humanities and social sciences, the application of psychoanalysis as a means of illuminating the complexities of identity and subjectivity is now well established. However, despite these developments, there is relatively little work that attempts to grapple with popular culture in its manifold forms, some of which, nevertheless, reveal important insights into the vicissitudes of the human condition.

The "Psychoanalysis and Popular Culture" book series builds on the work done since 2009 by the Media and the Inner World research network, which was generously funded by the United Kingdom's Arts and Humanities Research Council. It aims to offer spaces to consider the relationship between psychoanalysis in all its forms and popular culture that is ever more emotionalised in the contemporary age.

In contrast to many scholarly applications of psychoanalysis, which often focus solely on "textual analysis", this series sets out to explore the creative tension of thinking about cultural experience and its processes often drawing on observations from the clinical and scholarly fields of observation. The series provides space for a dialogue between these different groups with a view to creating fresh perspectives on the values and pitfalls of a psychoanalytic approach to ideas of selfhood, society, and popular culture. In particular, the series strives to develop a psycho-cultural approach to such questions by drawing attention to the usefulness of post-Freudian and object relations perspectives for examining the importance of emotional relationships and experience.

In *Post-traumatic Attachments to the Eerily Moving Image: Something to Watch Over Me*, Andrew Asibong takes as his focus the experience of television, film, life, and dreams, offering a compelling exploration of the deeply personal processes at work in traumatic recovery. Asibong traces the power and appeal of the moving image and its capacity to bring to life authentic feelings of nurturance and care. He argues that culture can be seen as 'a parental force', showing how images are moving in multiple senses, often underpinning senses of attachment, relatedness, selfhood, and recuperation. The potent intensities of moving image media are read throughout this book as 'enlivening' for viewers not just at the level of immediate experience in the auditorium or in front of our small screens, but also in terms of psychical life and its inscription in lived experience, whether remembered, fantasied, or repressed. Asibong shows how stretches of time and the shifting sands of attachment find anchors in repetition and familiarity, while also making strange our most beloved objects. The book is evocative, often beautifully so, moving seamlessly between past and present, and personal and shared experiences of trauma, politics, identity, and ideology. It offers a series of provocations and invitations to the reader to reconsider the uses that we make of moving image media, and to think proactively about the power of media to express the lived experience of raced identity in particular. Asibong's invitation to learn from experience and to take up the mantle of responsible re-visioning resonates clearly in a moment of profound cultural change, and provides a creative challenge to the reader, framing critical self-reflection as a key resource for our times.

Caroline Bainbridge and Candida Yates

About the book

What might it mean to seek out experiences of caregiving from screen media, especially at times in our lives when our access to the embodied care of living, breathing, human beings has been threatened, or is in danger of fading away altogether? Is it possible to think about such mediatised pursuits – often unfolding within the dire straits of environmental neglect – without judgment and even, perhaps, with something resembling gratitude? *Post-traumatic Attachments to the Eerily Moving Image: Something to Watch Over Me* explores how experiences of traumatic isolation and developmental impingement – in childhood and in adulthood, and in both familial and societal contexts – may create a desire in us to attach to certain kinds of screen media that we unconsciously believe are watching over us when nothing else seems to be. This book is about how a variety of viewers make psychical use of "eerily moving images", observed in film and television, and later taken into a traumatised mind, in order to facilitate their own idiosyncratic "working-through" of a disturbed experience of stolen caregiving. The book considers the possibility of a psycho-cultural recognition and reflection of both the general traumas of early environmental failure and the particular traumas of viewers racialised as Black, eventually asking how politicised film groups today might heal from the past and prepare for the future, through spontaneous discussion in the present of enlivening representations of potentially deadly vulnerability.

About the author

Andrew Asibong is a psychotherapist, trained in intercultural psychodynamic psychotherapy at the Tavistock Clinic, and registered with the British Psychoanalytic Council. He runs a private practice in North London, having previously worked as a psychotherapist in the NHS, a psychodynamic counsellor at the Guildhall School of Music and Drama, and a seminar leader at the Society of Analytical Psychology. A widely-published film and psycho-cultural theorist, he is the author of *Marie NDiaye: Blankness and Recognition* (Liverpool University Press, 2013), *François Ozon* (Manchester University Press, 2008), and the novel *Mameluke Bath* (Open Books, 2013), as well as the editor of *Sanity, Madness and the Family: A Retrospective* (Journal of Psychosocial Studies, 2018) and *Flaubert, Beckett, NDiaye: The Aesthetics, Emotions and Politics of Failure* (Brill, 2017).

Introduction
Something to watch over me

Father, don't you see I'm burning?

My dreams during the spring of 2020 were fantastically vivid. This one, from the night of Wednesday, 15 April, was no exception.

> *I'm trying to feed a little baby (it's been given to me for safekeeping) with a pipette. The baby is entirely wrapped in a plastic covering of some kind – in my notes I've written: "CAUL?" – so it's hard to see how to get the milk into its mouth. But I think I'll probably manage it. The baby is seemingly receptive to the challenge, and makes lots of eager, squeaking noises, to let me know it can smell the milk approaching.*

I thought immediately of David Lynch's film from the year of my birth, *Eraserhead* (1977). But I also felt that the baby I'd dreamed that night was an aspect of *me*, not just a piece of Lynch's film that had somehow got inside my mind. Perhaps it was both these things. Could a baby-part of me be making use of a memory of *Eraserhead* in order to communicate a message that might otherwise not have made it into representation? The baby in my dream wasn't identical to the baby from *Eraserhead*, and its plastic wrapping was different from the weird bandages of the baby in the film. But the dream indisputably possessed an *Eraserhead* "vibe", and I don't think it could have existed in quite the way it did without *Eraserhead*. My mind had taken something from that film (a film I don't even especially like), in order to create my dream's powerful vision, a vision I had trouble shaking off the next day, even after writing the dream down.

Once I thought about it some more, my dream's birth at a crossroads between my unconscious and the pre-existing cultural terrain of 1970s cinema started to feel even more complex than it had when I'd written it down initially. The day before, I'd watched episodes from three different television series. This wasn't an uncommon thing for people to find themselves doing in the spring of 2020, when physical movement had become suddenly, severely curtailed, and deep, collective anxiety felt omnipresent. But it felt

DOI: 10.4324/9781003185178-1

mildly excessive to me, even in the context of pandemic and lockdown. My first viewing was of an episode from the fourth season of the HBO series, *Six Feet Under* (2001–5), a show I was re-watching in order to complete the research for the third chapter of this book. In the episode I'd been watching, a woman dies of a virulent cancer that has rapidly spread through her body in a matter of months. Ignoring her alarming symptoms (as they feel too disturbing to be registered as real), the woman and her husband have instead focused their attention on the planning of holidays and the business of everyday life; she winds up on the embalming table at the Fisher & Diaz Funeral Home. My second viewing of that day was an episode from the Netflix series, *The Haunting of Hill House* (2018), which I'd begun watching in tandem with a close friend on the south coast. In this episode, a little girl must come to terms with the deaths of the entire litter of kittens she has recently rescued from a shed outside her house; years later, in the same episode, we will observe her at work in her job as a funeral director, embalming the body of her younger sister, who has apparently killed herself. As for my third viewing, this was the proverbial nail in that day's TV coffin. It was supposed to be the "lighter" option, an episode from the second season of the FX series, *POSE* (2018), which I'd begun watching in tandem with two close friends in the Midlands a few weeks earlier. In the episode, a narcissistic vogue ball diva, having taken up a new job as an S & M dominatrix, finds that one of her masochistically infantilised clients has died, in bondage, of a drug overdose, whilst she has been taking a cigarette break in the staff room. Filled with panic, the diva enlists the help of various ball friends, who assist her in "cocooning" the dead man, whose body she must keep with her, stuffed deep into the back of the wardrobe, for the rest of her life. I couldn't help but wonder whether my squeaking dream-baby, parachuted into my night-mind from a partial memory of *Eraserhead* – a movie I'd last watched over a decade previously – might not have been equally conceived as a result of my unprocessed feelings about the three different television shows I'd taken in that day. It seemed as if four different media experiences might have come together, from at least two different time zones of my mind, in the indelible dream-movie of one ghastly imperative that I really needed to hear at that particular time: *don't let the baby die!*

Freud's (1900) analysis of the dream of the burning child is well known and discussed often.

> A father had been watching beside his child's sick-bed for days and nights on end. After the child had died, he went into the next room to lie down, but left the door open so that he could see from his bedroom into the room in which his child's body was laid out, with tall candles standing round it. An old man had been engaged to keep watch over it, and sat beside the body murmuring prayers. After a few hours' sleep, the father had a dream that his child was standing beside his bed, caught him by the arm and whispered to him reproachfully: "Father, don't you see I'm burning?" He woke up, noticed a bright glare of light from the next room, hurried into it and found that the old watchman had dropped off to sleep and that the wrappings and one of the arms of his beloved child's dead body had been burned by a lighted candle that had fallen on them.
>
> (p. 509)

Freud seems reluctant to engage with the dream as an unconscious exploration of how it might have felt for the dreamer, himself once a vulnerable child, to have had to care, in turn, for a vulnerable child. He chooses (p. 510) to focus instead upon what the dream may tell us about "wish-fulfilment" (e.g. wishing the child alive again, or even wishing to sleep a little longer). The dreamer's traumatised relationship to caregiving – both as a father and, implicitly, as a former child – is treated as a mere detail that can be pushed aside in favour of a somewhat dogmatic presentation of the ineluctability of the pleasure principle. Lacan (1979) has rather more to say about the dream as an unconscious, post-traumatic facing up to a specifically parental duty, noting (p. 58) that the child-in-the-dream demands that the father *bear witness* to his failure to save his child from death. As Chapman (2016) puts it: "[P]erhaps the child is reproaching his father for not having done something sooner to prevent his death. And there is also the possible reproach that the father had entrusted the task of looking over his son's body to someone who was not up to the job".

As many of us know, especially if we're psychotherapists listening on a regular basis to the recounting by our clients and patients of their psychical life, traumatised people who have experienced significant levels of neglect in childhood frequently dream that they've forgotten all about a smaller creature (often a household pet) in their care, until it dies, or nearly dies. Whilst such dreams may well be rooted in some genuine, unshakable, unconscious guilt over their occasional remissness when small children to look after their animals properly, when analysed in more detail it usually becomes clear that the unbearable intensity of horror and regret over scenarios of potentially murderous neglect is linked to an emerging awareness, from out of the depths of their unconscious, of their *own* frequently appalling neglect at the hands of their parents or caregivers. Their dreams are an anxious communication about the awful centrality of caregiving – or rather, its failure – in their psyche, and their "guilty" dreams, in which *they* have become the negligent parent, are a desperate attempt to take on the guilt of their parents in these dreadful representations of abandonment and forgetfulness. The forsaken animals and babies in the dreams are, in other words, parts of themselves that have been left to die.

Something to watch over me

Moving images have always been obsessed with endangered children in need of protection. Emma Wilson (2003) picks up on a trend in a certain kind of contemporary arthouse movie to place at its centre the loss of an infant; but it seems to me that the figure of the lost, neglected, or abandoned child is everywhere in movies, once we start to take notice. It's not only in moving images of explicitly missing children – *Bunny Lake is Missing* (1965), say; or *Séance on a Wet Afternoon* (1964); or even *The Wicker Man* (1973) – that the dream of the lost, forgotten, or abandoned infant looms large. The dream is often wrapped in circles around many a disturbed adult protagonist's disconcerting behaviour. How, for example, can we watch *Psycho* (1960), without being curious and imaginative about Norman (Anthony Perkins) as a boy; his unrepresented relationship with his mother when she was alive; his abandonment to a world of insanity? How do any of Jane's (Bette Davis) or Blanche's (Joan Crawford) deranged acts of violence in *Whatever Happened to Baby Jane?* (1962) make any sense without our constant, appalled wonderment, as viewers, about their sacrifice, as little girls, on the altar of their father's narcissism, to the world of showbusiness? Hitchcock and Aldrich turn us viewers, whether we know it or not, into Ferenczi's (1949) child-analysts of adult patients; and the disappearance of children and childhood is as obsessive a theme in both *Psycho* and *Baby Jane* as it is in *Séance* or *Bunny Lake*.

The moving images I discuss in the course of this book all contain infantilised figures who find themselves both to be "disappeared", but also potentially "recovered", by forces that are both worldly and otherworldly. These infantilised figures are not always literally infants. As viewers, we latch onto the child-in-them and the child-in-us in order to do psychical work that is often profoundly transformative. Just as I approach Freud's dream of the burning child with a heightened awareness of the dreamer's potential anxiety around his own lost internal child, I've come to interpret the frequently obsessive attachments of many a viewer to the moving images of film and television as an expression of their unexplored feelings about experiences of intolerable vulnerability in childhood, or in some other environment of ongoing infantilisation. I myself felt compelled, from an early age, to focus on the shadows of endangered children weeping within the folds of pictures and dreams, whether those endangered children were clearly visible or not. I found that this compulsion to look for the lost child in the movies somehow seemed to help *me*. In focussing on the sound of ghostly crying, I learned not only to focus on the tears that were seeping from within my own psyche, but also on the unexpected figures of parental protection that began to emerge from out of the movies and, eventually, from out of my own, slowly emerging self.

René Roussillon (2011) writes movingly about the emotional experience of fearing, as an infant, that one may have reached the end of one's tether:

> These primary traumatic states share a certain number of specific features. Like helplessness, they give rise to experiences of tension and of unpleasure that have no representation (although perception and sensation may well be present) and no way out; that is, there is no internal course of action available (these have all been exhausted), nor can recourse be had to any external object (for these have all proved inadequate). Nothing seems to be available, and there is no hope left.
>
> (pp. 11–12)

This book offers a sustained reflection on some of our most creatively relational – or possibly "post-relational" – responses to intolerable feelings of traumatisation, hopelessness, and helplessness in infancy, childhood, adolescence, and adulthood. Specifically, it asks the question of what it might mean to seek to create experiences of emotional caregiving from moving images, consciously or unconsciously, passively or actively, at times in our lives when our access to the embodied care of living, breathing, human beings has been impoverished, threatened, or in danger of fading away altogether. The book seeks to explore how our experiences of neglect, restriction, and impingement – both at the family and the state level – may create a desire in us to attach to and internalise the imaginary characters and situations of very specific kinds of moving image which, at least at some level, we believe may be watching over us. These practices of attachment to and internalisation of certain moving images may, in turn, help us to generate our own dream-images of endangerment and caregiving which may, over the course of days, weeks, months, years, and decades, alter the structure of our thoughts, behaviours, and characters in ways at least as significant as certain forms of psychotherapy. In the chapters that follow, I explore how various viewers, including myself, have made use of certain kinds of moving images, observed in film and television, and later taken into our traumatised psycho-somatic systems, in order to reconfigure our disturbed, internalised representations of caregiving.

This book has been inspired by my growing conviction that I'm not the only person who has used movies, from an early age, to carry out a peculiar kind of child rescue operation. I began to suspect that, like the two bizarre protagonists of Jacques Rivette's *Céline and Julie go Boating* (1974), many of us had become obsessed, consciously or unconsciously, with the sucking of strange film-sweets that would enable us to travel into dream-houses, traumatically frozen in time, in order to retrieve forgotten children who had, for one reason or another, been condemned to die. These moving images became our therapy, our way of making contact with forgotten parts of ourselves, until more help could arrive. Whilst some of these movie "trips" could be described as ghoulish, neurotic, or perverse, akin to the compulsion of gothic heroines like Eleanor (Julie Harris) in *The Haunting* (1963), or the governess (Deborah Kerr) in *The Innocents* (1961), to return to the site of original trauma – the haunted house – to die there again and again, many of the trips were weirdly enlivening, putting us in touch with an energy, an aliveness we feared lost forever.

Strange days?

In the spring of 2020, when the Covid-19 global pandemic reached the place where I live, I was moving into the final phase of writing this book, which had been slowly gestating for several years. From one day to the next, we faced a new reality. This reality felt, in some ways, dreamlike and unreal: hospitals suddenly overflowing with the dead, dying, and gravely ill; expected sources of income to pay for food and shelter suddenly vanished, or in danger of vanishing; the freedom to leave one's home, if one was lucky enough to have a home, dramatically curtailed for an unspecified length of time. It was no longer legal to seek embodied emotional care or connection with anyone living in a different household, and if you were unfortunate enough to be living with people who had the power to do you harm, your chances of being emotionally or physically violated, even killed, under the new "lockdown" became critically increased. National leaders and governments – parental figures in the collective unconscious, whether we liked it or not – refused, for the most part, to be held accountable in any way whatsoever, abdicating from all responsibility for the provision of either truthful information about the confusing situation we found ourselves in, or the material resources necessary to care for the sick, vulnerable, and dying.

Something I noticed at this time was that the drastic and unprecedented situation of collective danger, uncertainty, isolation, and confinement felt, for many, weirdly familiar. For many of the people I continued to treat (now online) in my capacity as a psychotherapist, it didn't seem to feel *that* strange to wonder on a daily basis if grave danger might be around the corner. The suffering of insufficient embodied emotional care seemed to be a condition many of us had been born into. As for the systematic disavowal of reality by those who were supposed to be watching over us, this was a situation that many of us were only too used to. The conditions were ripe for a strange re-living, in a collective social context this time, of a situation that had already been encountered, usually in childhood, as a more private horror. I began to realise that many of us possessed early training in forms of physical and emotional deprivation that, for others, were altogether unprecedented; with this realisation came both a strange satisfaction and an intensification of sadness. The numerous ways in which our lives and relationships had genuinely improved since the original isolation of our childhoods became, for many of us, a source of immense gratitude. But alongside the real relief at the fact that things had got significantly better over the years, that we now had access to forms of human love and connection that had been simply out of the question back then, surged an old, reawakened sense of dread that had perhaps never, in truth, been truly overcome. Many of us found ourselves during this period turning for comfort to familiar ghosts of connection – to certain kinds of moving image – with a renewed intensity we hadn't suspected was possible.

For those of us who had access to moving images, there seemed to be a suddenly exaggerated dependence on those images for emotional survival. Communities of separated friends, lovers, and family members found themselves utilising films – and above all television series – as a means of staying connected to themselves and each other. This was the era *par excellence* of synchronised, simultaneous Netflix viewing. People began to explore and to mediate their relationships with people both inside and outside their household via an intensified connection to the imaginary scenarios found on television. Material coming up for discussion in online therapy sessions was suddenly inflected with references to films and shows in a way that hitherto had been merely intermittent and sporadic; now it was occurring in every other session, with many clients seeming to be clinging onto the series they were finding especially powerful with an unprecedented emotional intensity. The experience of relating to ourselves and to each other via screens became more intense still by virtue of the fact that, for many of us, visual contact with anyone outside our household could take place only via Zoom, Skype, FaceTime, and the like, converting us into sometimes ghostly moving images, entering each other's homes without needing to knock at the door or climb the stairs, instead slipping straight into living rooms to pick up where we'd left off the previous day. The new, computerised, online framing of relationship upon which we came to depend at this time robbed us of warm bodies to hold; but it offered us other kinds of interaction, insight, and means of expression, all those freezing, stuttering, missed communications notwithstanding.

If I knew what I was doing...

When I first presented my tentative ideas about how certain moving images of vulnerability and caregiving might potentially be used by children, adults, and teenagers in dire need of help, I was sometimes left with the concern that I was being viewed by some of my academic or psychoanalytic colleagues as, at best, sentimental, and, at worst, downright irresponsible. I couldn't be claiming that movies could be any substitute for the human care and interaction of a parent, counsellor, or therapist, surely? Five years later, having written the book that emerged as a result of this concern, I've come to realise that I'm not interested in prescribing any kind of substitute for human relationality. My interest is, rather, in analysing the behaviours we turn to when good enough human relationality isn't, or seems not to be, readily available, noting that these behaviours are not *necessarily* "perverse", and do not *always* destroy us. Unless we can take seriously the role of the moving image at times when, for whatever reason, living, breathing, human love is in short supply, we perpetuate a system in which our choices about who (or what) we latch onto are either venerated as "healthy", or else censured as "pathological". And those of us who have found ourselves, for one reason or another, deprived of ideal experiences of relating, are then locked out of psycho-cultural discussions of relating altogether.

The era ushered in by the start of the pandemic of 2020 and, in the middle of that pandemic, the defiant street-based and online resurgence of the Black Lives Matter movement, confirmed the hypothesis that had led to my decision to write this book in the first place: when we feel afraid of death, dying or – perhaps even worse – the possibility that we may be dying inside, and when we don't feel we have sufficient containment from other human beings to help us make it through these fearful feelings, intensely emotional interactions with certain kinds of moving image may help us to stay connected to the endangered aliveness within our psyches. If psychotherapy involves, for many of us who practise it, a passionate commitment to the warding off of deadness in both our patients and in ourselves, we cannot afford to ignore the multiplicity of cultural methods through which such an endeavour may take place. We need to be prepared to join up those methods, to make links between the disparate techniques to which human beings in desperate need have turned in order to stay in touch with their split-off and neglected child-parts.

Kuhn (2013, p. 2) quotes D.W. Winnicott as having remarked that, "if I knew what I was doing, it wouldn't be research". I've written this book not as much in my capacity as a film scholar and psychotherapist as from my emerging sense of myself as someone who has survived thanks, in part, perhaps – my hypothesis is tentative – to my discovery, internalisation, and ongoing emotional use of moving images. I still don't really know what I'm doing – but, in doing it, I feel transformed. I've found it helpful to step away from the environment of the university, an environment in which I'd existed for the whole of my adult life, in order to get these words written. I've found it helpful also to step away, for the time being, from most forms of institutionalised psychotherapy. Full identification with the professionally organised communities-supposed-to-know of academia and psychotherapy – communities of which I'd been a well-rewarded member – seemed to be blocking my capacity to observe unselfconsciously emotional phenomena in myself and others. I needed to stop aspiring to the status of expert, and instead accept that here, at last, was a project I could allow myself truly to *play* with. It's taken me a long time to realise the truth of Serge Daney's (2007) words (discovered thanks to Grant and Keathley, 2014), when he writes: "It's one thing to learn to watch movies 'professionally' – only to verify that movies watch us less and less – but it is another to live with those movies that watched us grow up and saw us – prematurely hostage to our coming biographies – already entangled in the snare of our history" (pp. 20–21).

I write tentatively, experimentally, and experientially, then, as self-identifying orphan and *cinéphile*, of the sort referred to by Daney in the epigraph of this book, focusing on my *own* experiences with television and film, life, and dreams, and on those of the generous participants who have willingly and knowingly collaborated with me (notably for Chapters 3 and 4) on this uncertain research into shimmering forms of help and helplessness. I write, above all, with a conscious awareness of how much the very act of writing this book extends and deepens personal processes of recovery from the very kinds of relational trauma that I'm trying to describe and explore for the interest and benefit of others.

Chapter 1

It's a hard world for little things

Post-traumatic attachments to the eerily moving image: a theoretical framework

The devil finds work

In his autobiographical account of a lifetime of ambivalent spectatorship with (white) Hollywood cinema, the writer and activist James Baldwin (1976) describes how, one day in 1931, his little boy self came to be mesmerised, to the point of near captivity, by a moving image of Joan Crawford:

> Joan Crawford's straight, narrow, and lonely back. We are following her through the corridors of a moving train. She is looking for someone, or she is trying to escape from someone. She is eventually intercepted by, I think, Clark Gable. I am fascinated by the movement on, and of, the screen, that movement which is something like the heaving and swelling of the sea (though I have not yet been to the sea): and which is also something like the light which moves on, and especially beneath, the water. I am about seven. I am with my mother, or my aunt. The movie is *Dance, Fools, Dance*. I don't remember the film. A child is far too self-centered to relate to any dilemma which does not, somehow, relate to him – to his own evolving dilemma. The child escapes into what he would like his situation to be, and I certainly did not wish to be a fleeing fugitive on a moving train; and also, with quite another part of my mind, I was aware that Joan Crawford was a white lady. Yet, I remember being sent to the store sometime later, and a colored woman, who, to me, looked exactly like Joan Crawford, was buying something. She was so incredibly beautiful – she seemed to be wearing the sunlight, rearranging it around her from time to time, with a movement of one hand, with a movement of her head, and with her smile – that, when she paid the man and started out of the store, I started out behind her. The storekeeper, who knew me, and others in the store who knew my mother's little boy (and who also knew my Miss Crawford!) laughed and called me back. Miss Crawford also laughed and looked down at me with so beautiful a smile that I was not embarrassed. Which was rare for me.

DOI: 10.4324/9781003185178-2

This remarkable passage from one of Baldwin's lesser-known works, unexpectedly resurrected in Raoul Peck's documentary about Baldwin, *I Am Not Your Negro* (2016), focuses on a child's extraordinary responses to the perceived movements of a woman projected on the cinema screen. The young boy is unexpectedly stirred; and, in his surrender to this strange stirring, he experiences uncanny new attitudes towards the possibility of a new kind of relating. Drawn in by the images of Crawford's "straight, narrow, lonely back", little James, no longer knowing, or indeed, perhaps, even caring, whether it's his aunt or his mother who has accompanied him to the cinema, is fascinated by something on the screen that mysteriously takes him away. Crawford's haunting mystery seems to possess the child, subsequently migrating from the screen to the store, where it enters the body of a woman who is perhaps more approachable than Joan Crawford – she is a "colored woman", not a "white lady" – and seems, at least temporarily, so utterly reassuring that she seems capable of overriding little James's attachment to his own family home.

What might it mean for a moving image glimpsed – or created – on screen, during a moment of great receptivity or need, to interact with our subsequent experience of the world in such a way that we are tempted to add it to – or even, eventually, to choose it over – our existing, "real world" family attachments or socio-cultural affiliations, even for an instant? From a number of perspectives, we might say that any child, teenager, or adult who is so irrationally hypnotised by a particular set of images that they risk losing their "real-life" kin is courting disaster. Literature is full of negative examples of characters who seal their fate through their seeming inability to resist the allure of a certain kind of image generated by the cultural field. The romance-obsessed Don Quixote abandons his loyal niece and housekeeper in favour of a seemingly deranged life, in search of the images of medieval chivalry, kept company only by the slavish (we might today call him "co-dependent"), Sancho Panza. As for that voracious nineteenth-century reader of novels, Emma Bovary, she proves willing to forsake both doting husband and neglected daughter in favour of the hopelessly tantalising shadows of Romantic stereotype, hunted out in one extra-marital affair after another. In *Madame Bovary* and *Don Quixote*, Flaubert (2003 [1857]) and Cervantes (2003 [1605 and 1615]) offered us iconic and largely dissuasive examples of the fantasy addict. Victims of various kinds of relational trauma these iconic protagonists may be, but this doesn't change the fact that their obsessional turn towards a love-object picked up in a libidinally over-determined and make-believe world is fundamentally pathological. Like the children described in Freud's (1909) canonical essay "Family Romances", their task – which they spectacularly fail to achieve – is the attainment of enough emotional maturity to accept ordinary human relationships for what they "really" are. Firestone (1987), reflecting on his own clinical practice, makes the point clearly:

When deprived of love-food, an infant experiences considerable anxiety and pain and attempts to compensate by sucking its thumb and by providing self-nourishment in various ways. At this point in its development, a baby is able to create the illusion of the breast. An infant who feels empty and starved emotionally relies increasingly on this fantasy for gratification. And, indeed, this process provides partial relief. In working with regressed schizophrenic patients, my colleagues and I observed that some had visions and dreams of white hazes, snow, and the like, sometimes representing the wish for milk and nourishment. One patient described to me a white breast that he saw, and when I asked what came out of it, he said: "Pictures".

(pp. 37–8)

Kidnapped?

Children's literature often specifies the danger of the child's turning to an eerily white, spectrally glittering object in the wake of a gnawing resentment about the deficiencies – real or imagined – of their own family or caregivers. Little Edmund in C. S. Lewis's (2009 [1950]) novel, *The Lion, The Witch and the Wardrobe*, falls furiously into the clutches of the Turkish Delight bearing White Witch because he cannot find acceptance with his siblings; before him, little Kay, in Hans Christian Andersen's (2009 [1844]) fairy tale, "The Snow Queen", faced a similarly beguiling situation. Perhaps most hapless of all are the little girl protagonists of Lucy Clifford's (1882) terrifying story, "The New Mother", condemned to a homeless childhood, foraging for berries in the woods, and living in daily fear of the glass-eyed, tail-swishing "new mother", all because they wanted something more exciting – or merely less depressed – than their long-suffering mother of origin.

These cautionary tales of alternately sad and horrifying parent-replacement aren't confined to generations past. In Neil Gaiman's (2002), *Coraline*, the eponymous child heroine finds herself trapped in an uncannily inverted household on the other side of a wall in her own home, where an "other-mother" and an "other father", both with buttons where their eyes should be, encourage her to relinquish her original family relationships in favour of alternative kinship with them, kinship that promises, like a peculiarly parent-obsessed pornography, to be both superficially containing and soul-crushingly dead. It would seem that culture is widely in agreement regarding the fundamental inadvisability – we might even say madness – of a disturbed or neglected individual's going off in search of image-based substitutes for a sense of love and relationality, no matter how dismal the real-life alternatives might be. While the superhero genre allows for a temporary indulgence of our infantile desire to model our relationships on a set of idealised images of potency, a contemporary – and now thoroughly disgraced – cinematic comedian such as Woody Allen pokes repeated, self-deprecatory fun at Walter Mitty like characters who remain obsessed, long into adulthood, with idealised icons imagined to watch over them. Allen's most fully realised exploration of this psycho-cultural tendency is probably the pathetic cinephile schlemiel Allan in *Play It Again, Sam* (1972), whose constant hallucinations of a ghostly Humphrey Bogart advising him on matters of love and sex is played strictly for laughs. Meanwhile, in Allen's movie, *Manhattan* (1979), the neurotic and self-obsessed protagonist, Ike, protesting at an accusation levelled at him by his best friend, Yale (Michael Murphy) that he thinks he is God, indignantly splutters: "Well, I gotta model myself after *someone!*"

Shengold (1993) takes Allen's apparently humorous self-aggrandisement very seriously in his book-length study of Freud's concept of the "ego ideal", in which he explores the various ways in which Freud himself made persistent, passionate, psychical use of figures other than his biological parents in his construction of a set of internal imagoes through whom he could forge his own adult identity. Shengold shows how, for Freud, not only Biblical figures such as Abraham, Moses, and Joseph, but also fictional characters such as Oedipus and Hamlet became the source of a quasi-parental energy that he would utilise (in some ways counter to his own argument in "Family Romances") to facilitate his own emotional maturation. Shengold suggests that Freud was far from alone in this repeated deployment of figures – frequently fictional – from outside his own family for the purposes of personality development and growth:

> In this book I want to focus on the universal need for parents that gets partially transformed as we lose the sense of parental omnipresence – an inevitable loss which can make us feel orphaned even when still fully parented. The need soon begins to shift to include figures from the past, from literature, and, most important for healthy development, others beside the parents from the present. This partial displacement functions to shore up our sense of identity, to provide continuity with our past, to become part of our psychic picture of ourselves. These substitute figures usually consist of great people from history, mythology, fiction, and contemporary life as well as more ordinary others whom we ephemerally endow with a kind of narcissistic greatness because their emotional propinquity fulfils our need for central importance
>
> (pp. 3–4).

Shengold's discussion is fascinating for the way it makes possible a respectful and non-pathologising exploration of how we may actually *need* to internalise certain fictional forms and figures in order to be "parented" in ways that facilitate our psyche's capacity to reach its full potential. The necessity of a novel, non-biological source for a new experience of being parented becomes greater, I would argue, the more deficient our "original" experience of being parented is. But these are precisely the circumstances in which our desperation for nurturing by fantasy figures may propel us into the arms of flimsy, insubstantial, or downright dangerous pseudo-caregivers. We may find ourselves in something of a Catch-22 situation, in which our starvation of actual parenting creates the conditions for an addiction to spectral stepparents, who can never feed us in the way we need to be fed. We may find ourselves in a circular complex of never-compensated nurturing, a complex in which we are doubly orphaned. What if, robbed of the chance to feed from a real breast in infancy, we end up getting deluded in later childhood, adolescence, and adulthood by a series of phony, phantom "breasts", thenceforth doomed to wander the earth in search of "milk" we expect, psychotically, to pour from the pages of books, or the screens of our televisions?

Contemporary psychotherapist Pete Walker (2014), writing about the development of complex post-traumatic stress disorder (CPTSD) in the children of dysfunctional families, empathically imagines a little girl, Maude, left to her own devices by neglectful and narcissistic parents who had already expended all their malignant energies moulding Maude's two older siblings into archetypal "golden child" and "scapegoat" roles:

> Maude became the classic lost child and was left on her own to raise herself [...] Over time, Maude numbed out into a low-grade dissociative depression, and felt extremely anxious and avoidant whenever she was in a social situation. At four, an eccentric aunt gave Maude a television for her room, and she was soon entranced. She was forced to develop an attachment disorder in which she bonded with TV rather than with a human being. Sadly, she is still lost in that relationship, living on disability in an apartment cluttered with an enormous amount of useless hoarded material.
>
> (p. 17)

For Walker, as for a persistent and persuasive critic of technology-inflected alienation such as Turkle (2013), the attachment path Maude is forced down is not in any way a helpful one. The aunt's gift of a television is simply not an acceptable alternative caregiver in the absence of real, living, flesh-and-blood humans. Rather than being a salve for the already existing relational wound that has opened up in the little girl, the television, a ghoulish kind of wire-monkey babysitter, seems to finish her off, snuffing out whatever aliveness might have emerged beyond the wreckage of her family tragedy. Like the glass-eyed "new mother" of Clifford's (1882) terrifying story, Maude's television stares at her with eyes even more deadened than those of her original caregivers. Not even glamorous enough to lead her into the white, snowy wastes of Narnia, Maude's television instead condemns her to a lonely adulthood of decidedly less "cool" addiction: the cardboard box compulsion of the self-entombing hoarder. But is Maude's the only story we can tell about the shifting attachments of a neglected child in relation to the moving image? Is there no chance for a child as underfed as Maude to make use of fictional forms of caregiving in the way an apparently more exceptional child such as the little Sigmund Freud, as described by Shengold, could make use of Moses?

The key word to probe with regard to little Maude's relationship to her television and the moving images she watches on its screen is, I think, "moving". It doesn't sound, reading Walker, as if there's anything remotely *moving* about the images consumed by the deprived and neglected child Maude: on the contrary, all movement in her world appears to have stopped. She is, as it happens, the sibling Walker chooses to illustrate the trauma-related concept of "freeze", that third strand of the "four Fs" (the others being "fight", "flight" and "fawn") that he suggests are the key characteristics of survivors of CPTSD. And if we cast our minds back to the little children protagonists created by Andersen, Clifford, Lewis, and Gaiman, it would appear that their experiences in the uncanny new worlds they so willingly wander into are also characterised by a recurrent sense of loneliness, freezing, and solidification. But Hills (2013), recruiting the child psychoanalyst D.W. Winnicott to offer greater complexity to the situation, argues that

> [m]edia users are not drug users [...] Winnicottian theory enables a way of sensitively moving past commonsensical (and "passive audience") judgments which denigrate media users, whilst holding onto the tension between creativity and dependence, between the paradox of "did you create that or did you find it?" [...] Being a media user ... can ... be a matter of excited creativity, desired unity, and yet recognition of the self's change, difference and growth.
>
> (pp. 81–2)

Going further, Bainbridge (2014) explores the idea of certain film viewers as the potential beneficiaries of a truly therapeutic encounter, invited as they are

> to step into the emotional experience of the characters on screen that is made all the more seductive through the use of dream-like imagery, hand-held camera and extreme close-ups. The invitation is to experience these states as if they were our own; to take up the emotional lives of the other in order better to understand their experience and more clearly to grapple with dimensions of human nature.
>
> (p. 63)

For Bainbridge, who nevertheless insists (p. 53) on the importance of avoiding any conflation of clinical and cinematic provisions of therapy, real emotional engagement with some of the films of Lars von Trier really do "provide us with a means of contemplating the 'primitive' aspects of the inner world. They arguably reveal to us something of the interiority of self-hood as it is experienced in moments of madness and in the context of dreams, for example" (p. 63). Such reflections take us a long way indeed from the cautionary discourses that would have us view *all* serious engagement with the creatures discovered in the folds of fiction, film, and media more generally, as a sign that we've fallen into the arms of madness. Bainbridge instead makes the fundamental point, via reference to Winnicott's (1971) concept of "potential space", that it is precisely the cultural object's capacity to allow us a manageable distance from the overwhelming experience of actual madness that enables us "to contain the destructive and disintegrating force of the narrative material" and consequently to access "the *holding dynamic* of the cinematic encounter" (p. 65, my emphasis).

The monsters and wizards who help us to grow

In her fascinating record of observations of her own infant son, Victor, and his emerging relationship to the moving images of television, Marsha Kinder (1993) writes the following:

> When Victor was around a year old [...] I would listen to his pre-sleep monologues, which frequently consisted of a catalogue of names (Mommy, Daddy, Victor, Sister, Granny), as if he were listing members of a category or paradigm. Sometimes the list would include a fictional character from TV like Big Bird. [...] Gradually over the next six months as he began to pay attention to the television over longer stretches of time, he started taking pleasure in recognizing the images of certain characters who appeared very frequently, such as Michael Jackson in music videos and Big Bird on "Sesame Street". It was as if he were adding these figures to the catalogue of names he had recited in his stroller and of faces he had studied in the family albums. He had no trouble recognizing Big Bird as the star: the distinctiveness of his size, shape, and color made him easy to distinguish from other characters. Whenever the image cut away from Big Bird, Victor would ask with anxiety: "Where Big Bird go?"
>
> (pp. 26–8)

Victor's emerging attachment to Big Bird, to Michael Jackson, and others does not seem *frozen* to me; nor does it seem especially alienated. Instead, it seems marked by the curiosity of a surprisingly thoughtful – if still slightly anxious – kind. Later, Kinder notes that little Victor's interest in moving images begins to focus explicitly on emotion and relationality:

> The first movie that he watched obsessively was Gene Kelly's musical version of *Jack and the Beanstalk*, which softens the Oedipal conflict by adding a character who mediates between father and son [...] Victor was most interested in parent/child couples – fathers and sons, mothers and sons – naming and following them, and worrying whenever any of them disappeared from the screen [...] Following each viewing, he would ask many questions, especially about the characters' emotions and motives (for example, "Why was the man running after Miss Piggy?" "Why was she angry?"). If he had a book of the same story, after watching the film version he would want my husband or me to read it to him every night before bedtime – the sleep-bargaining ritual [...] This stage of obsessive repetitions through various signifying systems seemed to provide Victor with models for generating his own sentences and stories about events in his own life [...] as if [...] these narratives would assure him of continuity and equilibrium in the midst of growth and change.
>
> (pp. 32–3)

Whilst we might be tempted to try to gloss Kinder's observations of her infant son as mere elaborations on Freud's (1920) *fort-da* model for a 1990s television age, it seems to me that a new key component distinctly emerges: Victor, drawn consistently to film-and-television stories *about* intriguing new relationships, begins to constitute the televisual texts themselves *as* intriguing new relationships.

I found myself thinking about the potentially reparative function of transfigured parent fantasies one December afternoon in 2017, on my way home from seeing the musical play – based on the novel by Patrick Ness, which I hadn't read (nor had I yet seen J.A. Bayona's 2016 film version) – at the Old Vic Theatre in Waterloo. The experience of seeing the play had really shaken me up; yet I'd also found it incredibly, indescribably containing. As I walked north from the Strand towards Shaftesbury Avenue, I tried to work out what had just happened, not only to me, but also to the suffering characters in whose universe I'd just been immersed for three hours. I sat down on St Martin's Lane to scribble my emerging thoughts. The eponymous monster of *A Monster Calls* seems to materialise, not unlike the spectral, time-travelling detective of J.B. Priestley's (2001 [1945]) play, *An Inspector Calls* (which I'd gone to see in the West End during this same period), as a sentient, authoritative and – above all – *relationally resuscitating* being, from the yew tree outside the boy-hero's window. Through the power of the three embedded stories he narrates to the boy, the monster somehow connects the grief-stricken child to his own repressed emotions regarding his dying mother, his absent father, and his deeply resented grandmother.

The monster – and the nested stories he tells the boy – are not reducible to straightforward symbolisations of the child, the parent(s), or the traumatically complex bonds between them. All we can say for sure is that the mother's gradual *disappearance*, as her cancer starts physically to erode her, is somehow responded to, in the child's psyche, and in the universe of the film, by the monster's gradual *appearance*. Along with this inexplicable appearance comes the monster's strange set of relationship-focused stories and the miraculous development of new possibilities of feeling and relating within the child. The child's survival of an intolerable bereavement – psychically experienced as abandonment – rests on his discovery of a mysterious new object (the monster), who conjures up a series of strangely moving images, and who – through these moving images – is somehow able to hold it all together. The thing I couldn't fully grasp, even once I'd made some kind of cognitive sense of how the narrative worked for the characters, was why I too felt helped – *truly helped* – by the child's discovery of the monster, by the monster's guardianship of the child, and by watching their relationship play out between them. Something had shifted in me that afternoon at the theatre, this much I knew for sure. I suspected – though of this I couldn't be fully certain – that it had something to do with a change in the way I was unconsciously relating to the dead and dying objects (mother, father, grandmother) of my own psyche. I began to remember having felt like this before, almost always after having watched a certain kind of movie.

Thomas Ogden (1991) remarks, in a clinical vignette relating to the psychical damage caused in the child by excessive maternal projective identification – a situation in which a mother makes unconscious use of her child as an object who must suffer feelings that she herself is unable or unwilling to experience – that a breakthrough moment in his therapeutic work with a profoundly dissociated patient took place when the patient happened to catch *The Wizard of Oz* (1939) on television one evening:

> In that hour Miss R. described how terrified she had been of the movie when she was a child. She said that during the previous evening while watching the film she had been very moved at the end when Dorothy finds that the Wizard is a little, bald-headed man and in a rage of disappointment shouts at him, "You're a very wicked man". The Wizard says, "No, Dorothy, I'm not a very good wizard, but I'm not a bad man". The patient sobbed bitterly and said, "I'm like the Wizard. I wasn't as special as she needed me to be or as ugly as she needed me to be. If I wasn't a wizard, I was nothing to her".
>
> (pp. 100–1)

Ogden's example spells out in moving, psychoanalytic terms his patient's realisation – through hearing the wizard's plaintive self-defence – that she had been used by her mother as a sort of wizard, discarded when her magical function stopped working. There seems to be something about the emotional acuity of *The Wizard of Oz* – its narrative, its performances, its aesthetic – that causes it to surface with predictable regularity in discussions (clinical, academic, and informal) and cultural representations of profound longings, shifts, or realisations taking place in the internal world of a child or adult spectator. Alan Parker's moving divorce melodrama, *Shoot the Moon* (1982), features a memorable early scene in which one of the four neglected little girl characters, seemingly hypnotised by *The Wizard of Oz* in her parents' perennial absence, mouths the Witch's words in perfect synchronicity with Margaret Hamilton's iconic snarls. The writer Salman Rushdie writes of *The Wizard of Oz* as a "radical and enabling film" (p. 56), confessing, in the wake of his nightmarish *fatwah*, that "I've done a good deal of thinking, these past three years, about the advantages of a good pair of ruby slippers" (p. 19). There are numerous other instances of the movie being deployed by patients, analysts, and others to help them through a challenging emotional, psychological or existential situation.

Sergeant (2016) writes of how the film enables both the protagonist and the spectator to engage with a fantastically emerging "potential space" (cf. Winnicott, 1971):

> Just as Dorothy engages with Oz differently from how she engages with Kansas, using the dreamed world as a site to act out the repressed desires and phantasies, so too the spectator is positioned to engage with the space of Oz in a different way from how s/he might with other classical Hollywood cinema [...] As opposed to the Freudian insistence on the "polarised opposition" between the subject's inner world of phantasy and external reality, Winnicott's potential space allows phantasy to function as the primary meaning-making activity through which external space is engaged. The subject acknowledges rather than represses that s/he is phantasising in order to give the surrounding space subjective qualities that come out of the particulars of the game s/he is playing.
>
> (pp. 90–4)

This idea that "potential space allows phantasy to function as the primary meaning-making activity" is, to me, a crucial one: it allows us to hypothesise about the importance of discovering fantastical potentialities for ourselves inside the screen. And just as the representation of *new spaces* discovered and explored on film may permit new forms of meaning-making to emerge for characters and viewers, so too may the representation of *new relational opportunities*. One reason why *The Wizard of Oz* offers such a recurrent emotional toolkit of strangely moving images is, in my view, the sincerity of its communication that Dorothy (Judy Garland) has at last had the experience of being intimately known by a group of profoundly sensitive beings, even if we cannot technically describe these beings as human. When she says goodbye to the Scarecrow (Ray Bolger), the Tin Man (Jack

Haley), and the Cowardly Lion (Bert Lahr) in the film's closing moments – only to find that they've remained with her, in transfigured form, even when she's back in the black-and-white world of Kansas – something about an unshakable emotional connection is conveyed, without embarrassment, to the viewer. This connection isn't about the "real-world" ties of family belonging offered by Uncle Henry (Charley Grapewin) and Auntie Em (Clara Blandick), beloved though these real-world caregivers and the kinship ties they represent may be. By contrast, the new relationships encountered in Oz, relationships that are filtered through what Ogden (2010) might describe as "dream-thinking" (as opposed to "magical thinking"), facilitate emotional experience and insight that are truly transformative in their radical potentiality.

Writing about the defensive function of fantasy in individuals who have experienced significant relational trauma in their early development, Knox (2003), drawing on the work of Fonagy (1995) and others, makes a number of important points regarding the early erosion, through parental neglect, of those individuals' capacity to think about their own minds – and about the minds of others – in truly reflective terms:

> The reflective capacity to attribute beliefs, intentions and desires to another person becomes fully developed at about 6 years of age, but Fonagy *et al.* (1995) suggest that this process depends upon the availability of parent figures who themselves have this capacity to empathize with and imagine what might be going on in the child's mind (Fonagy *et al.* 1995). Such parents are able to respond to a child's intentions and wishes, recognizing that the child's behaviour reflects and communicates these. Through this process the child comes to understand that intentions and wishes are causal in the particular sense that they have an emotional impact on another person and thus that they are real. Parents whose own reflective capacity is impaired will not respond appropriately to the child's communications and do not provide the reflective interpersonal experiences the child needs to develop an understanding of his own mental states.

Knox notes that one of the outcomes of such parental emotional neglect may be the flight, via fantasy, into a dissociated fascination with unreal and idealised modes of relationality. She recalls Jung's (2016 [1913]) warnings about this kind of post-traumatic capacity for dreaming:

> He also identified that these fantasies frequently take on an infantile grandiose character, writing: "In other cases the fantasies have more the character of wonderful ideals which put beautiful and airy phantasms in place of crude reality" (Jung 1913: para. 404). Jung later increasingly recognized that this kind of defensive response may be

maladaptive and itself perpetuate the problem, in that a present-day difficulty activates a dissociated part of the mind, a complex, which then dominates mental functioning inappropriately and without self-reflection.

(p. 129)

Post-traumatic fantasying in a child can be a notoriously difficult phenomenon to categorise as either "healthy" or "unhealthy". Children's literature from Lewis Carroll to E. Nesbit has, for many centuries, been obsessed with narratives that explore the sane *and* mad dimensions of a child's flight into the unreal. Fantastical films from *Harvey* (1950) to *Possession* (1981) to *The Ghost and Mrs Muir* (1947) have been similarly preoccupied with asking at what point a friend or relative who seeks to intervene in a "disturbed" adult's imaginative processes may be said to be either responsibly caring or despotically controlling. Knox spells out the dilemma in clinical terms, when she reminds us that

[o]n the one hand, defences serve to fragment painful meaning, rendering it less unbearable by a process of dissociation and compartmentalization. On the other hand, defences are also attempts at repair, constructing new and less distressing symbolic significance which renders trauma less threatening to one's personal sense of worth and identity.

(p. 131)

It seems to me that one of the crucial questions to be borne in mind as we try to assess the "helpfulness" of a post-traumatic engagement with reparative film fantasy is the degree to which the engagement does or does not seem capable of generating links, thoughts, and truly reflective function – an emotional awareness of one's own mind as real and other minds as real – in the dreamer-viewer. What if the child of unreflective caregivers is able, through engagement with the found objects of film-fantasy, to make his or her way – at last! – to representations and realities of parental figures with a capacity to truly think and reflect? What if this child is able, somehow, to make emotional use not only of the dream-like characters encountered within their discovered film-fantasy landscapes, but also of the landscapes themselves, in all their fantastical potentiality, in all their openness to psychical connection? James Grotstein (2000) frames what may be at stake here, for the fantasying child, with especially poignant clarity:

Are not the protests of traumatized, abused, or molested children and their adult survivor counterparts a plaintive plea to regain their lost innocence? Is not the mechanism of idealization but a way to find an object that is worthy of being worshipped? […] Do we not need an object of worship – and to personify as well as mystify – in order to mediate the infinities and chaos of our unconscious mental life as well as of external reality and to represent coherence, balance, harmony, and serenity in the form of a unified cosmogonic explanation?

(p. 270)

Recovery of the lost good object

I find Klein's (1946) emphasis on the infant's (or adult infant's) developmental duty to find (or re-find) balanced goodness in the original parental figure to be distinctly unhelpful – and potentially maddening – for those of us whose experience of our original caregivers may have brought us close to death, for those of us for whom a "depressive position", classically conceived, would entail a maturational workout of Sisyphean proportions. I condemn the position of a senior British psychoanalyst who, during a seminar in the penultimate year of my clinical training, proclaimed to the group of nearly-qualified psychotherapists that if our patients' parents *hadn't actually killed them* during infancy, then it was up to us to help our patients to reconnect with whatever indubitable goodness in those parents had managed to keep them alive. This position seems, to me, to be at some level psychopathic, but it is, at bottom, a bold articulation of a basically orthodox Kleinian position. Having said this, Klein's insistence on the necessity, for psychical health, of some kind of recovered or discovered good internal object (cf. Brenman, 2006) remains, for me, fundamental. This recovery may indeed entail, in more promising circumstances, the infant's making emotional contact with the "whole" parent, realistically, "depressively" conceived. Alternatively, it may need to entail, in more challenging environmental circumstances, the infant's making contact with the *potential* parent, the parent as s/he *might* have been, had s/he not been irreparably damaged by her own trauma. This does not mean that the recovering infant needs to lie, idealise, or take flight into a fantasy of parenting that is entirely removed from either her own experience or from any humanly relational possibility.

In a provocative passage devoted to the "dethroning of Mr [and Mrs?] Reality", in which he critiques the dogmatism of some of the interpretive approaches of self-appointed "king" and "perhaps ... queen" (p. 4) of psychoanalysis, Sigmund Freud and Melanie Klein, Michael Vannoy Adams (2004), drawing on his preferred psycho-cultural guides, C. G. Jung and James Hillman, notes:

> in contrast to explication and amplification, active imagination is not an interpretation of the image but an experience of it. Active imagination is a deliberate induction of fantasy by the patient. Patients evoke images from the unconscious and regard those images as a reality just as real as

any other reality. The technique entails both observation of the images and participation with them. Eventually, patients enter the fantasy and engage the images in conversations – or in what Mary Watkins (1986) calls "imaginal dialogues".

(p. 15)

Whilst not seeking here to position myself within any particular school of psychoanalysis, analytical psychology, or psychotherapy more widely – my theoretical and clinical approaches remain unashamedly eclectic – this passage by Adams feels crucial to my construction of a discussion that seeks to assert not only the acceptability but also the necessity of an active openness to the "imaginal dialogues" offered by the figures and fantasies – especially in their most caregiving manifestations – of certain kinds of dreams and films.

When, in *The Wizard of Oz*, Dorothy and her "fantasy" friends reflect on what they have meant for one another at the end of the film, just before she returns to Kansas, there's a reason why both she and most viewers find themselves weeping at the poignancy of the words spoken and the looks exchanged. This is a scene of relational acknowledgement: each character recognises that they have been impacted and have had an impact on another person, and that their collective emotional worlds have been transformed as a result. For a child who has not had this kind of relational experience with the "real" caregivers or siblings within the family, is it clear that the cultural experience of witnessing such an emotionally generous interaction taking place on screen in Oz is necessarily an *unhelpful* retreat into post-traumatic fantasy? What Dorothy discovers, relationally speaking, with her new friends in Oz, is *not* entirely removed from her experiences of actual humans in Kansas; the film's final scene, in which she links the new to the old, makes this poignantly clear. Far from rejecting the desirability of ordinary relationships in the "real world", *The Wizard of Oz* cinematically sketches out some circumstances under which such relationships could actually *feel real* for somebody who is enabled, through exceptional revelations of emotional phenomena and her own extraordinary openness to those revelations, to make contact with the lost parts of those s/he loves that still dwell in a place of goodness.

Serge Daney (1999), writing about his childhood relationship to Charles Laughton's horrifying movie, *The Night of the Hunter* (1955), a film about two orphans on the run, is fascinated by the figure of the old woman played by Lillian Gish who, in the second half of the narrative, gives the terrified brother and sister a home. Specifically, he is fascinated by her indescribable relational function vis-à-vis the troubled children, noting in wonder that "ni une mère ni même une grand-mère, elle se contente de veiller" ("neither a mother nor even a grandmother, it's enough for her to simply keep watch", p. 24, my translation). The Gish figure has a simultaneously outlandish and protective function for both Daney and the child-characters within the film: she appears at the start of the film as a celestial head in the night sky, warning all children, everywhere, to "beware of false prophets which come to you in sheep's clothing, but inwardly they are ravening wolves". It isn't only for the orphans within the film that the Gish "watcher" figure performs such seemingly extra-terrestrial protection. It is also within Daney, the real-life child-spectator, who will later identify as an "orphan" in his own right, that the Gish figure can be psychically and emotionally internalised. The moving image of Gish twinkling in the night sky will return mysteriously, yet somehow beneficently, to haunt the abandoned child-figures (both intra- and extra-diegetic) at the centre of Arnaud Desplechin's strange family documentary, *L'Aimée* (2007), which tells the story of his father Robert's eerily disappeared mother Thérèse, snatched from Robert's infancy by a long stay in hospital, followed by her death from tuberculosis at the age of 36. Blending words read from Thérèse's hospital journal with the visual icon of Gish – archetypal cinematic saviour of (some) abused and neglected children – Desplechin's film insists upon the emotional reality of a ghostly protective presence that never was, a composite audio-visual conjuring of a wise old woman his father's mother would never live to be, living on beyond time and space in the heart and mind of a curious, transgenerationally traumatised, cinephile grandson.

The journey made by the orphan siblings over the course of the narrative of *The Night of the Hunter* is from the increasingly vacant eyes of their biological mother, played by Shelley Winters – who will eventually settle, totally dead, yet still uncannily moving, at the bottom of a lake – to the mysterious care of the protective old woman played by Lillian Gish, her eyes twinkling as brightly as the stars by which her face is framed in the film's bizarre opening images. Whilst the original mother, is strangely, disturbingly *absent* (even in life), once she is literally dead (if still moving underwater), the other woman who emerges to take her place, is fantastically, almost supernaturally *present*. The shift the children are required to undergo, as both they and the film develop, is thus a relational one: they must let go of a set of dead, dying, or deadening parental objects (a father murdered by the state; a deeply unreliable mother; a monstrous stepfather) in order to attach to an available, containing, and fiercely *alive* protectress. Both the fading absence of Shelley Winters and the emerging presence of Lillian Gish are bewildering in their intensity; therein lies, I suggest, their extraordinary capacity for relational transformation.

For the endangered child in need of a new caregiver, upon whose containing, thought-provoking, truth-eliciting figure s/he might learn to gaze without fear, it's not inevitable that they wander down a purely destructive and delusional path of hypnosis by a snow queen posing as a fairy godmother. A certain kind of cultural text – and it seems to me that cinema and television, even more than theatre and fiction, appear to offer themselves as peculiarly bountiful in this regard – may instead offer the child (or merely child-like) viewer mysterious guardians who don't merely stand in for mother, father, or even grandmother, only to crumble or growl, button-eyed and frozen, as soon as they are trusted. More trustworthy and – perhaps counter-intuitively – more "alive" caregivers might be found in the folds of the moving image, impossible to describe in normative relational terms; they may facilitate in the surrendering viewer an opportunity for a different kind of relationship within the contours of a new paradigm altogether. For this kind of viewer, the chance may have arrived, via a mysterious intra-psychical dynamic, through which they may be both met and – in a positive sense – hypnotically *held*, by a filmic representation that simultaneously encourages the viewer's reflection, both conscious and unconscious, on the process of holding itself. The child-viewer is thus allowed to relate to a hitherto inconceivable form of relating, and, in the process, reinvent himself, herself, or themselves, as a newly relational being.

The weird and the eerie

In Jennifer Kent's film, *The Babadook* (2014), a traumatised boy-magician, whose father was killed just before the boy's birth, can only give expression to his unrepresentable feelings via terrifying interactions with "Mister Babadook", a horrific picture-book figure through which literally murderous parent-child energies are channelled. These energies can eventually be exorcised at the end of the film, but only once they have been fully explored in the acting out by the boy, his mother, and Mister Babadook himself – of something that is utterly appalling. In Guillermo del Toro's film, *Pan's Labyrinth* (2006), the child protagonist is robbed not only of her father through his death during the Spanish Civil War, but also, effectively of her mother, as a result of the latter's depressed and depressing surrender to a sadistic fascist general, whom she has married and by whom she has become pregnant. The girl's precarious childhood existence is seemingly rescued through her cultivation of a new relationship with a fantastical faun, with whom she must try to understand, work through, and somehow transcend the appalling earthly familial nexus within which she is currently subjugated. Not only is this faun no less terrifying than Mister Babadook, but there is also no guarantee that either the girl or anyone she loves will thrive, or even survive, as a result of her engagement with the creature. It's hard for the viewer of either of these disturbing films to derive straightforward pleasure from the onscreen children's turn to the clutches of two peculiar new beings, seemingly magicked up at the interstices of a traumatised psyche and a beloved cultural object (in both cases, a book). What is indisputable in both movies, though, is the failure of one or both of the "original" parents to protect the child, and the child's subsequent (possibly deadly) gamble on whatever dubious insights the fantastical new creature may (or may not) offer.

In his final work, an analysis of two key strains of non-realist representation in culture, the "weird" and the "eerie", Mark Fisher (2016) departs from Freud's (1919) canonical preoccupation with familiarity and non-familiarity (the key hinge on which *Das Unheimliche* turns), and from Todorov's (1973) only slightly less paradigm-setting concepts of doubt and hesitation, upon which the French theoretical edifice of *le fantastique* was built. It is Fisher's compelling articulation of the "eerie", focusing, as it does, on the "failure of absence" and a mysteriously interlinked "failure of presence" (p. 61), that feels especially inspired to me.

> We find the eerie [...] in landscapes partially emptied of the human. What happened to produce these ruins, this disappearance? What kind of entity was involved? What kind of thing was it that emitted such an *eerie cry*? [...] The eerie concerns the most fundamental metaphysical questions one could pose, questions to do with existence and non-existence: *Why is there something here when there should be nothing? Why is there nothing here when there should be something?* The unseeing eyes of the dead; the bewildered eyes of an amnesiac – these provoke a sense of the eerie, just as surely as an abandoned village or a stone circle do.
>
> (p. 11–2)

It seems to me that many of the fictions (e.g. *The Shining* (1980), *Solaris* (1972)) Fisher chooses for his illustration of "eerie" art are movies haunted – although he doesn't dwell on this – by the inexplicable disappearance of one or more agencies traditionally depended upon by the vulnerable for caregiving. These caregiving agencies may be a loving parent, a beneficent state, or a coherent sense of self. The disappearance of caregiving is often not made conscious within the movie, so it can't be properly mourned by the characters. And in the wake of the caregiver's unacknowledged disappearance, ghosts emerge within the narrative.

Fisher doesn't investigate how a fictional character's peculiar occupation of an eerie landscape may be connected to introjected parental absence, trauma, or "deadness" that remains unarticulated by the narrative in which they find themselves. Nor does he explore how a character's – or a viewer's – discovery and naming of their own eeriness might enable them to move towards post-traumatic, post-normative, or even post-familial configurations of intimacy and kinship. He does, however, make one fascinating statement regarding the dynamic impact of the eerie on our potential for a radically new experience of self in relation to the world:

> The eerie also entails a disengagement from our current attachments. But with the eerie, this disengagement does not usually have the quality of shock that is typically a feature of the weird. The serenity that is

often associated with the eerie – think of the phrase *eerie calm* – has to do with detachment from the urgencies of the everyday. The perspective of the eerie can give us access to the forces which govern mundane reality but which are ordinarily obscured, just as it can give us access to spaces beyond mundane reality altogether. It is this release from the mundane, this escape from the confines of what is ordinarily taken for reality, which goes some way to account for the peculiar appeal that the eerie possesses.

(p. 13)

I want to develop further Fisher's suggestion that eerie films may provoke in the viewer or reader *eerily new modes of attachment*, not only to that film, but also to other people, and to the world itself. Viewers who themselves feel, consciously or unconsciously, that they've been deprived of sufficient amounts of caregiving, who feel that a father, mother, or entire facilitating environment may have mysteriously disappeared from their lives may, I argue throughout this book, be drawn towards precisely those moving images in which not only are comparable phenomena of parental disappearance represented, but in which parental disappearance is "irrationally" linked to the appearance of a variety of eerily new entities and spaces. These eerily new entities and spaces may in turn offer themselves up to orphaned or abandoned protagonists – and viewers – as available for some form of ambiguously reparative emotional engagement. The film may start to function as a bizarrely caring and uncaring object, a ghostly text travelling towards the viewer through the folds of time, in a manner that seems truly disquieting. The viewer may find that s/he becomes obsessed with determining the extent to which s/he feels cared or not cared for by the ghostly movie with which s/he finds herself compelled to interact. Does the film make sense? Can it be trusted? Do I understand its intentions within a clearly delineated cultural and aesthetic framework, or do I feel as if it may be trying to drive me mad?

Resurrecting the "dead" parent

Bessel van der Kolk (2014), recalling the work of nineteenth-century psychologist Pierre Janet, writes about one of Janet's traumatised patients, a woman named Irène, the adult child of an alcoholic family, whose mother had recently died of tuberculosis:

> In addition to amnesia for her mother's death, Irene suffered from another symptom: several times a week, she would stare, trancelike, at an empty bed, ignore whatever was going on around her, and begin to care for an imaginary person. She meticulously reproduced, rather than remembered, the details of her mother's death.
>
> (p. 179)

The physical death of Irène's mother has given rise to symptoms of psychosis in Irène – fixation on an empty bed, still caring, trancelike, for an imaginary person – but so too has the deadliness of the relational bonds that tied Irène to her mother and her father in life. Following treatment with Janet in the form of hypnosis, Irène is able to cry, reflect, and synthesise in words her emotional experience of what she has had to suffer: "My mother was dead, and my father was a complete drunk, as always. I had to take care of her dead body all night long. I did a lot of silly things in order to revive her. In the morning, I lost my mind" (van der Kolk, 2014, p. 179). Irène is apparently resurrected, in a way, through therapy with Janet, and she is able to leave her *own* psychical morgue-bed. Henri Rey (1997), meanwhile, suggests that the vast majority of patients in psychotherapy arrive at the clinician's consulting room with the unstated and unconscious desire to heal not themselves but instead to revive the dead or dying parental figures they carry inside themselves. And André Green (1986) elaborates on the idea of the patient whose internal world is dominated not by an actually, physically dead parent, but by a parent who is experienced as long-lost and ghost-like even in life, a parental object who does not protect, but instead haunts the child's psyche through the sheer ungraspability of their disappearance. Green devotes himself, like Janet, like Rey, to the technical problem of how to persuade this kind of patient to leave the dead parent's bedside, whether this involves disentanglement from an actual corpse or of an emotionally "disappeared" parent's spectral absence-presence.

For those of us who find ourselves, for one reason or another, in similar positions to Janet's patient Irène, or to Rey's or Green's "haunted" analysands, we may discover, to our surprise, that our psychical resuscitation depends upon shifting our petrified gaze away from the corpse (or empty space) of the original parent, and onto an eerily moving object, discovered in the field of culture, before we are able to enter into "living relationships" in their fullest sense. We may need to allow ourselves a transitional stage of experiencing something that may seem, at first glance, like disturbingly ghoulish play with a ghostly nursemaid, before we can be fully ready to give up the ghost. A film viewer's unexpected attachment to otherworldly moving images and outlandishly moving forms of relating may facilitate new thinking and feeling processes within that viewer's mind and body; it may liberate them from the ghostly relationships they carry inside. Eerily moving images may function, not unlike Kafka's (1990 [1904]) literary "axe for the frozen sea within us", as the means through which the traumatised viewer may begin to "snap out" of his or her addictive fixation on the hallucinated figure of a dead, dying, or ghostly parent, lying, shouting, or twitching in an unmade bed. Resuscitated viewers may start to recognise and feel, in the mysterious space between themselves and the screen, the moving revelation

of eerily shifting post-familial shapes which, now that they have been given shimmering representation, eventually lead to the birth of new forms of relating between the different parts of the psyche.

Film artists have long been consciously or unconsciously preoccupied with the potential for the moving image on a flickering screen to offer the isolated child spectator an opportunity for a genuinely transformational voyage through time, space, and relationality itself which, even though it might in some ways appear nightmarish, may also prove utterly necessary for the deadened child's traumatised self to become reconfigured in a way that may become, at last, psychically alive. Sometimes this preoccupation has taken the form of introducing an intra-diegetic child spectator, whose visceral relationship to the screen itself becomes a focal point of interest in the movie. One of the most iconic images of 1980s American family horror cinema is that of little Carol-Anne (Heather O' Rourke) pressing her hands to the family's flickering television set in Tobe Hooper's *Poltergeist* (1982). An equally iconic image, this time from 1960s arthouse cinema, is of the sick young boy (Jörgen Lindström) pressing his hand to an otherworldly cinema screen at the start of Ingmar Bergman's *Persona* (1966). In *Poltergeist*, Carol-Anne's fascination with the screen leads her to be sucked through a fantastical portal into occupation of a ghostly non-life within the television set itself. We may interpret the

various changes that her family is subsequently forced to undergo as, in some ways, necessary steps towards the collective recognition of past acts of violence and concealment which are now forced to be brought into the light. And when the boy at the start of *Persona* rises from his morgue-bed to touch the flickering screen in his room, a screen on which are projected the combined faces of Liv Ullmann and Bibi Andersson, he reaches, in the absence of actual care, for an image of relationality. There, on the screen, he finds not one but two mothers. The mothers are merged; one seems alive; one seems dead; but it's never clear which is which. Perhaps, if the child studies the two pseudo-maternal figures closely enough, if he manages to truly touch this flickering screen with the mysterious women projected onto it, perhaps then he will understand how he came to be in the morgue. The problem is, of course, that these two mothers can *only* be touched via a cinema screen. More infuriatingly still, whilst one is capable only of talking about herself, the other refuses to talk at all. Bergman's (1989) autobiography makes for a fascinating paratext. Actual emotional and physical contact between the child Ingmar and his mother seemed to be challenging, to say the least:

> I tried to embrace her and kiss her, but she pushed me away and slapped my face. (Mother's slapping technique was unsurpassed. The blow was

dealt like lightning and with her left hand on which two heavy wedding rings added painful emphasis to the punishment.) I laughed and Mother burst into tears. She sank, with considerable skill, on to a chair at the table and hid her face in her right hand while fumbling for a handkerchief in her bag with the other.

(p. 6)

But when the child discovers the cinematograph, something gratifyingly alive and dead seems suddenly able to be accessed, something fantastically moving that both is and isn't to do with the unavailability of Mother:

I loaded the film. A picture of a meadow appeared on the wall. Asleep in the meadow was a young woman apparently wearing national costume. *Then I turned the handle!* It is impossible to describe this. I can't find words to express my excitement. But at any time I can recall the smell of the hot metal, the scent of mothballs and dust in the wardrobe, the feel of the crank against my hand. I can see the trembling rectangle on the wall. I turned the handle and the girl woke up, sat up, slowly got up, stretched her arms out, swung round and disappeared to the right. If I went on turning, she would again lie there, then make exactly the same movements all over again. *She was moving.*

(p. 16)

The unseen playmate

This book is a tentative exploration of the possibility that, for many survivors of developmental trauma and emotional illness experienced in their real-world environments, imaginative encounters with uncategorisable onscreen figures and relationships may offer the possibility of psychical resurrection, through the internalisation of eerie modes of interpersonal connection. Whilst never seeking to idealise the viewer-screen dyad – which, as I've suggested, can potentially become a site of addiction (with the capacity to lead the viewer into even more immobilising forms of psychical "deep-freeze" than before) – I nevertheless want to suggest that, for some viewers, whose capacity for linking, both to others and to traumatised parts of themselves, has come, in either their familial or societal frameworks, or indeed both, under relentless attack, new opportunities for unimaginable and newly-risen forms of linking can arise through engagement with some of the strangely benevolent "kidnappers" who flicker onscreen as radically moving images.

R.D. Laing (2010) memorably describes a dishevelled and disorganised patient who appears to elude the onset of a mind-state some might describe as "schizophrenia" by becoming unexpectedly attached to a movie:

> However, one day she arrived punctually and amazingly transformed. For the first time in my experience of her she was dressed with at least ordinary care and without that disturbingly odd appearance in dress and manner that is so characteristic of this type of person but so difficult to define. Her movements and her expression had, unmistakably, *life* in them. She began the session by saying that she realized that she had been cutting herself off from any real relationship with other people, that she was scared by the way she had been living, but, apart from that, she knew in herself that this wasn't the right way to live. Obviously something very decisive had happened. According to her, and I see no reason to doubt this, it had arisen out of going to see a film. She had gone every day for a week to see the film *La Strada*.
>
> (p. 155)

What Laing goes on to suggest is that, despite the bleakness and violence of Fellini's film – a video copy of which, I suddenly remember, as I write this, I myself would watch, again and again, as a twelve-year old, in my bedroom, although I couldn't for the life of me fathom why – there was something about the *aliveness* of Gelsomina, the central character played by Giulietta Masina, which somehow set up home and watch inside his patient, Marie.

> [W]hat struck her most forcibly was that, though so despairing and unhappy, this girl [the film character Gelsomina] did not cut herself off from life, no matter how terrible it was. She never became an agent of her own destruction. Nor did she try to distort her simplicity. The girl was not specifically religious; she seemed not to have had, any more than Marie, a faith in a Being whom she could call God; yet although her faith was nameless, her way of living was somehow an affirmation of life rather than a negation of it.
>
> (p. 156)

Surveying the limited clinical literature (e.g. Sekoff, 1999, pp. 116–7) on seemingly transformative filmic experiences, I've noticed that when an analyst is struck by a lasting alteration in a patient, following that patient's encounter with a particular set of moving images, there is usually something about this set of moving images that is strange, hyper-real, or fantastical. The effect produced by the moving images in the bedazzled client's inner world is otherworldly; there is often explicit, dreamlike thematisation of a path or road ("strada") down which an orphan-protagonist must travel. Something diabolically brutal haunts one side of the path; above the other hovers the potential of a more benevolent energy. But the evocation of intense goodness and intense evil does not feel like splitting of the "paranoid-schizoid" kind described by Klein (1946). Instead of marking a psychotic retreat from or defence against deep emotional truth, it seems as if the fantastical road and its otherworldly presences shimmering on the screen instead signal the representation of something nakedly, extraordinarily truthful.

Kalsched (2013) offers a poignant account of a 40-something patient, Dellie, who comes to realise, through dreams and conversations experienced in the course of her analysis, that before her powerful transference love for her analyst, the only internalised relationship she carried in her psyche that felt emotionally nurturing and real was the one she'd known, as a pre-adolescent, with an otherworldly creature, apparently of her own invention, which she named The Pony. At the age of eleven, Dellie found herself compelled to abandon her imaginative inner relationship with the Pony, under pressure from her "gang of pubescent girl-friends" to "pull her away from her childhood world" (p. 72). The Pony must be left behind, despite the undeniable – we might say indispensable – emotional, psychical, and spiritual support it has offered the growing child, who has herself been forsaken by her traumatised and neglectful family. The consequences of Dellie's abandonment of the Pony are grave:

> If before she had been in pain – sometimes unbearable pain, alternating with the joy of her imaginative world with its special soul-animal – now she felt vaguely "above it all", abstracted, dispassionate, observing everything with a kind of intellectual curiosity, disconnected from all the pathos and innocent suffering and pleasure of the Pony's world which now, she started to believe, was morbid and infantile.
>
> (p. 72)

As the years pass, Dellie's states of mind become increasingly cut off from other people. It is not until her relationship with her analyst is about to begin, several decades later, that the Pony returns to her, in visions and dreams:

> On the night before her first analytic session, she was sitting in a small fellowship group at church, feeling desperate, spaced out, and alienated, with the old homesick feeling, when a voice clear as day said to her: "I never left YOU … you know". She knew immediately that it was the Pony, and her old dream came back to her.
>
> (p. 73)

What Kalsched's book insists, largely concurring with ideas set out by Ferenczi (1949) and Fairbairn (1952), is that, after intolerable experiences of childhood neglect and abuse, the psyche catastrophically divides. The part of the child that feels intense life, joy, and suffering is forced to take refuge underground. Winnicott (1960), in his canonical article on the false and true self, writes of a process whereby the true self must go into "cold storage" until conditions are safe enough for it to be retrieved in analysis. Kalsched's vignette, outlined above, suggests that the Pony, whilst banished for years, even decades, had remained technically accessible to Dellie, if only she could have found the right environmental conditions to tap into this accessibility. The Pony has continued to watch over her; she has merely taken her internal eyes off *him*. Kalsched is fascinated by this concept of a part of the self that has become the survivor's quasi-divine watcher. Conceding that this watcher, together with the otherworldly realm of the psyche in which it exists, can do as much harm to the individual as good, often taking on violent, persecutory, voyeuristic, and addictive dimensions, Kalsched nevertheless hangs on to the idea that, under the right conditions, its superhuman energy can be harnessed, even before therapy can be initiated, for the purpose of radical healing. The post-traumatic psyche can tune into an unconsciously containing and revelatory experience of watching and being watched.

Four years into her analysis with Kalsched, Dellie has another momentous dream:

> Robert Redford, the actor, comes to the town where I grew up. He sits alone along the right side of the highway by the Golf and Tennis Club my parents belonged to. He has come here to watch as all the mustangs eat their children. It's really the mothers eating the daughters, because the "mothers" (the mares) will not allow their fillies to get treated like this. Down in the valley I can see what's happening. [...] It goes on for a long time and is terrible to witness. I realize that this terrible carnage is only happening here. [...] I am overcome with horror and compassion.
>
> (pp. 74–5)

Whilst Kalsched, whose research focus is neither the moving image nor star studies, doesn't seem especially interested in the somewhat left-field appearance of Robert Redford in his patient's dream, he nevertheless picks up on the idea that the emergence of the dream-film-figure marks a crucial turning point in Dellie's unconscious realisations. Redford is, he says, an internal "watcher", "someone filming the scene but not involved on a feeling level" (p. 75): he is the representational means by which Dellie can become consciously aware of her own attempted psychical murder of the Pony. No specific Redford film is mentioned as having been internalised by Dellie, although I wonder if either *The Horse Whisperer* (1998) or *The Electric Horseman* (1979) may have been psychically inspirational. At any rate, it seems to me that something about her introjection of this film star allows her mind to generate an experience of *otherworldly observation* that is at once ghoulish and caring. In Dellie's dream, Redford has become eerily detached, quite different from his generally perceived star persona. His new unconscious function is to record, for Dellie's internal cinema, a system of parent-child sacrifice that is taking place in the horse community.

Communicating this information to Dellie in an iconic manner, through a dream-posture of disturbing watchfulness, he permits her both to see what she had hitherto not been willing to see (her own psychical murder, during adolescence, of the vulnerable and "soulful" part of herself), and once again to make emotional contact with this sacrificed energy, via the vivid revelation of his watchfulness: "'And yet the Watcher must have known the Pony was missing,' said Dellie, 'and so must have had something to do with bringing him back. He seemed to have knowledge of the split without being part of the split. When part of the self splits off, the Watcher seems to emerge'" (p. 76).

Might there have been a way that Dellie could have stayed less disconnected from her "pony-energy", even while it was in Winnicottian "cold storage"? Might her inevitable psychical split in the wake of developmental trauma have been less catastrophic? Hockley (2014) writes of a phenomenon within film spectatorship that he calls "the third image" (p. 1), a new, hybrid, internally generated representation in the psyche, created in the space between the viewer and the film. The concept is clearly connected to Winnicott's idea of the "potential space" that arises in the playful gap between the sufficiently creative infant and its "good enough" primary object. In the case of Dellie, a survivor of developmental trauma and (we can only presume), a person who has psychically internalised at least one moving image of Robert Redford, the "potential space" she discovers is a rather ghoulish one – it contains anthropomorphic visions of child-murder – and the "third image" she dreams is disturbingly uncaring (an ordinarily benign star simply sits and watches as the slaughter takes place). What Dellie's film-inspired dreamwork shows us, I think, is a desperate sort of symbolisation, one that makes sudden and essential discoveries through a representation of arresting eeriness. At the heart of that eeriness is Dellie's unconscious request, from the depths of her post-traumatic despair, for a radical form of witnessing. She is asking a ghastly version of Robert Redford to confirm for her, in dreams, what she already knows: that something appalling has taken place and needs, somehow, to be put right.

Child rescue by miraculous intervention

The psychotherapist Julie Bowden (GAA03, 2016) tells the story of one of her traumatised clients going to the movies. This woman had told Bowden in a session about having gone to see the film *Aliens* (1986) at the cinema. The client has excitedly perceived in the narrative of adult protagonist Ellen Ripley (Sigourney Weaver) – returning to outer space to do battle with a deadly alien and to rescue a small girl-child held hostage by the gigantic creature – a perfect onscreen recounting of her own psychical journey to travel back towards the horrors of her own childhood, and to retrieve the little child version of herself who is trapped in a paralysed state of post-trauma. This is no mere intellectual metaphor; the client is not marvelling at the cleverness of the filmmaker's narrative skills. No: as Bowden relates this, her client has come into contact, via the miraculously found film-object that is *Aliens*, with a visceral dream-vision of a process that she has hitherto struggled to put into either images or words. She must share this experience with her therapist. Her therapist goes to see the film; she too is shaken at a deep emotional level; she too must share the experience, first at a conference, then later on YouTube. Moving images are not, in this example, being used merely to explain or to illustrate psychical phenomena: they are instead beheld in stupefied wonder by the viewer who needs them, not only as the interpretive vehicles of caregiver-infant retrieval, but also as the providers of a genuine caregiving function in and of themselves.

Bowden's client has gone to the cinema, looking to the screen for something; she has ended up stumbling across flickering pictures of a sci-fi mausoleum that contains the internal figures of her own psyche: a monstrous alien; a long-lost child being held hostage; and an adult child – the protagonist Ripley – who, taking her courage in her hands, will set about releasing both the traumatised child and her own traumatised self. The effect for Bowden and her client is genuinely life-changing: something healing has been found at the heart of a trip to the movies. Thanks to the encounter with *Aliens*, a new dream has been allowed to be dreamt. Grotstein (2000), speaking of dreams, but finding himself speaking, seemingly inadvertently, in a filmic discourse, frames the situation brilliantly: "There is a dream audience who anticipates the dream and requisitions it from the dream producer in order to recognize its own problems and resonate with its own hostaged self – a self experienced as having become lost, like Sleeping Beauty waiting to be awakened by the Prince Charming dream" (p. 11). It is as if, for Bowden's client, the trip to the cinema has functioned as a voyage to the underworld. Instead of travelling back from Hades with Eurydice on her tail, the client has instead brought back a part of herself that had been given up for dead.

Moving images of fantastical child-rescue may be glimpsed in dreams, but they are also glimpsed in plays, novels, television, and films. Our culture tends to deride artworks and individuals who take seriously human encounters with eerie figures of this kind, whilst at the same time proliferating narratives and situations that revel in exactly this dynamic. Dexter Fletcher's film, *Rocketman* (2019), focusing on the neglected childhood, adult addictions, breakdown, and eventual recovery of the musician Elton John, is a film that, in its climax, engages explicitly with the moving imagery of the disintegrating adult Elton's fantastical and necessary reconnection with the inner psychical child he carries within him. He must reconnect with this inner child in order to come back from the brink of suicidality. Whilst some reviewers of *Rocketman* seemed almost viscerally repulsed by a denouement they variously described as sentimental and tacky, others expressed their gratitude and joy at being able to behold on screen an emotional experience they had hitherto been unable to find in visible form in the cultural domain. This radical division in spectatorial response towards the symbolisation of Elton's "inner child" in *Rocketman* seems to me, emblematic of a profound psycho-cultural ambivalence towards contemporary artworks that dare to show certain kinds of characterological rebirth without irony. Such cultural objects tend to split viewers into two groups: those who feel desperately and unexpectedly moved, shaken and grateful for having a feeling reflected back to them that they may have given up on ever seeing in symbolic form; and those who are actively contemptuous of such a "naïve" representation of psychical transformation.

This book seeks to understand how those who have engaged unashamedly with the rescuing potential of such eerily moving images may truly be said to have been palpably affected or even *helped* by their encounter. kitt price (2020) weaves a compelling thread between "Marlene", a fan who reaches out by letter to the precognition-obsessed playwright J.B. Priestley in order to share with him her own apparent capacity for dreaming the future, and Kay, an imaginary character from Priestley's (2001) play, *Time and the Conways* (first staged in 1937), showing how the link between the two women takes place at the level of a shared discovery of an eerie source of protective aliveness, travelling from the future, that is somehow capable of intervening in the present for the purposes of life-saving reparation. We find movies that spin around the fantasy of a potentially helpful presence emerging from between the folds of time occurring throughout film history, from the wave of afterlife- and angel-obsessed *films blancs* of the 1940s and 1950s (e.g. *A Matter of Life and Death* (1946), *It's A Wonderful Life* (1946), *Here Comes Mr Jordan* (1941)), to the time-travel blockbusters of the 1980s such as *Back to the Future* (1985), *The Terminator* (1984), and *Peggy Sue got Married* (1986). These particular movies aren't the ones that necessarily "helped" me or those I've interviewed for later chapters of this book; and I haven't included them here for prolonged analysis. But I mention them in passing to suggest that they might merit investigation in viewer-response terms, for their potential, via a fantastical aesthetic and a preoccupation with the imperative to rescue and repair, to reach out to a viewer in need; trapped and isolated in a neglectful "real life" environment. More recent films that turn on a post-traumatic temporal intervention, using experimental narrative and aesthetic to bolster their effect of eerie potency, include Gaspar Noé's *Irreversible* (2002) and Quentin Tarantino's *Once Upon A Time in Hollywood* (2019), both of which I personally find profoundly *unhelpful*, in emotional terms, depending as they do on peculiarly violent forms of privilege-laden disavowal in order to work their pseudo-magic. Again, though, they illustrate the intensity of a culture obsessed with the post-traumatic rescue of vulnerable human beings in grave danger, via a fantastical intervention in (film) time.

The comments section of YouTube is awash with the fantasies of ordinary people who seem to long for fantastical interventions via media-based miracles in either their own lives or the lives of others. Beneath an uploaded video (Santos, 2015) of the late British singer Nick Drake's song "Place to Be" can be found the following comment, from a user named "wayfaringshaman": "I wish *Doctor Who* would make a tribute episode for Nick Drake, kind of like the one they did with Van Gogh – where The Doctor took him to the future to see how much he's celebrated. I don't know, I've run out of things to cry to". "wayfaringshaman" expresses a desperately compassionate desire to intervene fantastically in Drake's ultimately fatal depression, to facilitate a visitation from the future that would somehow reach into 1974 (the year Drake took his own life) and offer him containing energies that would give him the strength to hold on. Chris Marker's time-travelling "ciné-roman" *La Jetée* (1962) is perhaps the ultimate filmic exploration of this deep yearning, depicted throughout the collective cultural domain, for a protective entity, emerging from out of the folds of the future, to save a part of the self that has been doomed to death. Ferholt (2007), writing about *La Jetée*, articulates the emotional opportunities afforded its viewer by the film's peculiar blend of emotional, temporal, and aesthetic experimentation:

> Like the play within *Hamlet*, or Gregory Bateson's description of play as embodying paradoxes of abstraction, *La Jetée* provides us with the sensation of a spiral of consciousness, the sensation that we are looking down on ourselves. Falling into the space of the film's opening we see our own lives differently when we leave – as, through film, we have glimpsed a future. Furthermore, because it has a future, a film is alive [...] You can live in film, but film also lives within you [...] With film we are able, for the first time, to see another actively looking [...] Because we become ourselves through the gaze of another that sees us, to see that the other can look as we look, and therefore see us as we see others, is to see ourselves seen through another. It is to finally have that possibility of turning around just fast enough to see oneself [...] As Marker showed with *La Jetée*, film is love.
>
> (pp. 26–7)

Filmic and televisual images that find a way of "saving" an endangered, dead, or dying child, or an infantilised adult, through a miraculous loop in time, appear to be all around us. My sense is that more of us are unconsciously – and often quite desperately – identified with these endangered, dead, and dying children or infantilised adults than we care to admit. The psychical *use* we make of the moving images, in which the abandoned and rescuing figures proliferate, demands to be explored with both intellectual and emotional seriousness. In this book, I argue that certain kinds of eerily moving image can be used as an unexpected resuscitator for the trauma survivor's alive-dead psyche. Halfway between the human and the non-human, such moving images are imbued with an unexpected energy that can help the viewer to re-experience his or her internal representations of self, other, and relationality itself, in a psychically productive and enlivening manner.

Trying to teach aliveness through film

The images I focus on are from movies and television that find courageous (and often shocking) ways of somehow *intervening* in the dissociation that takes place in a human mind in the wake of developmental trauma. All of them revolve, sometimes obsessively, around an exploration of post-traumatic "watching", of the kind evoked by Dellie's dream of Robert Redford and the horses, or by Bowden's *Aliens*-client. They offer up dream-like allies and protectors as a key component of their network of moving images, watchers whose function is to look after the shards of fragmented child-being that have been scattered after the violations of psychical or physical assault. These pictures also tend to transgress the boundaries of linear time in their determination to whisk vulnerable characters, especially children, out of the potentially deathly clutches of neglect or abuse. Their combination of emotional insight, spectral watching, and time travel makes them susceptible for use by certain individuals as psychical objects that are themselves healing and protective. The cultural generators of dreams, fantasies, insights, and, in some cases, an ongoing sense of being held in the world by a robust internalisation of a moving image, these pictures start to function in individual and collective psyches as urgently needed symbolisations of a hitherto unthinkable "primitive agony" (cf. Winnicott, 1974): pain has been unconsciously known, but not yet truly lived. Weighty and long-lasting in their bizarre, psychodynamic effect on the viewer, the moving images I explore offer themselves up for an internalisation that is, in some ways, on a par with Dorothy's climactic recollection of the otherworldly alliances she and Toto forged together in Oz. If they terrify, they do so in order to retrieve a more honestly vulnerable aspect of the hypnotised viewer; if they appear to rupture, they do so in order more fully to repair a psyche that has already been far more violently ripped, long before the moving image came along to reveal the damage.

By the time I began to teach film studies at university in the mid-2000s, I'd already started to realise that something peculiar happened in both my mind and in my body when I watched certain scenes from these kinds of movies. I understood that the situations that tended to shake me most tended to depict what I would now call unexpectedly cosmic nurturing, a sort of archetypal caregiving, bestowed upon a supremely abandoned human in need by an uncanny figure who has travelled some distance, often through time, to find and recognise the vulnerable being in question. The transformative scene would usually be constructed through a daringly and idiosyncratically "alive" linkage of various vitality forms (cf. Stern, 2010), blending music, movement, and image in such a way that an impression of joined up, attuned, "total" viewer-screen interaction would feel unbearably – but healingly, regressively – intense. I found myself desperate to share scenes like this with my students. Across a range of wildly dissimilar modules, I would find ways of incorporating class discussions of uncanny, time-travelling moments of empathic, quasi-parental caregiving by angelic figures. An MA module I regularly delivered on contemporary American cinema would find me asking students to reflect on the closing moments of Barry Jenkins' film, *Moonlight* (2016): the blending of Chiron's (Trevante Rhodes) belated embrace with his long-lost friend/lover Kevin (André Holland) and the memory of his child-self "Little" (Alex Hibbert) being taught to swim, held by the gentleness of the waves and his long-dead mentor Juan (Mahershala Ali). Another module would gravitate every year around a particular sequence from the middle of Stephen Daldry's film, *The Hours* (2002). This was the sequence in which the viewer suddenly realises that the morose, deathly, dying poet Richard (Ed Harris), a character from the strand of narrative set in the 1990s, is none other than the bright, playful – but already deeply anxious and precociously mature – little boy Richie (Jack Rovello), young son of depressed and possibly suicidal Laura (Julianne Moore) from the 1950s part of the film.

The way in which the film reveals the desperately alive child from the past and the desperately dying man from the present as two fragments of the same human being, through the meaningful montage of two stories we previously had no reason to believe were connected, would sometimes cause me momentarily to lose control of my pedagogical train of thought during my teaching of the class. Immediately prior to the film's revelation that the 1990s adult Richard and the 1950s child Richie are the same character, we viscerally experience another fantastical bridge through time, as the 1920s Virginia (Nicole Kidman) connects to the 1950s Laura, via the fantastical object of her novel *Mrs Dalloway*. In the 1920s strand of the film's narrative, Virginia has been attempting to create her central character, all the while fighting against a debilitating depression. Her dreaming of Mrs Dalloway in her mind and through her pen temporarily "saves" her from sinking, just as the character (now published in novel form) "saves" Laura from killing herself in the 1950s Los Angeles hotel room. As Philip Glass's musical score swirls more and more loudly, the water of Woolf's world literally invades the air and space of Laura's hotel room: contact has been made between one suicidally depressed temporal dimension and another; a miracle has been achieved. Meanwhile, in the 1990s, Clarissa (Meryl Streep) strives to extend a lifeline to Richard via dialogue, empathy, and shared memories; but her efforts are ultimately unsuccessful. The only mode of reaching out in the movie that definitively "works" is the one performed by the cultural object (the novel

Mrs Dalloway) that travels three decades forwards through time to touch a traumatised woman from the future.

When I was teaching *The Hours*, I came to believe that the film might, for certain viewers, be performing a rescuing function comparable to that which the novel *Mrs Dalloway* plays within the film for the depressed character, Laura. Richard can't make visceral contact with his child self, Richie; and his friend, Clarissa, can't reach him through their conversation. The film in which they all appear, however, bridges the folds of time in a way that electrifies the viewer, offering him or her jolts of aliveness and psychical linking that remain inaccessible to most of the characters themselves. None of the theories available to me – mostly Deleuzian in flavour – regarding film as potential "time machine" (e.g. Rodowick, 1997), or as a somehow corporeally vivifying tool (e.g. Shaviro, 1993) seemed quite able to grasp the complexity of the emotional and deeply *personal* phenomena I felt I was living through when I watched *The Hours*. My sense of the psychical energy that was being released in me, and in some of my students (e.g. Farress, 2018), through our viewing and discussion of these central sequences was of a simultaneously ghostly, liberating, and protective beneficence. Reaching for a passage from Wright's (2000) Winnicott-inspired article on how "to make experience sing", which the group would then read and discuss together in the context of what we'd been watching, helped, to some extent, to make sense of just how moving we all seemed to be finding the representations of recognition in these particular frames of film. Wright edged us towards the exciting hypothesis that the especially moving scenes were somehow recognising and claiming us as their orphaned children. Our intuitive sense that something infantile in us was being generously nurtured by the movie itself had found a welcome support in psycho-cultural theory.

As I was teaching these strangely rewarding classes, noticing myself and others swept up in what felt like momentous and yet also deeply thoughtful responses to the material, it seemed to me a waste to leave our discussion of what was happening at a purely intellectual level of enquiry. At times, such as when the students and I listened together to Cat Stevens' "Wild World", after having read the funeral scene in Ben Rice's (2000) novel *Pobby and Dingan*, in which little, dead Kellyanne's "imaginary" friends are buried to that same, beautiful song, it felt as if we were hovering, Rivette-like, on the edge of some kind of group sorcery, reaching into imaginary and imaginal circles-within-circles, managing to pull gloriously real life out from within an intradiegetic dream. And yet the context of a university seminar didn't feel, at least not then, like an appropriate framework in which to explore my deeply felt – and growing – sense that we, as a group, were actually thinking, talking, and dreaming about the unexpected retrieval of something sacred in ourselves. I think that I was starting to become aware of a certain "unspeakable" quality in my own responses to some of these film sequences; and I had enough psychoanalytic understanding, even then, to realise that is this was probably related to something traumatic in my own life. I wasn't yet ready or willing to look at the whole story head on. Instead, I published two scholarly articles (Asibong, 2015a and Asibong, 2015b), which skirted around the issue in a somewhat oblique and highly intellectualised fashion, all the while claiming to be clear and direct.

Beyond the intellectual defence

I'm sometimes puzzled by how little academic writing on our emotional investment in the moving image, both as individuals and as societies, really dares to look at the (sometimes horribly) wounded parts of ourselves and our communities that gravitate, for psychical survival, towards certain cultural objects. It feels as if Ian Suttie's (1988 [1935]) landmark (psycho)analysis of the cultural "taboo on tenderness", echoing Ferenczi's (1995) cry at the psychoanalytic taboo on spirit, could be very usefully applied to an academic and psychoanalytic *Weltanshauung* defined by "objectivity" at all costs. Some theorists, in the semi-legitimised autoethnographic turn of recent years, have begun to experiment with including the subjective self in their studies of object-attachment and fandom. Stacey's (1993) important work on female film stars and their spectators and Kuhn's (1994; 2002) autoethnographic explorations of her own early relationship with cinema have both had an impact on my decision to approach my own filmic material through the lens of my own "irrational" emotional attachments. Perez's (2008) analysis of his lifelong relationship with both film versions of *Imitation of Life* deepened my growing commitment to an exploration of film attachments that could be at once theoretical and emotionally open: "*Imitation of Life* is the cultural artifact that has chosen me – named me – inspiring trauma and reverie" (p. 119). Perez is especially compelling in his articulation of a troubling split at the heart of his relationship with the films' images:

> I lay in bed, head aching, stunned that I had been reduced to convulsive sobs by a movie with such racist (and formulaic) machinations – a movie I found entirely transparent, or so I thought. I would return to this film, and its more famous remake, repeatedly as a teacher, race scholar, and queer fan. These repeated returns added to my pain and anger, but they also reinforced the more ineluctable pleasures for me of *Imitation of Life*. My difficulty in deciphering that pleasure, my inability to compartmentalize it, compels an incessant return to the source.
> (p. 120)

Sprengnether's (2002) fascinating collection of autobiographical essays, entitled simply *Crying at the Movies*, explores the very personal relationship between her own traumatic experiences, from her witnessing, aged nine, of her father's death by drowning, to a range of childhood, adolescent, and adult sexual and emotional intensities, seemingly beyond the capacities of language until juxtaposed with her account of a related film-watching experience. Fisher's (2014) *Ghosts of My Life* hints at the existence of a writer whose own emotional health is a key factor in his choice of cultural objects, even if he prefers to place his emphasis on collective melancholia rather than on any specific investigation into how – other than through the seemingly unshakable existence of capitalism – such a mass depression takes shape in the first place. When he writes that "[i]n 1982, I taped [the group Japan's hit song] "Ghosts" from the radio and chain-listened to it: pressing play, rewinding the cassette, repeating", the reader is tantalised: what *was* it about that song that drew Fisher in so? Even if I can feel a sort of wordless identification with the siren-like experience he evokes, might it be possible to find language for this pull towards something so hopelessly, glamorously spectral?

In the exploration that follows, I want to keep on asking the same uncomfortable question from a number of different angles: what is really going on with us (with me?) when we find ourselves grabbing at images we think might save us, begging them to, please, hold us tight? How do we "get real" in our writing about our own thoughts, spirits, and internal objects, whilst at the same time remaining committed to the rigour of psycho-cultural analysis? This book is an attempt to offer a simultaneous theorisation, personal exploration, psychodynamically inflected analysis, and politicised contextualisation of the various emotional uses made of certain kinds of moving images by people who have found that they are in serious emotional and/or physical danger. Whilst I situate my project within a wider landscape of writing emerging from the intersections of film and media studies, psycho-cultural studies, and clinical psychoanalysis, I accept that much of what I am attempting here may feel unacceptably hybrid to some academic readers. I've found points of commonality in Plantinga's (2009) research on "upsetting" film, in Lubecker's (2015) writing on the "feel-bad" film, and in Laine's (2011) study of "feeling cinema"; but here I'm allowing myself to travel into terrain in which I expose my own emotional processes to the reader's scrutiny and compassion. If, like Walker (2005), I invoke the concept of a "trauma cinema", this is at the same time to freely admit myself to being a traumatised spectator. If, like Fisher (2014), I draw on theories of haunting and "spectralities" in my explorations of my viewing practices, this is to acknowledge without reservation that I myself am haunted, and that there are clearly demonstrable psychical and psychosocial reasons for this.

Kuhn's (2013) edited volume *Little Madnesses* – together with so many of her previous writings on the psycho-cultural and emotional functions of the moving image – is a key text in the emerging discussion of a spectator who *feels* as s/he watches and plays. Grant's (2020) hypnotic video-essays enable us, like Kuhn's best work, to build emotionally satisfying bridges between psychoanalytic concepts relating to object-use and a willingness to acknowledge the author's own emotional states during her engagements with the potent cultural objects she is exploring. As for me, I'm trying to accept the powerlessness of my early surrender to eerily moving images. This powerlessness has had, at times, a genuinely traumatic quality. But over the course of its development, it may have edged towards becoming something that's, to paraphrase Hallward (2001), *absolutely post-traumatic.* This idea can't be proven, only played with; but, in order to proceed with my playing, I must be willing to operate in a realm that isn't merely cerebral.

In the shadow of ongoing injury

This book takes as its premise the hypothesis that there may be something in many spectators' uses of particular moving images that is akin to a child's relationship with an especially helpful toy or "transitional object" (Winnicott, 1971). In this sense, it has a great deal in common with the recent academic "turn to object-relations" in screen studies and psycho-cultural theory. Bainbridge and Yates's (2014) edited collection of essays on media and the inner world considers the recurrence of compulsive, paranoid, anxious, or otherwise vulnerable modes of spectatorship at the heart of an ongoing academic and clinical conversation about our often rather messy psychical uses of the moving image. Wright's (2009) work on mirroring, attunement, and self-realisation as these play out in creative and spectatorial phenomena makes for a crucial intervention in our capacity to think about artistic and religious experiences as new/old spaces through which our earliest interpersonal relationship – the dynamic between ourselves as infants and our primary caregivers – may be re-experienced and, perhaps, reconfigured. Rignell's (2016) writing uses Winnicott to think through a viewer's potential emotional and ethical metamorphosis through a series of "encounters" with the later films of Michael Haneke.

The ideas of Winnicott are alive and well in these fascinating writings about our psychical use of moving images: the Winnicott of play, transitional objects, and potential space. In this book, though, it's also the Winnicott (1974) who writes of our *fear of breakdown* who demands attention, the Winnicott for whom a terror of falling over the edge, the terror of falling and falling forever, is never too far away. bell hooks' (1991) much-quoted sentence – "I came to theory because I was hurting" – is foundational for me. Her important work on "oppositional spectatorship" (1992) and "teaching to transgress" (1994) never baulks at the challenge of acknowledging the author's own emotional pain, together with an unrepentant recognition of the cultural object's psychical importance to the racially traumatised, partially dissociated, or intolerably fearful viewer. I seek to examine my own – and others' – fundamentally *agonised* use of moving images, to offer an account of psycho-cultural activity that insists on the psychically transformative and politicisable potential of the genuinely post-traumatic moving image.

How might the viewer use a filmic encounter not just for comfort, or even insight, but in order to save their own psychical skin? The remainder of the book takes this hypothesis of a strangely containing, half-alive, mysterious film-skin seriously, testing it out, in conjunction with psychoanalytic theory and close readings of audience testimony, on a number of cinematic objects. Arguing that what we hear, if we listen carefully to viewers, all the while thinking both clinically and culturally, is no less than a cataclysmic revelation and disinterment of our internalised deadness, I test out a number of seismic encounters with moving images, using a range of different methodological approaches. This book synthesises psychoanalytic and psychosocial reflections on object-related fantasying with simultaneous analysis of spectatorial practice, examining different viewers' creatively and destructively idiosyncratic use of the same moving images over time. Using a number of different research methods (psychodynamic theory; auto-ethnography; semi-structured interview; groupwork; close reading of filmic/televisual material; politicised mourning and curative/curational film-ritual), I explore the ways in which developmentally traumatised individuals make conscious and unconscious use of hauntingly moving images over the course of a lifetime, in order simultaneously to play with and de-toxify their internal worlds, worlds which may be experienced as dead, damaged, or dying. I ask whether spectators' psychical uses of moving images may, in some cases, enable new, more "alive" forms of thinking, dreaming, feeling, and relating to become possible, and I attempt to clarify the conditions under which such internal transformations might optimally occur.

I seek to describe new relationships that are created between the survivors of trauma and the moving images they find and use to do intense emotional work-play. I place at the book's heart a very specific question, posed in each chapter from a different angle, and examined via a number of different methodological approaches: how do survivors of different forms of affliction – from early relational trauma to racialised state violence – make *conscious and unconscious* use of particular moving images in such a way that hitherto damaged parts of their psyche may "become alive" (cf. LaMothe, 2005)? The question has serious implications, not only in the realms of film and media theory, but also (and arguably far more importantly) for those involved in innovative film curation, psychotherapeutic clinical practice, and parental and pedagogic caregiving. The next chapter of this book explores my own idiosyncratic use of a number of films for something that retrospectively felt like my own psychical survival, eventually zooming in on the way in which two of the films to which I seemed most passionately attached – two "misfit sequels", *The Curse of the Cat People* (1944) and *Twin Peaks: Fire Walk with Me* (1992) – offered me fantastical representations of my own family's traumatised and traumatising zones of deadness. Chapter 3 focuses on the various psychical uses made by a number of different viewers of the television series *Six Feet Under* (2001–5), examining how this traumatised "secret society" of watchers became gradually conscious of a paradoxical aliveness at the heart of a literally funereal televisual landscape. Finally, in Chapter 4, I shift the focus from individual to collective spectatorship, moving from the universal traumas of early environmental failure to the particular traumas of a specific socio-political group living today. In the chapter's analysis of how a predominantly Black film society emerged out of the context of unusually high levels of physical, emotional, and structural violence, I explore how the group used eerily moving images of racialised vulnerability *together*, in order not only to heal from the impact of past and present wounds, but also to prepare collectively for an uncertain future in the shadow of ongoing injury.

Chapter 2

I just wanted to tell you that everything's going to be all right

My life in the bush of film-ghosts: an autoethnographic analysis

The kindness of strangers

When I was ten, I first turned for help to the combined television and VCR in my bedroom. It was the autumn of 1988 and my two older sisters had just left home very suddenly. The first sister, who was eighteen, had gone away to university. The second sister, who was fifteen, had been taken by the social services into "care", as a result of the violence and threats of murder from my father which had always been a regular part of our family life. The secondary school I'd just started at was a brutal, humiliating, racist place, and my parents offered me no strategies for survival there, the only pupil racialised as Black, often struggling for recognition by the thousands of white eyes around me as fully and indisputably human. Nor did they offer any conversation about the family's recent implosion. My father, a frightening (and frightened), highly educated, West African man with a history of severe, disavowed trauma, and my mother, a white, equally highly educated, Cornish woman with a transgenerationally prescribed capacity for the abandonment of her children in times of extreme danger, had no known connection to Merseyside. We'd settled abruptly in 1982 in the skinhead-infested town on the other side of the river from Liverpool – the eccentrically-named "One-Eyed City" of Birkenhead – without family, friends, or community. Unlike Jung (1963), whose famous dream of the Liverpool "rain, fog, smoke and dimly lit darkness" eventually leads his wandering psyche towards a "little island [which] blazed with sunlight, on [which] stood a single tree, a magnolia, in a shower of reddish blossoms", our traumatised family had no flowering symbol of aliveness to illuminate our journey through the "dirty, sooty city" to which we'd migrated in waking life, at least none that was immediately apparent.

When I was eleven, I tried running away. I managed to stay for a few days with a family I vaguely knew and hoped would foster me, having observed my middle sister's apparent orchestration of her own fostering. I didn't get fostered; but I do remember being engaged with by my new parental figures during that week in a way I've not forgotten. The father, Maurice, taught me

DOI: 10.4324/9781003185178-3

to ride a bike and did my homework with me; the mother, Andrea, checked in with me every day about how I was doing. We all watched *The Wizard of Oz* (1939), and we talked about it afterwards. My own parents turned up together at the school gates one evening the following week – an unprecedented move, never to be repeated – wearing awkward, unnatural grins. They took me straight to McDonald's and promptly blocked all access to the other family. I'd been offered the combined television and VCR shortly after my sisters' twin departures, and now I turned back to this object with renewed hunger. I'd clocked from the outset its unstated function as a kind of robot-pacifier, embodying my parents' lack of capacity to provide any kind of attention or care. But I didn't mind. It was a cheap player; erratic, it chewed up videotapes it didn't take to. My parents, busy, in any case, with the maintenance of their mutually dehumanising, "interracial" marriage, weren't interested in which movies I watched, and paid little attention to the strange new babysitter who now took such enthusiastic charge of my cultural diet.

Internal horror-show

In his essay in Kohon's (1999) edited volume on Green's (1986) "dead mother complex", Bollas (1999) reflects on his therapeutic work with Antonio, a young man seemingly afflicted by a perpetual, post-traumatic, sulky resentment towards his childhood, his parents, and relationships in general. What is noteworthy, for Bollas, is how his patient Antonio needs to create internal representations of an outlandish kind in order to do justice to the intense affect of his complex and divided psyche:

> The price he paid for years of childhood revenges against his parents, all of which were purely internal, was to cultivate a genre of horror fantasies that could scare him witless, although increasingly he realised that they also amused him. Or more pertinently, when he had a bad thought he would set up cinema within himself, popcorn stand included, and sell tickets to the other portions of the self which in states of carefully deployed innocence could walk into an unfolding scene of horror to their extreme fright. But as with the horror film addict, such scenes were also exciting, and of course it was a great relief to have survived.
>
> (p. 94)

Bollas's analysis suggests that the only way Antonio found to offer himself psychical symbolisation of both the awfulness of his Italian family's move from Sicily to England during his childhood and also the fact that, for various reasons, "he felt deeply harmed by both parents" (p. 95), was to "convert [bad thoughts] into a trailer for a feature film that was soon to follow, and he could darken the self like a cinema dimming the lights to better see projected images" (pp. 95–6). Bollas turns to the metaphor of horror cinema projection in order to convey Antonio's compulsion to facilitate a strange *watchfulness*, similar, in some ways, to the kinds of watchfulness we discussed in relation to Kalsched's patient Dellie in Chapter 1. However, Bollas fails to develop his ideas about the potential pertinence of his patient's relationship to cinema itself, which is never actually mentioned. What's clear, though, is that part of Antonio's post-traumatic pathology involves an addiction to the creation of images and experiences (both inter- and intra-personal) which force a horrified self into the position of spectator. Some dreadfully real violation or loss, previously – and maddeningly – invisible, needs now to be watched compulsively; and perhaps by dint of (someone, something, anything) *watching in the right way*, slides of Antonio's blank, internal horror may be able to be developed and processed.

Watching the films which, in 1989, I started habitually to record from late-night Channel 4 and BBC2, kept me in touch with the memory of watching videos with my sisters before their sudden disappearance. The machine had previously belonged to the family, and we three siblings would run to it whenever our father was out of the house. We used to watch two feature-length music documentaries, about The Beatles and Michael Jackson respectively, over and over again; these were my sisters' choices. But once I was on my own, I felt pulled towards strange fiction films emerging from the more eccentric fringes of American independent cinema. Looking back, I think that perhaps my immediate fascination with the 1970s "New Hollywood" during my adolescence had something to do with trying to get back to the "other side" (the other side of my birth, that is); back to a fantasised, intermittently glamorous ghost-world; back to what I dreamed my family might have been before I'd come into the world; back to when they'd all lived in 1970s America. With less luck on my side – more freedom to roam the streets, say, or a greater capacity for psychosis – my unconscious search for my family's mysterious phantoms might have led me to stumble into some terrifying real-life version of Scorsese's *Taxi Driver* (1976), or Kubrick's *The Shining* (1980). Instead, my quest led me towards the foundation of an otherworldly and – in strictly relative terms – *safe-ish* home in my bedroom, amongst increasingly peculiar moving pictures. I think that these pictures kept my mind alive until other people – and my own slowly individuating self – could take over, far away from the physical family environment.

The moving images towards which I gravitated were definitely not always necessarily nurturing of my developing pre-adolescent psyche. I found my way towards many films which were horribly unsuitable for a child of my age. At the same time as being mesmerised by mysterious scenes of cinematic caregiving and relationality, I was also hypnotised by *re*-traumatising (if not uninteresting) movies about gender, sexuality, violence, and addiction, films like Richard Brooks' *Looking for Mr Goodbar* (1977) and Brian de Palma's *Dressed to Kill* (1980). Analytic thinkers from Bion (1959) to

Brown (2005) have shone useful light on the potential for trauma to generate a compulsive resistance in the survivor to thinking and linking. There's always a danger of merely revelling in blank, blind horror. This dangerous aspect of my own emerging cinephilia is undeniable, and it's important to acknowledge it here. But I want to spend more time exploring the aspects of my teenage watching that felt more alive.

In search of something real

Moving images that make no attempt to conceal or disavow the trauma inherent in the "making and breaking of affectional bonds" (Bowlby, 2015), but instead, not unlike fairy tales in Bettelheim's (1991) canonical analysis, find enchanting ways of representing it, may, rather than re-traumatising the viewer, instead offer him or her an emotional shelter that enables new kinds of thinking and feeling to develop in the psyche. A meaning-generating process may take place. Bion (1962) describes this as "alpha-function", the conversion of undigested (and as-yet-indigestible) psychical phenomena into images which may be used in order to think and to dream:

> If the patient cannot transform his emotional experience into alpha-elements, he cannot dream. Alpha-function transforms sense impressions into alpha-elements which resemble, and may in fact be identical with, the visual images with which we are familiar in dreams, namely, the elements that Freud regards as yielding their latent content when the analyst has interpreted them. Freud showed that one of the functions of a dream is to preserve sleep. Failure of alpha-function means the patient cannot dream and therefore cannot sleep.
>
> (pp. 6–7)

Some of the eerie movies to which I began, in the late 1980s, to become attached, before my tentative entrance in the late 1990s into intimate adult relationships, or my ambivalent embrace in the late 2000s of psychoanalytic psychotherapy, may have helped me, prior to the properly reparative and relational work of both these pursuits, to learn both how to dream and how to sleep. The shadow side of my teenage viewing habits notwithstanding, I found myself regularly entranced in my bedroom by scenes that spoke to me of things that seemed giddily, emotionally, and ineluctably *real*. This sense of realness struck at the wooden heart of a vague impression I sometimes had of not being fully alive, of being merely a Pinocchio-like character, fabricated for the purpose of containing the psychical projections of irreparably damaged minds, both within and without the family group. The filmic depictions of a certain kind of emotional connection on screen, all of which were, in one way or another, fantastical, offered me an opportunity to glimpse real alternatives to the family blueprint of deadened feeling and narcissistic relating. The words of Michael Eigen (1999) resonate intensely for me:

> Larry lacked a background of successful bursts of shared aliveness with real people. Can one jump-start this capacity out of the blue? How can one get practice, if one never begins? Aliveness needs a lifetime of practice if one is to learn to navigate its destructive aspects. But one has to start somewhere.
>
> (p. 77)

Van der Kolk (2014) outlines a number of therapeutic methods developed to help trauma survivors to reconfigure their experiences in such a way that something of their internalised sense of isolation and paralysis may shift. The goal of these therapies is not to deny, disavow, or distort the reality of what has actually been suffered; but instead to facilitate a breach in the mind-body's debilitating experience of helplessness, terror, and abandonment:

> In my experience, physically reexperiencing the past in the present and then reworking it in a safe and supportive "container" can be powerful enough to create new, supplemental memories: simulated experiences of growing up in an attuned, affectionate setting where you are protected from harm […] an alternative memory in which your basic human needs are met and your longings for love and protection are fulfilled.
>
> (p. 300)

Certain modes of spectatorship – and the mind's subsequent interactions, in dream, play, conversation, or fantasy, with that remembered experience of spectatorship – may facilitate precisely the kind of "reexperiencing" to which van der Kolk is alluding here. He deploys Bion's (1962) concept of "containment" in order to convey the flavour of what he's proposing. At the heart of the psychical encounter with the "new, supplemental memories" (e.g. a film character's experience of radical protection in the midst of a larger framework of abandonment, trauma, and neglect), a renaissance may take place at the seat of the self, a renaissance that is generative of new ways of thinking, feeling, and relating.

A number of recent researchers (e.g. Szykierski, 2010; Brown, 2012) have suggested that it was Bion's personal experience of mind-shattering trauma during the First World War, combined with as-yet-unresolved relational conflicts from early childhood, that led him to formulate a theory of a healing relationship between an object that has the capacity to "contain" and a fragmented psyche that, under good enough circumstances, has the capacity to be "contained". The traumatic roots of Bion's (1962) theory of the "container-contained" dynamic helped him to understand how, in the absence of human shielding from environmental violence or toxic psychical projections, the surviving individual will need to find new representations, objects, and relationships in order to develop, or re-develop, a mind capable of thinking. Building on Bion's idea that a traumatised, shattered, or dissociated individual's emotional contact with a dream, or with a dreamlike representation generated by another person, might be conducive to that individual's experience of feeling "contained", and to the subsequent development of a new – or renewed – capacity for thinking, Lia Pistiner de Cortiñas (2017) suggests that the analyst can try to bind together the patient's associations into a kind of "artificial dream":

> I am developing what is implicit in Bion's contributions to clinical practice, namely, the idea that analysts need to enrich their equipment for the investigation of psychic realities with stories, dreams, myths, narratives, etc., to form a "verbal picture gallery" able to provide models that can be used for different aspects of emotional situations [...] These ideas give a new value to the function of "constructions" in psychoanalysis (Freud, 1937d). The construction of a model, an "artificial dream", using the tools of symmetry and analogy, makes the relationship [e.g. with the parents during infancy] more evident, rather than just the related objects (for example: breast, penis) which anchor the relationship. In psychoanalysis we need to have tools for discovering and showing the patient the relationships of which he (or she) is not aware, due to dissociations and difficulties in symbolization.
>
> (p. 247)

Reflecting on how a patient she names Maria, a patient who could neither play nor dream, who "seemed to live in a kind of museum world, a kind of immobile atmosphere where nothing is alive" (p. 248), eventually came to use William Wyler's disturbing abduction movie, *The Collector* (1965), as a means of describing her own psychical reality, Pistiner de Cortiñas argues that "this model [the film] allowed us to think and ask what stayed locked up, immobilised, and what was the danger of getting out of this immobilised, isolated situation" (p. 249). Another Bion-oriented therapist, Cartwright (2010), writes of a particularly film-like dream in a "borderline" patient, a dream that appears to shift both the patient's sense of herself and of the transference relationship into new, representable territory:

> *She was kissing a man, it was like she was in some Hollywood romantic movie. She recalls the thought while she was dreaming: "this was the best kiss". But when they both turned towards the camera their faces looked ravaged and bloody.* I said the last image in the dream was difficult for

me to think about. Amelia agreed. I asked her about the Hollywood romantic aspects of the dream. She said, "It was me being romantic, but at a distance, in a movie" [...] The "bloody kiss" excited and intrigued me in the sense that I felt like a witness to something beautiful unfolding, the birth of her own experiencing, despite the difficulty of the image. It appeared to be her "dead alive" self in a thinkable form, with all its trauma [...] Some understanding that the "dead alive self" is the best way that some patients are able to generate a sense of coherence is important. In the face of a fragile ability to create mental representations this strangely represents some sense of hope.

(pp. 245–7)

Both Pistiner de Cortiñas and Cartwright show how in a certain kind of "deadened" patient, it's by channelling a specifically cinematic part of their traumatised mind that something resembling both symbolisation and aliveness seems to get mobilised. Despite – or perhaps because of – the unpleasantness of the moving images involved, the patient gradually finds herself with a greater capacity for thinking, feeling, representing, and relating to the unpleasantness she has already lived.

Too sad to think about

Sometime around 2000, I found myself crying unexpectedly at the final scene of Anand Tucker's film *Hilary and Jackie* (1998), a movie about the relationship between the cellist Jacqueline du Pré (Emily Watson) and her sister Hilary (Rachel Griffiths), a film which, taken in its totality, didn't necessarily strike me, when I first saw it, as anything to write home about. But the scene that made me cry felt like something else entirely. In the scene, the child Jackie is playing on the beach with her sister Hilary when she comes across her own adult self, a well-meaning ghost from the future. The adult ghost Jackie speaks to her child self, saying: "Jackie: I just wanted to tell you ... that everything's going to be all right". Something shockingly generous seemed suddenly to have materialised, not just between the characters on screen (different parts of a single self, communing, on the beach, across time, space, and the frontier between life and death), but also between the scene and me. It was as if the film had transformed into an aged, kindly grandparent, sharing an enlightening revelation of what it meant to stay alive, *truly alive*, even after a part of you has died. I felt as if a long-lost part of my own child-self had been found and was now being addressed and acknowledged by an entity swooping in from another dimension. I was being talked to, communed with, by a kindly, spectral memory from the future, helpfully captured on a movie camera. It was a deeply mysterious feeling, utterly moving, as if fragments of my shattered self were coming together after far too long apart.

I felt compelled to tell my mother about the scene when I next saw her, even though it had been many years since I'd tried to communicate with her about any experience that might be described as personal, emotional, or meaningful. Playing her Elgar's cello concerto when she came to visit me in my apartment a few weeks after my encounter with *Hilary and Jackie*, I attempted to describe the scene from the movie, and the beginnings of how I'd felt about it. Her reaction to our conversation was helpful, insofar as it shone a light on what our interactions of this kind may have been like when I was a child or infant. Not feigning ignorance about the kind of aesthetic or relational intensity I was relaying to her so much as quietly stating her opposition to any kind of discussion of it, she simply murmured: *"It's too sad to think about"*. We spoke no more about it.

Of supreme importance in the creation of the powerfully "oceanic" feelings that were surging up within me was, I think, the music by Edward Elgar, permeating both this scene and the entire film. The combination of the music with the creation of a fantastical, temporally porous dimension on film – all filtered through such emotionally honest images of caregiving between a vulnerable part of the self and another part that is protective and alive – created a symphony of elements that were playing, in tune, in me, together. The result felt like an experience, taking place inside my mind and body, of linking, protection, recognition, and repair. Stern (2010) writes compellingly about the ways in which various art forms – *especially when they work together in concert* – may be unconsciously experienced by the viewer or listener as mimetic of a primitive set of moving interactions with an ideal caregiver. Stern notes that "when parent and infant play, the stimuli for the baby come from the mother's eyes, face, body, and voice. Parents are a 'sound-light show' for the baby, a spectacle to play upon their states of arousal" (p. 107). A baby's experience of being adequately held and seen is intimately connected to the non-conscious, non-verbal range of sounds, images, and movements that it experiences as a multimedia bath of relationality through which its guardians operate in order to care for and communicate with it. As babies, as patients in therapy, and as people interacting with an art form, there's something about the object's capacity to blend aspects of sound, movement, and image, in a combination that reflects and responds to our need for recognition – a two-way dynamic Stern calls "attunement" – that doesn't just *improve* our sense of being real, but upon which that sense of being real is utterly dependent.

When art forms are able to arouse us in this way, via their creation of what Stern calls "vitality forms", we light up inside; something in us comes (back) to life. Film, says Stern, can be immensely, especially enlivening:

> Cinema is the ultimate mixed art form. It can create vitality forms through its own unique means as well as simultaneously through any of the other art forms that operate under its roof – music, the movement and gesture of the characters, theatrical effects, visual-scenic effects, language, and narrative. These can operate in various combinations. [...] The point is that a cinema has its own techniques to create vitality dynamics. When these are combined with the vitality dynamics elicited by the simultaneously acting other modalities in the film, the effects can be extraordinary. Something like Wagner's "totality" has been approximated.
>
> (pp. 89–98)

The potency of that scene at the end of *Hilary and Jackie* arose, for me, I think, from a kind of double-fusion, a longed-for coming together of already intertwined vitality forms which then combined with dialogue that was unabashedly relational and object-seeking. I'd been allowed to watch and participate in the journey of an eternally protective dimension of Jackie's imagined self, travelling through time and space to witness, reassure, and watch over a child-part that had been thought lost forever. Form and narrative worked together to spin a hypnotically containing film-dream for a viewer who was, without realising it, still frantically searching for a reparative experience of holding.

Icarian games

Ogden's (2017) discussion of moments in his clinical practice when he has found himself engaging with patients about literature and film expands on Pistiner de Cortiñas's and Cartwright's therapeutic willingness to share in their patient's post-traumatic use of re-animating symbols. Far from being a performative or academic indulgence in which the analyst might narcissistically or co-dependently collude with a patient's intellectual false self, such instances of "talking-as-dreaming" mark, for Ogden, an opportunity for truly creative play, in which the book or film under discussion helps to facilitate the emergence of thoughts and feelings which would otherwise remain repressed in both patient and analyst. His conversation with a patient, Ms L., about J.M. Coetzee's (1999) novel, *Disgrace*, cracks open a fertile space *in both of them* for thinking about relational losses that hitherto could not find a frame:

> In my work with Ms L., I had, for more than a year, been unable and perhaps unwilling to think/dream/remember and keep alive in myself the enormous (unimaginable) pain that the patient's father and the patient had experienced in relation to the death of his first wife and their daughter. I was astounded by my inability to have kept alive in me the emotional impact of those deaths. At that point in the session I was able to begin to dream (to do conscious and unconscious psychological work with) what I now perceived to be the patient's feelings of "disgrace" for being alive "in place of" her father's wife and daughter and in place of the parts of her father that had died with them.
>
> (pp. 104–5)

Ogden's discussion of the "talking-as-dreaming" that took place during sessions between himself and a male patient, Mr B., is even more remarkable in terms of the light it shines on the therapeutic potentiality that may emerge from the play between two people over a symbolising movie-object. Crucially, the conversations with Mr B. take place shortly after Mr B., who "grew up under circumstances of extreme neglect" but "nonetheless [...] tenaciously clung to the hope that his parents, particularly his mother, would see what was happening without his having to tell them" (pp. 107–8) has a revealing dream about relational deadness. In the dream,

> there was a single horrifying image of a shabby wax figure of a Madonna and infant in a wax museum. What was most disturbing about the image was the vacant stare that each was giving the other [...] The session that I will describe occurred shortly after the Madonna-and-infant dream. It was a period of analysis in which the patient and I were beginning to be able to talk to one another in a way that held some vitality, and yet this way of talking was still so new as to feel brittle and, at times, a bit awkward.
>
> (p. 108)

Mr B. asks Ogden if he knows the Coen brothers' film *Raising Arizona* (1987). What follows is a fascinating – and quite unprecedented – bout of "play" between the two men, as they talk-and-dream together about the movie. Ogden surprises both himself and his patient when, giving more information than has been requested or is strictly necessary, he admits to Mr B. that he has seen that movie "a number of times" (p. 109).

> Mr B. moved his head on the pillow in a way that conveyed a sense of surprise that I had responded as I had. It seemed clear to both of us that we were in uncharted waters. As this emotional shift was occurring, I had in mind a number of thoughts about the transference-countertransference. Mr B., in asking me a direct question, had dared to make himself less "invisible", and I had, without conscious intention, responded in kind. Moreover, he was inviting me to join him in talking about the work of two brothers, the Coen brothers, who made extraordinary things together. Making something (becoming someone) with one's brother was an experience that the patient had missed out on with his own brothers. Perhaps his introducing them into the analysis reflected a wish to have such an experience with me.
>
> (p. 109)

Mr B. begins to talk excitedly to Ogden about his thoughts and feelings regarding *Raising Arizona*:

> "I'm sorry for getting so carried away". (The patient's voice was full of the excitement of a child.) I asked, "Why not get carried away?" (This was not a rhetorical question. I was saying in a highly condensed way that there had been very good reasons for the patient as a child to feel that it was dangerous to talk with excitement in his voice, but that those reasons were true to another reality, the reality of the past, which for him often eclipsed the reality of the present.)
>
> (p. 110)

Not only is the relational tone between Ogden and Mr B. beginning to shift in important ways, but they also find themselves coming together towards an emotional joint analysis of the representation of caregiving in the film's final scenes.

> Mr B. excitedly interrupted me to say, "Yes, his dream at the end has it both ways. I want to believe he's looking into the future. No, it's a softer feeling than that. It is a feeling of *maybe*. Even for such a screw-up as Cage, if he can imagine something it might happen. No, that sounds so trite. I can't find the right way of putting it. It's so frustrating. If he can dream it, it has happened in the dream. No, I can't say it the way I mean it".
>
> (p. 111)

My experience of trying to talk to my therapist, F., about the cultural objects that had emotional significance for me underwent great shifts in the course of the therapy. Early in the relationship – I would say for the first two years – I felt that F. resisted or refused my attempts to introduce conversations about movies and television into our sessions. Initially, I thought this might be because he didn't know or wasn't interested in the objects I would obsessively reflect on. Later, I reflected that he perhaps felt it would be poor analytic practice to encourage the proliferation of such material. Whatever it was, my frequent ruminations about irrational feelings of "responsibility" towards the character of Brenda (Rachel Griffiths) in the television series *Six Feet Under* (2001–5) went largely unremarked upon, whilst my announcement that my mood was significantly improved on days I held in mind the protective influence of Simone Simon's character in *The Curse of the Cat People* (1944) was met with what felt like bewilderment. But somewhere along the way, things between F. and me began to shift. There was a deepening of our therapeutic relationship more broadly, of course, but what I want to mention here is the way in which the shift manifested at the psycho-cultural level. F. seemed to loosen up around the discussion of cultural objects. The effect of this loosening up on my emotional experience of him and of our relationship was enormous. A number of instances stand out in my mind, all examples of an Ogden-like "over-sharing" of his own experience of the cultural object in question: a seemingly off-the-cuff remark about *his* impression of the libidinal (and anti-libidinal) screen personae of Jessica Lange; an involuntary cry of surprised amusement that my conservative father would own a record by Grace Jones.

Trivial though these examples might sound, they dramatically altered my capacity to relate to F. as a whole person, living, like me, within a wider cultural field. In engaging with me through these objects, F. wasn't simply indulging an infantile part of me that was "addicted" to film (and pop music) culture; he was engaging with the idiosyncratic way in which my psyche had found to make sense of unbearable feelings. Looking back, it was as if he had tuned in, via a growing receptivity to the emotional significance of certain objects in my response to early trauma, to Bion's (2005) remark that "[t]he analyst, in the midst of the noises of distress, the failure of analysis, the uselessness of that kind of conversation, still needs to be able to hear the sound of this terror which indicates the position of a person beginning to hope that he might be rescued" (p. 21). It might not have seemed like it at first, but the sound of *my* terror took the form of talking about movies. It had to be listened to. When, several years into the therapy, I found myself talking, for perhaps the tenth or twentieth time, about the indescribable importance to me of the fragmentary bond between the protagonists Brian and Neil in the final scene of Gregg Araki's film, *Mysterious Skin* (2004), a crucial moment occurred between us. When I momentarily forgot the name of one of the two boys, F., quite out of the blue – I have no idea if he had seen the film or had merely internalised it through my repeated evocations – supplied the missing name: "Neil".

F.'s gentle and unexpected proffering of that name "Neil" at the moment it found itself blanked out of my mind feels a little like the therapeutic equivalent of Alison Bechdel's (2006) autobiographical recollection of her far-from-perfect father's surprising capacity to indulge her, from time to time, in "Icarian games"; these were those moments when she would soar above his body, arm-wings outstretched, balanced deliciously on his feet. The feelings of intimacy and containment little Alison experiences with her father Bruce in those moments are as indisputable as they are uncharacteristic, rare, and short-lived. They pave the way beautifully for the novel's denouement, in which, shortly before his suicide, Bruce takes his daughter (now a young woman) to the cinema to see Sissy Spacek as Loretta Lynn in *Coal Miner's Daughter* (1980). A little later comes the unforgettable final page: it's a memory-image of Bruce standing patiently on the floor of a swimming pool, ready to catch his little, learning-to-swim daughter, as she leaps, full of trust, into the water. It seems to me that in all these "Icarian games" – between Ogden and his patients, between Bruce and Alison, between F. and me – something crucial is enabled in the non-narcissistic willingness of the "parent" to join the "child" in a shared space of moving revelation.

Maps to the stars

During my second year as a patient in twice-weekly psychoanalytic psychotherapy, at the age of 31 – the age of both my parents when I was born – I dreamed I was in the attic bedroom of my late 1980s early adolescence, my

combined television-VCR by my side, when I heard the doorbell ring downstairs. Hovering at the top of the stairs to see who was at the door, I heard, to my amazement, the distinctive voice of my therapist, F., trying to gain entry to the dark and barricaded house. He was here to see me and to find out how I was doing, but also to remonstrate with my parents for their shocking neglect of me in my formative years.

There was something of the feel of the iconic arrival of Father Merrin (Max von Sydow) at the afflicted house in the film *The Exorcist* (1973) that permeated the dream, but with none of the horror implied by that association, merely a kind of acknowledgement of the seriousness of the situation at hand. In the dream, I certainly didn't feel like little Regan (Linda Blair). I didn't feel frightened; I was, on the contrary, immensely excited and relieved that I was going to be helped. One thing seemed especially clear in the dream: it wasn't me who was to be "exorcised", but instead my parents would be politely, but firmly, confronted by a power greater than themselves.

Upon waking, I felt deeply grateful to my unconscious for having shown me this dream. It was as if my family and I were being offered some kind of real and retrospective intervention via time travel, a visit from a supernatural social services that would actually alter my emotional reality within this sickly group in which I'd been trapped and immobilised for so many years. The dream felt like proof to me – my first, in a way – that the past wasn't simply fixed and frozen in aspic for all eternity, and that whilst real events had most certainly taken place and could not be changed, there existed folds in time through which modification of the psychical experience of those events could genuinely occur in the present. But I also felt – and I remember this eerie sensation distinctly – as if the dream and its core image had been waiting for me, waiting for a time when I would be able to receive the care and understanding they had to offer. I felt so deeply comforted.

The kind of operation in which psychical help arrives for the already traumatised psyche from the future, from the past, or from some indescribable loop in time is, in my view, something the post-traumatic psyche is always unconsciously both grasping to access, by any means necessary, and at the same time furiously resisting, whether or not formal psychotherapy or treatment has begun. Guntrip (1968), himself a former patient of both Winnicott and Fairbairn, wrote of just how challenging it is for the patient in recovery to be able to let go of the abandoning part of the internalised parental object in order to take the hand, psychically speaking, of the therapist:

> Thus a female patient who had had physically cruel treatment by her mother as a child, dreamed that she was being hurried along a road by her father who was cross and nagging her, when she saw me on the other side of the street, pulled her hand out of his and dashed across the road to me, refusing to return when he shouted

at her. On another occasion she reported a dream that her mother had been beating her when I arrived and drove her mother away. Then later I had to go off on business (the end of the session) and she burst into tears and ran after her mother who began beating her again. A bad object is better than none, she could not be alone and her relation to a cruel mother was her most deeply rooted object-relationship.

(p. 203)

The fear of change, of growth, of "abandoning" the abandoning parents, is not too great for Guntrip's patient to make an *initial* move towards self-rescue, at least in one of the dreams. But the bid for long-lasting escape is hampered, in the second dream, by a sense of betrayal by the new object, the therapist, as he ends the session. The abandoning part of the original parental object retains its primacy after all, and the self-harming, intra-psychical dynamic within the patient begins again. If we were to conceive of the therapy as a kind of exorcism, we might say that the exorcist finds himself up against an extremely resilient set of demons in the patient: whilst the demons, or "bad objects", are willing to depart momentarily, in one night's dream, say, leaving the patient free to form new relationships with an external world of human beings, they are ready to return to possess the patient in a heartbeat.

It was Fairbairn (1952), Guntrip's long-term therapist before he found his way to Winnicott, who first framed analysis explicitly in terms of exorcism with his arresting declaration: "It becomes evident, accordingly, that the psychotherapist is the true successor to the exorcist, and that he is concerned, not only with 'the forgiveness of sins', but also with 'the casting out of devils'" (p. 70). Fairbairn had long been concerned with the patient's seemingly perverse unwillingness to accept the opportunity for freedom from possession offered by the therapist-exorcist, and had concluded the following by way of explanation:

> The child not only internalizes his bad objects because they force themselves upon him and he seeks to control them, but also, and above all, because he *needs* them. If a child's parents are bad objects, he cannot eject them, even if they do not force themselves upon him: for he cannot do without them. Even if they neglect him, he cannot reject them: for if they neglect him, his need for them is increased [...] There is now little doubt in my mind that the release of bad objects from the unconscious is one of the chief aims which the psychotherapist should set himself out to achieve, even at the expense of a severe "transference neurosis": for it is only when the internalized bad objects are released from the unconscious that there is any hope of their cathexis being dissolved.

(pp. 67–70)

For both Guntrip and Fairbairn, the therapist's challenge seems to be a quasi-mythical one. In some way or another, never fully articulated by either of them, except in relatively vague formulations about the therapeutic relationship needing to be a reparative one, the therapist must rise up in analytical vigour and vitality to challenge and overpower the spectral parental deadness that has been so indefatigably internalised by the patient. But isn't such a challenge beyond the capacities of the therapist alone, or indeed of any human being? It seems to me that the patient's eerie colonisation must be met with an energy that is equal in potency, an energy of fantastically caregiving aliveness. In the wake of devastating relational trauma, there are surely limitations to the therapeutic capacity of "good enough" caregiving and "ordinary" dreaming. But if the patient, struggling to take in the "unintrojectable new objects" (Lussier, 1999, p. 158) needs something more akin to angelic care, won't s/he have to wait for the arrival of a new world?

Green's (1986) landmark essay on the psychical complex of the "dead" mother spelled out in the starkest possible terms what might be at stake in the analytic treatment of a patient who, during infancy, experienced their primary caregiver as somehow ghostly in their emotional absence, devoid of the sort of aliveness and curiosity about their child's emotional reality that Winnicott had spelled out as a prerequisite for "good-enough" mental development. According to Green, such patients come into therapy the bearers of a kind of inner "tomb", within which lay the badly buried corpse of an un-mourned parent, the so-called "dead" mother, physically present but psychically inaccessible, blankly and unrepresentably lost to the child for reasons beyond his or her grasp. The internal worlds of these borderline orphans are cluttered with the still moving carcasses of abandoning caregivers, endlessly reproduced in the present-day relationships of the compulsively repeating adult children:

> The dead mother refuses to die a second death. Very often, the analyst says to himself: "This time it's done, the old woman is really dead, he (or she) will finally be able to live, and I shall be able to breathe a little". Then a small traumatism appears in the transference or in life which gives the maternal image renewed vitality, if I may put it this way. It is because she is a thousand-headed hydra whom one believes one has beheaded with each blow; whereas in fact only one of its heads has been struck off. Where then is the beast's neck?
>
> (p. 158)

Herculean efforts would appear to be required of both patient and analyst. Eshel (2017) states the situation well when she asks: "Can analysis provide the enormous counter-forces needed for freeing and extricating these patients from the powerful, gripping, destructive forces of the black hole, of the "dead" mother? And can the analyst (when not a remote observer) survive and influence in this devouring, annihilating world of deadness?" (p. 24).

Ferenczi (1995), writing his clinical diary of 1932–3, revealed an increasing preoccupation with the same key questions. How, he asked, can a psychotherapist facilitate a healthy, living capacity for emotional attachment in people who have themselves partially "died" out of loyal sympathy with the parents who failed them, parents who themselves felt compelled to "un-know" what needed to be known? Ferenczi's account of patients who appear to have split into hybrid creatures composed of partially "dead" and partially "alive" material, as the direct consequence of physical and emotional injuries, abandonments, and betrayals sustained in infancy is consistently fascinating:

> A child is the victim of overwhelming aggression, which results in "giving up the ghost", with the firm conviction that this self-abandonment (fainting) means death. [...] Someone who has "given up the ghost" survives this "death" physically and with a part of his energy begins to live again; he even succeeds in re-establishing unity with the pre-traumatic personality, although this is usually accompanied by memory lapses and retroactive amnesia of varying duration. But this amnesic piece is actually a part of the person, who still is "dead", or exists permanently in the agony of anxiety. The task of the analysis is to remove this split.
> (p. 39)

Frozen out by the mainstream analytic community in London and Vienna in the 1920s and 1930s, ridiculed and censored in the decades that followed his death in 1933, Ferenczi is one of the only well-known analysts who dares – in the private pages of his clinical diary – to dwell on the real ontological implications of the turn to a psychotherapeutic discourse of the seemingly fantastical:

> To what extent do those who have "gone mad" from pain, that is, those who have departed from the usual egocentric point of view, become able through their special situation to experience a part of that immaterial reality which remains inaccessible to us materialists? And here the direction of research must become involved with the so-called occult. Cases of thought transference during the analysis of suffering people are extraordinarily frequent. One sometimes has the impression that the reality of such processes encounters strong emotional resistance in us materialists; any insights we gain into them have the tendency to come undone, like Penelope's weaving or the tissue of our dreams.
> (p. 33)

Reiner (2017), reflecting on compelling clinical evidence to support Ferenczi's scattered suggestions that certain kinds of traumatised patients may generate a sense both in themselves and in their therapist of the existence of a relational realm of connectedness which seems post-human, picks up on the pioneering analyst's fleetingly mentioned concept of the "astra":

> Ferenczi's idea of the astra delineates a response to early trauma and emotional abuse in which the child escapes the painful, emotionally deprived earthly self to seek comfort through contact with an all-knowing, omniscient part of the mind. He called it the astra, the Latin word for stars, essentially a dissociated state in which the infant's real self exists far away "in the stars". The emotional bond to the mother, already damaged by her absence or neglect, is thus further severed by the child, as is the bond to his (or her) own feelings.
>
> (p. 135)

Reiner neither praises nor idealises the traumatised adult/child's turn to a fantastical plane of mental representation. Indeed, she is wary in the extreme. She is clear about the price the individual pays for the passage into seeming transcendence of the trauma-situation, taking a clear clinical position in which she distances herself, more unequivocally than does Ferenczi himself, from the notion that there might be a psychically truthful or healthy dimension to this kind of post-traumatic "astral" flight:

> According to Ferenczi, the infant in contact with the astra represents an omniscient self associated with "God", a saviour and divine container. Communication with this state is later commonly viewed by the individual as spiritual enlightenment, a relationship with God. In some sense this is true, for it aims to save the child from unbearable pain. However, this "divine" container cannot really contain feelings, it contains the *fragments* of feelings, and so the child is "saved" only from *experiencing* the terror of such a disintegrated state, which continues to loom throughout his life.
>
> (pp. 135–6)

Reiner's warning about the dangers of this kind of post-traumatic exit strategy could not be expressed more starkly:

> Their capacities for intuition seemed to me to be rare "gifts", and yet ones which also have serious negative effects on mental development. Their escapes to the astra were disengagements from feelings too painful to bear, and disengagements from mothers unable to help them bear those feelings. I had to wonder why the rage, terror, and dissociation accompanying these early traumatic events result in violence, suicide,

or psychosis in some, and in others serve as means, however ineffective, of gaining access to higher truth. I had to walk a fine line, honouring these intuitive gifts while interpreting the damaging implications.

(pp. 138–9)

It feels hard to find our way out of a sort of clinical impasse. We're told by the likes of Guntrip, Fairbairn, Eshel, and Green that certain kinds of relational trauma lead to the development in children and in adult-child patients of an internal "deadness" that cannot be challenged by ordinary therapy, such is the patient's near-supernatural commitment to the preservation of a ghostly object. These analysts hint at the need for a kind of connection with the patient that could be somehow equal to the power of the phantom, only with an opposite energy of aliveness. Ferenczi's tentative suggestion that relationally traumatised patients may be led to make contact with "astral" planes of connectedness as a result of their unmooring from human care is held at bay by the likes of Reiner, even as she is struck by the genuineness of seemingly telepathic links made between analyst and patient in the transference and countertransference: for these links are apparently not conducive to a robust or relational container for thinking. Everywhere we turn in the clinical literature, the post-traumatic hydra seems to grow a new head.

Ferenczi (1995) himself seems open, to me at least, to a more prolonged period of exploration, one which he himself was unable to undertake. He admits the severely problematic dimensions of the "astral" route of self-soothing, but is at the same time unwilling to give up on the fundamental conviction that clinicians should hesitate before dismissing the patient's post-traumatic generation of something angelic:

> The astral fragment helps the individual by driving it insane. For many cases there is no other kind of possibility, the last pass before death or suicide. Astra also produces dream images and fantasies of happiness [...] In addition to the capacity to integrate the fragments intellectually, there must also be kindness, as this alone makes the integration permanent. Analysis on its own is intellectual anatomical dissection. A child cannot be healed with understanding alone. It must be helped first in real terms and then with comfort and the awakening of hope. We must stop despising suggestion when faced with the needs of purely infantile neurotics. Kindness alone would not help much either, but only both together.
>
> (p. 207)

Intrinsic to the unconscious mind of the child (or adult child) who has survived serious developmental impingement or assault is, for Ferenczi, the unshakable hope that real help may be available in the form of radical recognition from some external source. In order for this recognition to "stick", to be properly integrated within the survivor's traumatised mind-body system, the unacceptability of what has taken place must in some way be framed or symbolised by a simultaneously kind and authoritative interaction, itself broadly supportive of the idea of linking phenomena that may in some way be transcendent or "fantastical". Kalsched (2013) expresses beautifully the potential of what could happen within a therapeutic relationship that's receptive to the traumatised (but not psychotic) patient's generation of mysterious linking symbols within the transference, when he describes an important shift in his work with a man he names Richard, whose dream of a dolphin "starts in a 'desolate' situation and ends with a numinous image of aliveness" (p. 64):

> The inner world also opened up, for both of us. He not only met something new from me. He also met something new inside himself. Our new experience *in relationship* brought a buried child and leaping dolphins out of his unconscious in a dream. These symbols of his liberated energy confirmed *the birth of new life inside him and the return of his soul*. I was also "re-animated" by his material. [Daniel] Stern's way of saying this is that in "moments of meeting" a transcendent dimension (*kairos*) intersects what is otherwise a one-dimensional linear progression of time (*chronos*). *Kairos*, he says, is a "coming into being of a new state of things…a moment of opportunity that escapes or transcends the passage of linear time (Stern, 2004: 7) [...] Between me and Richard, we could say that something from another dimension flooded into the space we created within the inter-subjective field.
>
> (p. 69)

Different people, different ways

My relationship with the films I'd begun to discover on videotape as a child in the late 1980s, immediately after my sisters' departures and my own attempted escape, crystallised through a seemingly irrational fascination with particular sequences or scenes, which I would watch over and over again. Oftentimes, these would be scenes of great tenderness and care, buried at the heart of a movie that was otherwise rather cruel. I loved the scenes of ambivalent caregiving in Brian de Palma's *Carrie* (1976) between Carrie (Sissy Spacek) and the reluctant gym teacher Miss Collins (Betty Buckley): the moment at the glittering prom among the stars, when Carrie grabs Miss Collins to hug her – in a weird visual echo of the time she grabbed her at the start of the film, naked and bloody and screaming – exercised a strange and slightly shameful fascination over me. I adored the sequence in David Cronenberg's *The Brood* (1979) that shows traumatised little Candy (Cindy Hinds) being escorted through the snowy Canadian wastes back to Dr Raglan's (Oliver Reed) "Somafree Clinic", a monstrous guardian-sibling on either side of her. One scene from a *non*-horror film that haunted me with comparable levels of intensity came from the opening few minutes of Hal Ashby's film, *Being There* (1979), a film I never really grasped or cared for in its totality, at least not as a child, but which I knew my father found inexplicably amusing. In the scene that obsessed me, Chance (Peter Sellers), a middle-aged gardener with learning difficulties, is being told by Louise (Ruth Attaway), the woman who has brought him his meals all his life, that their employer has just died and that she – a maid who has no formal responsibility for him – is leaving too. He will have to fend for himself. Chance doesn't seem to be listening to Louise. He seems fixated instead on the television show he was watching before she came into the room. The show is *Sesame Street*.

It's the episode in which Big Bird has gone into a lonely and resentful rage because of the arrival of the new baby, Cody. Big Bird has barricaded himself into his room, instructing Buffy, Susan, and the others not to bother him. Buffy [Sainte-Marie] manages to gain provisional entry into Big Bird's hideout, where she proceeds to sing him a song ("Different People, Different Ways") which she hopes will make it clear to him that he is still loved – and very much – but that baby Cody also requires love, a love which the adults may express with a heightened sense of urgency because of the infant's extreme vulnerability. Chance can't take his eyes off the scene from *Sesame Street* while Louise continues to talk to him and, all the while, Buffy's song to Big Bird – which gradually metamorphoses into a tender duet – can be heard over *his* scene, the scene from *Being There*, a scene which somehow *cannot* transform into something relational, at least not for Chance and Louise.

What used to make the scene so powerful for me, I think, was that even though emotional contact between Chance and Louise seems out of the question, some kind of unspeakable link *is* created between Chance and the long-ago television scene, and, in turn, between the long-ago television scene and me. Caregiving, blocked in the "real" world, must, as in a fairy tale (via the archetypal godmother), find an ingenious route of travel. It finds its way from Buffy's strange, hauntingly warm song, a musical scene from children's television embedded within a fictional film about an adult with the mind of a (dissociated) child. The song travels from Buffy's regretful, communicative heart to Big Bird's bruised and offended one; and, from their reparative, utopian world of *Sesame Street*, onward it journeys to the chilly world of Chance and Ruth; finally, from that filmic world of 1979, it flies into my attic bedroom, a decade later, in Birkenhead. The transmission of tender energy was allowed to take place, against all the odds.

I found myself wanting to watch the sequence again and again. The larger story of the television-addicted, idiot savant Chance didn't really grab me, at least not consciously; it was only much later that I would latch onto *Being There* as a whole object, in all its class-conscious, race-conscious, psycho-spiritual abundance. But still, that strange, early scene, of the abandoned Chance listlessly watching Buffy and Big Bird singing together, somehow served as a powerfully emotional reminder that I wasn't on my own, that real connections did exist.

It's impossible from watching only the *Sesame Street* scene in *Being There* to deduce precisely what is actually going on in the embedded scene with Big Bird and Buffy Sainte-Marie. The experience of watching Chance instead forces the viewer to absorb a string of what Laplanche (1987) might call "enigmatic signifiers", some visual, some aural flashes here and there, but flashes which combine to produce a very powerful feeling of sadness, curiosity, and wonder. It was only years later, trying to track down the full song on YouTube so that I could write about it, that I discovered the full scene from *Sesame Street*, from an episode first broadcast in 1977, the year of my birth. Reading some of the excited comments beneath the clip on YouTube (ЛУбНиН, 2013), I realised I hadn't been the only one to derive immense – and surprising – personal comfort from the scene. A user named "Fishbeast Productions" says: "I'm mildly obsessed with this, ever since seeing it on *Being There*", to which another user, named "Manu", replies: "Dude, I've had the same thing for a month now ever since I saw the movie. It's my go to getting high song, there's something cool in the vibe". A third user, "Jim Fields" adds: "Fucken [sic] exact same thing with me. It's such a weird minor key. It's happy and haunting at the same time and I saw it watching the movie and I then I had to hear it on YouTube. Thanks, God, for the internet!" The declarations of stunned recognition keep on being posted, with ever-mounting enthusiasm: "Welcome to the club!" (a user called "row"); "Same – holy shit!" ("Zachary Doyon"); "Me too!" ("peace love"); "Same here: amazing film and song" ("Moses Gavron").

The fantastical building of bridges

Why does this scene from *Being There* provoke such powerfully emotional responses in so many viewers? I don't think it's just about the situation it depicts. In my case, it's clear that the scene offered me, at the level of its manifest content, some unsolicited awareness about the traumatic losses I'd been obliged to sustain, as well as some previously intolerable knowledge about the theft of my own childhood, and the kinds of caregiving I myself had missed out on. But, as with the scene at the end of *Hilary and Jackie*, several other elements come together to create a sensation of vertiginous poignancy for *many* viewers, regardless of specific circumstances. The central role of Buffy Sainte-Marie's song, "happy and haunting at the same time", feels indisputable. There's something, for me, of Proust's (1996) "little phrase" in it, the sense of a musical communication, seemingly from another dimension, that is at once ineffable and inextricably connected to a deep feeling of vulnerable connection to another human being. For Swann in love, the haunting melody, the "little phrase", is mysteriously linked, musically, to an indescribable evocation of his perception of a real, human relationship with Odette, whilst simultaneously seeming to stand in for all relationality in the universe. The effect is cosmic, anaesthetic, synaesthetic: it unblocks constricted airways; *it actually helps Swann to breathe.* In the same way, that scene from *Being There* would make me gasp with simultaneous sadness and pleasure, connecting me somehow to a form of breathing that had been banished and blocked from the suffocated household in which I found myself for as long as I could remember.

But there's something else too, and this is the multi-tiered way in which Buffy and Big Bird's performance of vulnerable reconciliation is nested within *Being There*'s larger narrative. The nesting effect – the scene-within-a scene – heightens an experience of what I want to describe as a kind of *anti-traumatic bridge-building* in the mind of the viewer. Writing about the power of certain kinds of performance in the generation of a powerfully therapeutic "meaning-making" effect in film and in life, Bruce Eadie (2020) is concerned with the insertion of fictional interludes (often performed by the traumatised subjects of a film) within certain trauma-focused documentaries:

> These fictional interludes (or "fictional"-films-within-the-documentary) are not fictional in the sense of fictitious (untrue or a lie) but closer to fictive; they emerge from the imagination or perhaps the unconscious or are provocations that have the power to reconfigure understandings of what might be conventionally described as the "real" world. Perhaps better still, we could think of them as alternative frames of experience that interact with and modify other frames of experience which appear more straightforwardly non-fictional. It is the carrying over to documentary of one of the oldest literary techniques, the frame story or the story-within-the-story, where the inner story has the power to modify the outer story or to reveal a "truth" in the outer story that would not have emerged otherwise. It is in the dynamic encounter between the frames that insights ("truths" or meanings about a real non-fictional world) become available.
>
> (pp. 172–3)

Drawing on the potentially seismic function of both the play-within-the-play subplot in Shakespeare's (2006) *Hamlet*, and on the "baits of falsehood" extolled by Freud (1937) (referring to a different subplot in *Hamlet*) in his "Constructions in Analysis", Eadie explores the fascinating idea that where blankness or non-representable experience lie, it may only be via the careful planting and cultivation of "fictive" material *within* the larger frame of "reality" that a jolt of (sometimes bodily-experienced) meaning-making may be created in the psyche that observes at the intersection of the two dimensions. In the same way, when we find ourselves watching Louise – who is watching Chance, who is watching Buffy and Big Bird – we unwittingly take part in a series of *fantastically nested observations* that are taking place simultaneously between different media, different couples, and different generations.

The televisual scene of Buffy's caregiving in *Sesame Street*, embedded in the scene of Chance's spectatorship in *Being There*, embedded in the "real life" scene of video-watching in viewers like me, produces, I would argue, an even more profoundly intersectional jolt than the one evoked by Shakespeare, Freud, and Eadie. For the intersection is tripartite. Three different levels of the representation of abandonment come together, condensed through Big Bird and Buffy's duet, nesting one within the other. The effect is vertiginous in the manner of certain Russian doll narratives, not unlike some of E.T.A. Hoffmann's (2011) fantastical deployments of metalepsis in his *Serapion Brethren* fictions, or those created by Potocki (1996) in his dizzying *Manuscript Found in Saragossa*. The three bridges that are built *here* – between Buffy and Big Bird; between Buffy-Big Bird and Chance; and between Buffy-Big Bird-Chance and the viewer of *Being There* – feel, to me, like these quintessential Russian dolls, but also like the unconscious (re)construction, in the viewer's mind, of three (or even four) different generations, coming together to care for one another, through the sharing of different perspectives and times. A ghostly (great) grandmother (Buffy) emerges out of the past to talk to her adopted child (Big Bird) about abandonment and its reversal. A blank (grand)son (Chance) listens, fascinated, to his ancestors' magical song-dialogue. And a (great) grandchild/viewer struggling in the present, addressed by them all, takes part in this eerie conversation taking place between different levels of a newly discovered screen-family, all the while making unconscious links to his or her own tangled tower of generations. Mightn't such a film-facilitated gathering resemble a survivable journey, beyond familial deadness, through the revivifying "astra" evoked by Ferenczi and his followers?

Perezhivanie of the playworld

Certain films can feel enlivening in a way that feels palpably therapeutic – even without representing anything especially profound – to a troubled viewer struggling with the absence-presence of a panoply of familial ghosts. This kind of enlivening is experienced in the body, and it derives, I think, from the way the film's transversal and interlinking structures make a creatively insane use of overlapping worlds. The overlap triggers something madly alive, buried deeply within the viewer's psyche which, in a flash, becomes conscious of itself as coming back from the dead. There's a sequence in Jacques Demy's *The Umbrellas of Cherbourg* (1964) when Geneviève (Catherine Deneuve)'s mother (Anne Vernon) invites her daughter's suitor, Roland Cassard (Marc Michel), to the family home for dinner. Roland begins to sing – as is well known, this is a film delivered entirely through song – his backstory of a failed love affair with a young woman named Lola. As he sings, strangely familiar images (familiar, at least, to the cinephile) of an abandoned shopping arcade in Nantes suddenly start to cascade onto the screen. And we suddenly realise, in a crazy jolt of joyful recognition, what has happened: Demy has created a madly beautiful dream-bridge to his earlier film *Lola* (1961), a film in which Roland Cassard himself had been the protagonist.

With the delivery of Roland's song, the viewer has the weird sensation of travelling to a past life of sorts: the past Roland of *Lola* is glimpsed from the perspective of a future world in which everything is different, in which speech has been replaced by songs. And yet the two worlds are connected; they speak to each other; they communicate, via a privileged moment of magical, inter-filmic recollection. Something comparable happens in the insanely time-bending, Priestley-esque, portmanteau horror movie, *Dead of Night* (1945), when, in the film's terrifying, penultimate sequence, the hapless architect of the connecting frame narrative, Walter Craig, finds himself suddenly propelled *into* the individual stories of the various guests, each of whom has had a turn at telling a different unsettling tale of ghostly precognition. Watching that sequence in *Dead of Night* for the first time in my early twenties, I remember feeling as if I was high on some kind of trauma-shifting drug, in which the boundaries of self were being dissolved, not psychotically, but in such a way that it really was possible to make contact with the dream-worlds of others. I could be admitted, under special circumstances, into an apparently fictional landscape and, once inside that world, I could even *knock on the doors of the dream-worlds of characters living in there*. When, at the end of *Dead of Night*, Walter breaks into the world of the third story, and then keeps going, trying to gain access to the dream-story within *that* story – *"Peter! Let me hide in the room in the mirror!"* – I feel as if I'm witnessing the architectural construction of a link beyond language, a foray into what it might mean to travel into a woken-up ghost of a psyche that's finally allowing itself to be known.

Beth Ferholt's (2007 and 2009) pedagogical analysis of "film-play" in the study of imagination in work with children offers a helpful framework within which to try to understand what may actually be happening to viewers like me, when we experience moments such as Roland Cassard's sung *récit*, or Walter Craig's climactic darting through the dreams of the storytellers, with such a vertiginous sense of therapeutic boundary-dissolution. Ferholt analyses experiences of supremely dynamic aliveness – *perezhivanie*, as Vasilyuk (1984) names it – in children who are allowed to *play* with fictional figures and sequences that have magically left the confines of their ordinary framing narrative and have travelled into the "real" world. Later on, these children create their own play about their experience of the "playworld". Ferholt shows how these kinds of structured play-experiences offer children an opportunity for the growth of unknown or forgotten forms of psychical aliveness and internal regeneration:

> Through the children's play about the playworld, I also saw more clearly than ever before that it is in wild juxtapositions that this allegiance to the integrity of the "unreal" world, an integrity of that which appears to be outside the scope of consideration, is upheld. In children's play, embodiment of imagination does not depend upon set forms, but upon a truthfulness to an essence of the imaginary. And this truthfulness is found in the irresolvable contradictions which multiple perspectives reveal as they rub against each other.
>
> (2007, p. 11)

Earlier in her essay, writing specifically about the children's interactions with situations from *The Lion, the Witch and the Wardrobe*, Ferholt notes that

> The children began to stay in from recess and after school to sit in the White Witch's castle and recount the dreams they'd had the night before about Narnia and their classroom, or to draw pictures in which they saved members of their family who had died, or were deployed in Iraq, from the White Witch, or simply to spend a few extra minutes sitting on the floor of the wardrobe amongst the soft fur coats.
>
> (pp. 7–8)

In allowing ourselves – whether we are children, adults, or something in between – to experience the mind-altering borderlands *within* and *between* fictional landscapes, we may allow ourselves access to previously locked compartments of stories, dreams, and traumas that have been planted, without our permission, within the layers of our own psyches. I'm suggesting that there are eerily moving images that reveal not only the structure of the secret that a traumatised child-viewer has been carrying *for* a traumatised parent, but also the structure of a secret about the child-viewer's attachment *to* that traumatised parent. In the mysteriously moving reactions some of us may experience when "playing" with seemingly innocuous filmic "meta-" moments, such as the ones I've been describing in *Being There*, *The Umbrellas of Cherbourg*, and *Dead of Night*, we may be beholding the start of a process of intra-psychical excavation that has as much to do with the appreciative glimpsing of our own "ghosts in the nursery" (Fraiberg, Adelson, and Shapiro, 1975) as with our aesthetic admiration of an impressive cinematic display of metalepsis.

In the final section of this chapter, I want to consider some of the different openings I discovered through the repeated viewing, during my late adolescence and early adulthood, of two particular films, both of which have played important developmental roles for viewers, not only in their original historical context of production, release, and distribution, but also in the present day. I want to reflect on how I engaged with these films as audio-visual recovery rituals, conscious or unconscious, turning to them again and again, climbing into the ghostly nurseries they sometimes resemble, not in a spirit of ghoulish self-burial, but rather as a form of *astral excavation*, passing through the membrane of these films, as through a looking-glass, to retrieve fragments of my temporarily deadened child-self. I want to try to make emotional sense of my own use of these two sets of eerily moving images, over a number of years, seeking to articulate in as clear a way as possible how I was seeking to make visible my own panoply of internal ghosts. Something emerges, I think, about a child's glimpsing and grasping, in a privileged moment of aesthetic clarity, his parents' forgotten parents, his family's disavowed demons, and his own temporarily lost good objects. These films enabled a tripartite, time-travelling, transgenerational connection to be forged in the psyche of the receptive viewer I was starting to become.

You mean all this time we could have been friends?

Nemerov (2005), analysing the B-picture, *The Curse of the Cat People*, produced by Val Lewton in 1944, positions the movie in the same way he positions many of the deeply moving "horror" films Lewton made for RKO between 1942 and 1946, including *I Walked with a Zombie* (1943), *The Ghost Ship* (1943), and *Bedlam* (1946): as an eerily poetic meditation on social forms of grief and affliction prevented from making their way into public discourse in the United States during the period of production. Nemerov's focus, throughout his book on Lewton, is on World War Two, and the multiple forms it assumes in Lewton's dreamlike, overlapping film universes. In his exploration of *The Curse of the Cat People*, though, he pinpoints the film's preoccupation with a certain kind of marginalised child. How might the filmed consciousness of such a child shine a light on the darkened zones of disavowal perpetuated by the obsessively normative adults around her? The movie charts the unbearably touching friendship between Irena (Simone Simon), the ghost of a Serbian immigrant (whose tale of troubled, traumatised, racialised sexuality had formed the basis of the earlier film, *Cat People* (1942)), and a lonely little girl, Amy (Ann Carter), whose parents and schoolmates endlessly castigate her for her over-active imagination and penchant for daydreaming. Nemerov captures the politicised potential of Amy's capacity for friendship with Irena when he states:

> Only one character within the film recognizes the dead person's presence: the little girl Amy. Hearing Irena's song, she peers through the

frosted windows and prepares to go outside. Going out alone to meet Irena, she is the audience's surrogate, the only figure that can lead us to a confrontation with death [...] the otherworldly child who knows more than the adults, the little girl on whom Bing Crosby's blandishments of the home front – "Accentuate the Positive" – are completely lost. Children in wartime films often are not quite Americans, not quite fully assimilated to the wartime ethos of optimism and normal-as-can-be. Too imaginative, too curious, they sense the presence of death in ways that adults alternately busy with the eggnog and card games, the big-band soiree, or screwing that lug nut onto the fuselage of a B-24 found depressing and impolite.

(p. 38)

Amy is a six-year old girl who lives with her parents, Oliver (Kent Smith) and Alice (Jane Randolph), and their compliant Jamaican servant, Edward (Sir Lancelot), in Tarrytown in upstate New York. Amy is constantly getting into trouble with her parents, first, because of her tendency to daydream, and second, for her social exclusion by mocking classmates, for which Oliver blames her. Amy begins to look for other forms of emotional connection, eventually finding new relationships in two unlikely places. First, she begins to frequent the house of an aged, narcissistic actress, Julia Farren (Julia Dean), who lives with her adult daughter Barbara (Elizabeth Russell). Julia takes a shine to Amy, but refuses to acknowledge her own daughter Barbara, whom she claims is an "impostor". Second, Amy makes friends with the ghost, Irena. Irena is the spectral form of Oliver's dead first wife, the tragic anti-heroine of the earlier film *Cat People*. Amy knows nothing about either her father's first marriage to Irena or the bizarre events of the first film, which focused on Irena's belief that, if sexually aroused, she was in danger of turning into a large cat. Oliver is increasingly enraged by Amy's earnest insistence that she is now friends with a dead woman whom she never knew. Eventually fleeing the family home to seek refuge with Julia Farren, Amy is nearly killed by Julia's jealous, rejected adult daughter, Barbara; but she is saved when Irena's soul appears to merge with that of Barbara, visually announcing the possibility of alliance and solidarity amongst the film's three pathologised women: Irena, Barbara, and Amy.

When I discovered the strange universe of Lewton's 1940s B-movies in my late teens, I became instantly obsessed with their depiction of perversely neglectful environments that are inexplicably pierced by fantastical moments of connectedness, taking beleaguered protagonists and viewers into new emotional spaces from which there can be no return. I became fixated on sequences in which a world of intolerable – but normalised – deadness is pricked by a moving image of real horror; a horror that somehow gives rise to the flow of empathy. There's the moment in *I*

Walked with a Zombie (1943), when the naïve, white American nurse Betsy (Frances Dee) is confronted one drunken, sunny afternoon at a Caribbean café terrace by calypso singer Sir Lancelot's horrifyingly dreamy ballad, "Shame and Sorrow for the Family". In that instant, weirdly reminiscent of David Lynch's *Mulholland Drive* (2001), Betsy is forced to take in a musical communication of indigestible transgenerational trauma. There's the deranged sequence in *Bedlam* (1946), in which the wilfully apolitical heroine Nell (Anna Lee) is confronted in London's Vauxhall Gardens by the dreadful sight of the Gilded Boy's (Glen Vernon) painful death on stage for the amusement of depraved, upper-class spectators, including her own idiotic patron. And then there's that nightmarish scene in *The Seventh Victim* (1943), on the New York subway in the middle of the night, when wholesome protagonist Mary (Kim Hunter) must behold the sight of the man she's watched, just hours before, being murdered, now being propped up on the train, as if he were still alive, between two ghoulish devil worshippers who sit on the seat opposite her, acting as if butter wouldn't melt in their diabolical mouths. I found myself returning to these movies, and specifically to these dreamlike moments, again and again; they seemed to envelop me in something unspeakably warm. But of all the movies, including the original *Cat People* of 1942, it was *The Curse of the Cat People* that felt like it was shifting my experience of myself in the world. *The Curse of the Cat People* works towards the production of new alliances, new awareness, and new feelings that cannot be blanked out by the pathologically normative injunctions of the film's adult characters. Like Ferenczi's (1995) "wise baby", the child of trauma who intuits the source of the parental sickness that abuses and oppresses him or her, the child who has been forced, from infancy, to serve as his or her mad parent's psychiatrist, Amy is miraculously able to see into her family's unconscious and to make friends with its traumatised contents. *Through the figure of the ghost, Irena, a new and differently "dead" mother can be called, connected, and communed with.*

A third of the way through the film, Amy comes across a photograph of Irena in a drawer. Her mother, Alice, concedes that the woman is beautiful. She tells Amy that the dead woman's name is Irena; but she doesn't elaborate on Irena's identity, or on what she meant to her and Oliver in their traumatic pre-marriage story. When I first saw *The Curse of the Cat People*, this photographic revelation to Amy of an Irena who was supposed to have been erased but refuses to disappear was paralleled by *my* excitement at the dead Irena's unexpected and incongruous return from *Cat People*. Even though I'd seen Simone Simon's name in the opening credits, I couldn't actually believe that she'd be back. How could she return from *Cat People*? And in a film as different as this one? It was this unnameable thrill that I felt – the thrill of a new and yet familiar person returning to me in a way I couldn't possibly have foreseen – that the film takes and "runs with", in the form of what Amy does next. For Amy somehow recognises that, in Irena's illegal return to a space in which she has no leave to remain, something *real* is taking place; she recognises that her mother, Alice, is hiding something from *both* of them; and she recognises that it's precisely this poorly hidden thing that – if she can face it, connect with it, survive it – will bring her, Amy, into *aliveness*, the state that is refused by her parents. Running into the garden, she throws her ball, calls out Irena's name, and Irena appears to throw the ball back to her. This moment in the film always marked the start of the film's apparition to *me*; its meeting of *me*; its throwing a ball back to *me*. This was the moment the film came out of the darkness for me. This was the moment I recognised, with my body – not just my mind – that, in some strange way, I was starting to feel like Amy; and that the film, in some equally strange metamorphosis, was beginning to function fantastically for me, almost as if it itself were the ghost, Irena.

Patricia Polledri (2012) writes compellingly about post-traumatic mental states of lonely, adult enviousness, states that are always rooted in an intolerable childhood experience of isolation and emotional starvation. Describing her patient "Sally", Polledri writes: "Sally was left without a picture, or a symbol of herself, in relation to a life-sustaining object" (p. 69). *The Curse of the Cat People* achieved the miraculous feat of establishing Irena in both Amy's psyche *and* mine as nothing less than the viable representation of a life-sustaining object. During the sequences in which Amy and Irena begin to "bond" with one another, there's a wonderful evocation of the child's "encapsulated containerlessness" (as Polledri, following Gallwey (1991), names the post-traumatic situation of being left without an internalised, life-sustaining object) at last finding itself mended by the arrival of an adoptive parental object. This new foster mother is not only willing to serve as the child's emotional "container", but will underline and accentuate, in every conceivable way, the child's new *claimed, connected, coupled* identity, within a secure and stable parent-infant dyad. When Irena first utters the phrase "Amy and her friend" – this was the title Lewton originally wanted for the film itself – Amy is ecstatic: "Oh, I *like* the sound of that! 'Amy and her friend! Amy and her friend!'" And from this point onwards, every interaction between Simone Simon as Irena and Ann Carter as Amy seems to have been filmically constructed with the aim of creating in Amy – and perhaps also in the tragically "containerless" viewer – an internalisable representation of *child-self in relation to a containing parent-other*.

The sequences in which Amy and Irena play together in the enchanted back garden – Irena teaching Amy to count by means of fantastical numerical figures in the form of humans; Amy conversing with Irena about the different personalities of her three "children" (dolls); Irena sharing a mystical spell with a sceptical Amy; Irena lighting up the entire wintry garden with snowy sparkle – would envelop me with something that felt ineffably warm. It wasn't just sentiment, it wasn't just whimsy; it was like some sort of fantastical *wrapping* (cf. Anzieu, 2016) for my skinless psyche. Allowed to play with Amy in the company of her helpful, communicative, spectral guardian, I think I was gaining access to a powerfully reparative glimpse of "astral" recognition; and it really wasn't as complicated as all that.

The voice of love

There's already been so much written on David Lynch's work, especially his *Twin Peaks* creations, by both scholars and fans – the most significant, from a trauma recovery perspective, being Courtenay Stallings' (2020) book *Laura's Ghost: Women Speak about Twin Peaks* – that I'll keep these final thoughts on his film *Twin Peaks: Fire Walk with Me* (1992) very brief. I've long experienced the movie as some kind of monstrous child – or perhaps anachronistic ancestor – of *The Curse of the Cat People*; a close relative, in any case, who has seemed to watch over me with at least as much intensity as Lewton's B-picture. The story of Laura Palmer (Sheryl Lee), the spectral teenage focus of the original television series, *Twin Peaks* (1990–1), is well known. Found dead, wrapped in plastic, and floating downriver in the small, fictional, Washington town of Twin Peaks, Laura must have the mystery of her horrific murder solved by an idiosyncratically intuitive FBI agent named Dale Cooper (Kyle MacLachlan). The follow-up movie from 1992, *Fire Walk with Me*, constitutes what is known as a "prequel", and tells the story of Laura's last seven days alive. Very much like *The Curse of the Cat People* in relation to *Cat People*, *Fire Walk with Me* has a somewhat freakish connection to *Twin Peaks*, its "parent" text, belonging to an entirely different genre, and vibrating on a totally alternative frequency. The tone has shifted utterly, the old characters uprooted and relocated in what feels like a grotesquely transformed terrain. *Fire Walk with Me* has none of the "damn fine coffee" humour (if this is what it was) so prevalent in the often arch and self-consciously ironic television series, instead opening up, through a fearlessly sympathetic engagement with Laura's lived reality as the victim of rape and murder by her own father Leland, a Ferenczian portal into the world of horrific abuse within a patriarchal family unit. Furthermore, the movie offers us a fantastically transcendent dimension of reality, in which Laura's fragmented, traumatised self will either be annihilated or saved. Like Amy, Laura must negotiate a trauma-world of demons, angels, and eccentric messengers, which emerge out of an imaginal – but not imaginary – realm. When I first saw the movie in 1993, shortly after its release, I rejected it. I don't think I wanted to see so *mad* a revelation of the madness at the heart of a family.

But little by little, in my later teenage years, I began to let it in. As I did, the film began to work on me in much the same way as Lewton's "cat people" sequel, via precisely the same two elements of much-needed representation: a fierce recognition of parentally-buried phantoms emerging from the crypt; and the conjuring of forms of love and connection *beyond* the "encapsulated containerlessness" of Laura's traumatically-induced psychical state.

I began to allow *Fire Walk with Me* to take up residence inside my mind roughly a year after I saw it, around the same time as I first watched a comparable – but far less alive – film, *Looking for Mr Goodbar* (1977). Theresa (Diane Keaton), the young woman who's brutally murdered at the end of *Goodbar*, will never understand that the murderer *is*, in so many ways, her father. The toxically masculine dangers she runs headlong to meet in the addictive "singles' bars" are, in a way, eroticised embodiments of a danger she's known all her life: her father's misogynist hatred of her. *Looking for Mr Goodbar*, a slightly deadened (if still fascinating) movie, will never really *show* us this transpersonal connection between Theresa's father and the man who ends up stabbing her to death; nor does it seem interested in facilitating our thinking about such a disturbing link. But in *Fire Walk with Me*, Laura's fantastical recognition of what's happening to her *before it happens* felt to me as if it was being deployed in the service of the revelation of a profoundly emotional truth. Certain sequences worked on me – and still do – with the potency of a thunderbolt: Laura hiding in the bushes outside her house, watching in terror as she sees her father Leland emerging from it, an emergence that can mean only one thing: he *is* the rapist demon B.O.B.; they are one and the same; the split between the two entities she's been forced to construct in order to preserve her traumatised psyche from too much truth is just that, a construction, an artifice; and within the folds of *this* film, the split can be removed. The film forced – and still forces – me, along with Laura, to *wake up*, to face the reality of a horrific continuity that we'd prised apart in an earlier state of defensiveness, to keep ourselves from knowing the whole truth.

The penultimate sequence, featuring Laura's annihilation by her infanticidal, incestuous father Leland, showed me images I couldn't unsee. But rather than being traumatised (or re-traumatised) by these images, I think that I took them in as helpful pictures of a simultaneously archetypal and deeply personal familial horror. This won't have been the experience of everyone who watches *Fire Walk with Me*, which could be a "triggering" film for viewers who find the representations of abuse in the film too close – and perhaps too irresponsible – for comfort. It may be that it's precisely the absence of gendered mirroring between my experience and that of Laura – I'm not a woman and I've not been a victim of the kind of murderously sexualised violence to which she is ultimately subjected – that has allowed me to introject dimensions of the film's representations of horrified recognition as oddly comforting. I can only put it this way: when I watch certain scenes, I feel as if they are trying to help both Laura and me to engage in a form of thinking that's been silently prohibited. This form of thinking isn't, for me, about literally understanding either of my parents to be a rapist or a murderer, but rather about being willing to surrender to a new conceptualisation of my family – of my entire childhood situation – as being, in a way, *possessed*. The contortions of Sheryl Lee's face and body in the scenes when she gazes, appalled, yet freshly alive, at what she is now recognising in her father – in the bushes in front of the house, or at the dinner table when he tells her to wash her hands – felt, to me, like gifts to a representationally impoverished psyche. I was being offered a visualisation of grimaces that I already carried inside, invisible and in embryonic state; I simply needed help with carrying these appalled expressions all the way to the muscles of my face. It's the generosity of the film's audio-visual depiction of Laura's "cracking up" (cf. Bollas, 2011) that's stayed with me, accompanying me in difficult moments with no less warmth than the images of Irena in her joined-up play with little Amy.

The film's representations of emotional connectedness have managed to live in me with corporeal immediacy. The scene in which Laura begs her best friend Donna (Moira Kelly) *to confirm that she is indeed her best friend* is a scene that helped me to articulate, without embarrassment – and I truly believe for the first time – a truth about the desperate need for (and the possibility of) real loyalty and warmth between humans beings in trouble. When the Log Lady (Catherine Coulson) speaks enigmatically to Laura outside the Bang Bang Club about the existential repercussions of "this kind of fire" – and when Laura subsequently enters the club to listen to and weep before the song of the singer played by Julee Cruise – I've continued to feel that I'm being touched by communications that are travelling towards me from a place of genuine concern. I still do feel this. It doesn't matter to me what the intentions of the screenwriters or the director of the film were: the important thing is that the film's representations, its existence in the world, made me feel less alone. The fantastical bond the film establishes between Laura and Dale Cooper, the man who will later investigate her murder, is, of course, the ultimate bridge of caregiving between dimensions. The presence of Dale's extraordinary love and support in the universe, despite and beyond the horror of Laura's neglect and abuse, feels both indisputable and non-negotiable. Can *we* grasp the existence of this love and support, even as Laura herself cannot, at least not in this life?

Laura's last, long laugh in the film, after her death, when she finds herself in the Red Room with Dale and with other figures from the imaginal realm, plays out over a piece of music by Angelo Badalamenti entitled simply: "The voice of love". The scene begins with Laura and Dale looking at each other, eyes meeting in mutual recognition, him standing next to her. This isn't a connection that's either nameable or prescriptive. Slowly, Laura looks down, and her gaze becomes very serious; a deep sadness begins to enter her face. And that's when we see it: the birth of truly confident *insight* into what has taken place, manifesting on, flooding into her face. Badalamenti's music begins to rise; the light on Laura's face changes, becoming bright white. The angel that was lost earlier in the film – it simply disappeared from the picture in Laura's room – now returns, rather as Ferenczi (1995) tells us that the supernatural being he names "Orpha" appears to watch over the different fragments of the trauma victim. I watched this scene years before I'd read Ferenczi, of course, or even heard his name. Dale sees the insight on Laura's face; he watches her nodding head; he smiles and acknowledges that he can see what is going on for her. And then Laura begins to laugh, her head nodding with greater and greater insistence. For me, Laura's laughter in that incredible scene, her streaming tears *as* she laughs, and the birth, at last, of her *authority* over her own experience, conveyed a madly beautiful – and utterly necessary – recognition on the screen that was watching over me during my own adolescence of something in my own life that hadn't yet found its way into thought, feeling, or representation. I wanted to get up from my bed and touch the close-up of Sheryl Lee's face on my television screen, just like the boy at the start of *Persona* who gets up from his morgue-bed to touch the screen-face of Liv Ullmann.

Laura's authoritative laughter signified, for me, her recognition of her own ineluctable involvement in forms of transgenerational violence, trauma, narcissism, and abandonment, that will remain forever beyond the reach of perfect linguistic articulation. But just because something is beyond language does *not* consign it to a realm of non-representation. I was glad and grateful to *see* this kind of metamorphic recognition on screen; it served as an example; and Laura had to go through it before I did. Whilst Freudian and Kleinian forms of psychoanalysis tend to withhold the therapist's stated belief in a patient's stories of the harm done to them by their caregivers, often preferring to speak instead of the pathological manifestations of the patient's unshakable "grievance", films such as *The Curse of the Cat People* and *Fire Walk with Me* not only seemed to *believe* me: they made my own belief possible in the first place. More than that, they offered me forms of protection and encouragement without which I don't think I'd ever have made it to anything resembling a clear-sighted assessment, years later, in psychotherapy, of my past and present. It doesn't matter to me whether or not this assertion seems sane. The important thing is that it's true.

Chapter 3

May I be alive when I die!
Psycho-televisual regeneration six feet under: an audience study

I felt a funeral in my brain

For a long time, I wondered what *Six Feet Under* wanted from me. Could a television series actually *want* something from a person? It seemed unlikely. And yet I felt something somehow demanding about the characters – and indeed the entire universe of the show – every time I tried to make total sense of their comings and goings. It was as if the price to be paid for the comfort that each individual episode offered me was the strangely guilt-ridden feeling that I was also responsible for holding it all together afterwards. *Six Feet Under* is a "critically acclaimed", generically hybrid television series, created by Alan Ball. It ran from 2001 to 2005, mixing family melodrama, black comedy, art-house experimentalism, soap opera, and supernatural fantasy, following a small group of characters through a number of banal and borderline experiences over a period of five years. I was haunted by the worry that, no matter how much I thought about the series' characters and the world in which they existed, I could never quite do them justice, never give them the containing meta-representation within my mind that they needed and deserved. Mark Fisher (2016), writing about the fictional planet Solaris, captures some of what I felt about that show:

> What does Solaris want? Does it want anything, or are its communications better thought of as automatic emissions of some kind? What is the purpose of the visitors that it sends? You could almost see the planet as a combination of externalised unconscious and psychoanalyst, which keeps sending the scientists undischarged traumatic material with which to deal. Or is the planet granting what it "thinks" are the wishes of the humans, grotesquely "misunderstanding" the nature of grief, almost as if it is an infant gifted with great powers?
>
> (p. 115)

The sensation of a failed, quasi-Sisyphean *duty* towards imaginary, televisual creations felt, for me, especially intense towards the eerily fragmented character of Brenda, played by Rachel Griffiths. I felt, on repeated occasions, that I couldn't find peace until I grasped what it was that I was failing to fully understand about her. It was like being tormented by a riddle to which there was no answer. My misplaced guilt with regard to Brenda began in a strangely shame-laden way. I'd bumped into a colleague and her partner at the arts cinema in town. Somehow, we found ourselves discussing *Six Feet Under*, then (in 2005) in its fifth season, airing on British television on Channel 4, and drawing to its close. The thing was, even though the show had been running for five whole years, I'd only just started watching it properly. I'd caught an episode or two, here and there, possibly on French television in 2003, but I didn't really know who the characters were. I'd formed the erroneous impression that the character of Nate's (Peter Krause) first wife Lisa, played by Lili Taylor, was one of the main characters, and I was puzzled by her absence from this fifth season. "Who's this new character, Nate's new wife – Brenda?" I heard myself asking my colleague and her partner. "What's her story? Has she replaced Lisa?" My colleague smiled knowingly; but her partner didn't miss a beat. "*New* character?" he exclaimed. "Brenda's been in *Six Feet Under* for the past five years!" I felt embarrassed at my ignorance, but also confused. *How* could Brenda have been in the show since the first season? So she *preceded* Lisa? It didn't make any sense. But *why* didn't it make any sense? I felt my mind getting into a tangle, a familiarly "compulsive mentation" (cf. Sekoff, 1999, p. 113), frequently normalised among academics; it felt physically uncomfortable. Brenda tantalised me, both with her seeming refusal to be known, and with her strangely undead quality; she seemed to frustrate all my mental attempts at mourning or "closure". Years later, I'd link my "Brenda headache" to my mother's habitual, oddly triumphant exclamation at the height of any argument that had arisen from some misguided attempt on my part to try to engage emotionally with her: "You don't *know* me!" And, later still, her written command, printed in capitals, in a Word document chillingly entitled *The Last Straw* and attached to a business-like email – "I wish you all the best with your life, love and ambitions. But PLEASE DO NOT COME TO MY FUNERAL. Mummy" – seemed unconsciously designed to provoke in me an internal quest for meaning that would be both painful and frantic.

Inevitably, my new favourite object, *Six Feet Under*, died on me a few weeks after the conversation at the cinema with my colleague and her partner. I rushed out to buy the DVD box set, curious and excited to find out how the story had begun five years earlier, and by what curious twists and turns of character and narrative, we'd arrived at the final season entry-point at which I'd arrived. Just as my colleague's partner had foretold, I discovered Brenda, to my horror, in the opening episode. Unrecognisable as the lonely yet intermittently warm and genuine person I'd been fascinated by in the fifth season, in this pilot, I found an icy, pathologically narcissistic, dead woman. I think, in retrospect, that this shock of moving backwards, at rapid speed, from my experience of the sporadically "alive" Brenda at the end of the show, to the "corpse" Brenda at the beginning, may have structured my onward journey with the entire series. It all became, for me, about somehow making sense of Brenda's miraculous resurrection. So many aspects of the show felt impossibly personal to me, but this was the nub: the realisation that, in obsessively watching this programme, I was engaged, despite myself, and a full three years before my psychotherapy was to begin, in a televisual fantasy about a "dead mother complex" that gets somehow reversed. Trying to get hold of the alive-dead Brenda (daughter of a "replicant", her deliciously appalling psychotherapist mother in the show is played by the iconic *Blade Runner* star Joanna Cassidy) still feels slightly maddening, a task beyond my cognitive capacities. At the same time, it feels terribly important, like a dream I can't quite get hold of upon waking, but which needs, nevertheless, to be analysed against all the odds. This peculiar "duty" to re-assemble Brenda – together with her various fictional and meta-fictional, child and adult, alive and dead selves – in *Six Feet Under* is, perhaps, what led me to the research project of this chapter. I needed to know if other people – and not just academics! – were capable of becoming as painfully committed in their responses to the show as I had. At the same time, I wanted to know if other people also experienced that grateful sense of containment I'd so frequently felt *when I'd just let myself be held by an individual episode*, without worrying too much about solving the (non) mystery of the entire show.

Ghosts of our lives

Michael Eigen (2004), an analyst whose work has long sought to synthesise observations by Klein, Winnicott, and Bion in relation to his patients' repeated descriptions of their sense of diminished psychical aliveness, of feeling at least partially deceased, writes that "the sense of being dead has become a popular clinical theme. More people than in the past now seek help for feeling dead. Although feeling dead is a central complaint of many individuals, it is not clear where this deadness comes from or what can be done about it" (p. 4). The more I thought about my own electrified response to *Six Feet Under* in the autumn and winter of 2005, a time in my life when, aged 27 to 28, I really was starting to feel as if I might, in some strange way, have given up the ghost, the more I started to wonder if this television series itself might have constituted a strange kind of psychotherapy for the zombified viewer I then was, precisely by revealing, triggering, and offering a working-through of some of my own internal deadness. What if the deadness – both physical and psychical – around, between, and inside all the characters in the series was somehow generative of a form of new aliveness within this deadened viewer? My experience of watching *Six Feet Under*, together with some of the intensely "alive" reactions reported on the many fan postings on YouTube and on the HBO website, have led me to suspect that a radical *de-phantomisation* might have been effected in many viewers through their obsessive internalisation of the series.

Already back in 2005, long before I had begun my own therapy, or my training as a therapist, I was dimly aware that the way in which I was "feeding" on the show, at a time of great existential discombobulation, felt reminiscent of how I'd "fed", ten to fifteen years earlier, on films and videotapes, as a younger adolescent. I was also aware that the series was prodding – and, in some ways, reanimating – the "dead" psychical objects and relationships from childhood that were still moving inside me, although I didn't yet have the language to describe that process. The literal deadness around which the show obsessively turned (in the form of the corpses being prepared for viewing at the funeral home) seemed to provide concrete representation for the emotional zombification not only within the protagonists (variously explored as depression, addiction, dissociation, and other trauma-related conditions), but also still lodged, as-yet-unanalysed, within me. At times, it felt as if very powerful "shocks" from the Californian world of *Six Feet Under* were being sent to my world of the English East Midlands, shocks that were meant to awaken me to the sheer intensity of the trauma I was still carrying inside me. Ogden's (2017) patient, Ms L, exclaims to him during a session in which the two of them are enthusiastically discussing J.M. Coetzee's novel *Disgrace*: "There's something about what's happening *between* the characters and *in* the characters – no matter how awful it is – that is oddly right!" (p. 103). In the same way, the stuckness and suffering these characters of *Six Feet Under* underwent really was troubling to me at times – but it did feel *oddly right*.

One of the paradoxes inherent in my first experience of *Six Feet Under* was the way it appeared to offer me, when in a vulnerable and perhaps "regressed" spectatorial state, an experience of some sort of containment, precisely *through*, rather than despite, its seeming revelry in the representation of psycho-spiritual brokenness. I came to suspect that I was drawn to it in a child-like way, as a signifier of radical, pseudo-parental honesty – a bit like the monster in *A Monster Calls* – a symbol of trauma-related sensitivity that I was searching for, but had not yet found, in flesh-and-blood figures of authority. Speaking to others who'd seen the show, and who had reacted in comparably intense ways, I began to suspect that I'd not been alone in the sheer extremity of my response. Two key questions now quickly emerged for me. First: were these other people's reactions to the series invariably linked to earlier, possibly unconscious, experiences of abandonment and bereavement, which were now being made conscious and offering themselves up for processing? Second: had these people felt deeply, movingly *helped*, as I had, by the fictitious ghosts of *Six Feet Under*, or had they, on the other hand, felt abused or neglected by something spectrally insensitive, boring, or obscene? Throughout the series, ghosts from within the narrative are experienced in very different ways by the intra-diegetic humans who engage with them. Sometimes, they are felt as benevolent energies, wise, kind, and ineffably healing. At other times, the ghosts are persecutory, spiteful demons, goading the haunted individual towards self-hate, self-harm, or even self-destruction. On still other occasions, we find the ghost's effect on the person it haunts to be difficult to assess, perhaps seeming initially "positive", but soon afterwards feeling unhelpful, abandoning, disappointing, or bland. In the same way, real-life audience members can be affected very differently by engagement with this series *as* ghost. Not everyone is in the same emotional boat; not every crossing of the Styx is a positive one; nor is the "crossing" even necessarily experienced in so grandiose, mythopoetic, or archetypal a way. In this chapter, I try to understand just how "helpful" the fantastical ghosts of *Six Feet Under* might be said to have been to a community of real people, self-identifying as survivors of trauma, who have chosen to engage with the series. I also allow myself to document the acting out of my long-standing compulsion to achieve forms of intimacy with others by persuading them to watch and discuss moving images with me, a compulsion that lies, in part, behind the conception of this book.

Recognition of something real

Twenty years after the airing of its pilot episode, *Six Feet Under* finds itself intermittently lauded in both popular and academic culture, whilst never quite gaining the persistent, mainstream, hyperbolic recognition of shows like *Twin Peaks* (1990s), *The Sopranos* (2000s), or *Game of Thrones* (2010s). It's sometimes difficult to square this somewhat measured cultural response to the series with the earnest proclamations of many a fan that, despite having consumed vast amounts of television over the course of their lives, there is simply *nothing that compares* to *Six Feet Under* in terms of how much the show has personally affected their lives, or how much it's worthy of respect in simultaneously aesthetic and emotional terms. Having said this, there have been a score of excellent articles and chapters, both scholarly and journalistic, on the televisual legacy and intellectual implications of the series. Roughly half of these can be found in Akass and McCabe's (2005) important edited volume, which covers a wide range of formal, ethical, and political issues raised by the series, including its deployment of the fantastic, its engagement with self-help culture and the American Dream, and its representations of mothering. Many of the articles, both in and out of Akass and McCabe's book, focus specifically on the centrality of death, funerals, and mourning in the series' narrative. A large minority of the other articles concentrates on the ground-breaking ways in which the series represent women and gay or queer male characters.

Various exceptional pieces of writing on *Six Feet Under* draw out and explore diverse aspects of the show's trauma-soaked, sometimes barely articulable singularity, all engaging explicitly with the emotional and ontological dimensions of the series that push it into the realms of what we might call extreme aesthetic experience. Munt (2006) movingly captures the sheer enormity of the programme's impact on the viewer's sense of existing in the world:

> The last episode of *Six Feet Under*, containing the final sequences that show the accelerated lives of the main characters rushing toward their deaths, is unique in serial drama. These mini-narratives have no dialogue; they are staccato dream-like scenes that depend on the interpretation of a knowing viewer who can interpret the visual shorthand. They also address an audience who will record and replay the images in slow-mo on VHS or DVD, lingering on those speedy glimpses of the Fisher family futures. This is a unique breaking of form, showing the yet-to-be uncanny future, breaking the temporal frame of the series, opening up the future space, and the pluperfect tense. And with the death of *Six Feet Under* the viewer dies with it, her only enduring hope is to join HBO's community forum, on bulletin boards like "David and Keith"; the thread is still live, and the fans are still touching their imaginary friends.
>
> (p. 275)

Anderson's (2008) research on "post-traumatic television" singles out *Six Feet Under*, making clear that "its approach makes *Six Feet Under* the only text of this thesis that I contend does not deny or repeat trauma, but that rather attempts to work through it" (p. 98), noting elsewhere that "while *Six Feet Under* acknowledges the value of some aspects of psychology, it critiques traditional psychoanalysis as an absolute solution to weighty issues like trauma" (p. 110). Anderson concurs with my own pursuit of the therapeutic potential of the "eerie" when she writes that "*Six Feet Under*'s ghosts create the ideal counseling/confessional environment, a perfect opportunity for a discourse with the self" (p. 105). Shoshana and Teman (2006) develop, through careful exploration of the show's situations and characters, their intriguing concept of a "life-self" and "death-self" as sketched out among various paradigms of being, whilst Probert's (2019) psychoanalytically-inflected discussion of the representation of sex and sexualities in Season Two underscores the way in which *Six Feet Under* refuses to draw back from the depiction of an unconscious, post-traumatic kernel at the heart of a variety of different (but mostly compulsive) sexualised practices, relationships, and dynamics.

Relatively few of the pieces of published writing devoted to *Six Feet Under* directly investigate the cognitive, emotional, or ethico-political impact the show has made – and continues to make – on those viewers who engage wholeheartedly, even obsessively, with it. It's on this small body of audience-focused research that this chapter attempts to build. A short, autobiographical article, by Rosie Swash (2014), published in *The Guardian*, is candid in its admission of the powerful effect the series had on the writer: "Ten years ago, when I watched the show, I would often dream about the characters. There was something about *Six Feet Under* that got to me on a profound level. It was the same with the final scene [...] Somehow, for a moment, everything else seemed pointless". Rhiannon Bury's (2008) book chapter, based on close analysis of material posted on the *Six Feet Under* website fan page from June 2004 to August 2005, finds fans becoming immensely heated and hostile towards one another as a result of emotional disagreements over the notorious "That's My Dog" episode (4:5), in which David is abducted. And an article by Drew Grant (2011) documents how he turned to the show during a profound depression, following the end of a relationship:

> I went through the entire show in about a month and a half, which is actually a pretty solid feat, considering that the show had 63 episodes, each an hour long. I told my concerned friends calling to check up that I was fine, I was hanging out with my friend Brenda, or Claire. (Ha.) I ordered in Chinese at night, slept all day, told my parents I was sick, and continued to buy meds I wasn't prescribed from shady guys on Craigslist. I don't think I knew it at the time, but I was watching "Six Feet Under" in the hopes that I'd get depressed enough to kill myself. Fortunately, that's not the effect the Fisher family had on me. This dark little family who dealt with mortality every day, whose business was literally trading in death (including their own) slowly, over the course of those painful six weeks, taught me more about appreciating life than the past four years of my own had.

Walters (2011) teases out the racialised and gendered dimensions of "third-wave cultural activism" as they unfold on the series website's multiple and involved discussions of the various episodes' funerals. Brickman (2008) weaves together the different strands of specifically queer fandom as they emerge in response to various characters on the show. Schiappa, Gregg, and Hewes (2004) demonstrate that viewers who've engaged closely with the series have been changed at a profound level in terms of their attitudes towards death and dying. Bacle (2016) explores the way in which she used the show to help her mourn the death of her brother. Finally, Amber Segal's (2016) remarkable dissertation focuses on "generative mourning in a fragmented world" (p. 2). Segal, who dedicates her essay to her two older brothers, "for not being David or Nate" (p. 2), uses *Six Feet Under*'s multiple representations of art and creativity as intra-diegetic responses to death and dying, in order then to pose, at least implicitly, the question about what it might mean for real-life spectators to introject, creatively use, and *mourn* the show itself, drawing on Freud, Klein, Segal, and Winnicott to construct an exploration of the "potential space created by the cultural experience of watching television", which then "allows for a creative relationship between the object and its audience" (p. 3).

Tales from the Fisher & Sons Funeral Home

It may be helpful for the reader who has never watched *Six Feet Under* to have a sense of the narrative that unfolds over its five seasons. Each season is divided into twelve or thirteen episodes of around 50 minutes, and there are 63 episodes in total, the finale running for 90 minutes. In the opening episode, Nathaniel Fisher (Richard Jenkins), the 50-something owner of Fisher and Sons Funeral Home in Los Angeles, is killed on the afternoon of Christmas Eve 2000, when a bus crashes into his hearse. He was on his way to pick up his eldest son, Nate (Peter Krause), from the airport. Nate, unaware of his father's death, has just met a woman named Brenda (Rachel Griffiths) on the plane from Seattle, where he lives. Upon arrival in Los Angeles, they have sex immediately, in an airport store cupboard. Nathaniel is buried by his three children Nate, David (Michael C. Hall), and Claire (Lauren Ambrose) and his widow Ruth (Frances Conroy), but his mourning by the family seems, in some strange way, perennially half-hearted and incomplete. Instead, his ghost appears on a regular basis to the various characters, sometimes helping them to make sense of emotional and existential quandaries, but at other times merely tormenting them.

Nate, originally intending to be back in Los Angeles just to spend Christmas with his family, ends up staying permanently, joining his younger brother David in the day-to-day running of Fisher and Sons, and pursuing what feels at times like an oddly masochistic relationship with Brenda, an intellectually intimidating and emotionally avoidant massage therapist, the daughter of narcissistic psychotherapists and, in childhood, the literally barking subject of a well-known pop psychology book, *Charlotte, Light and Dark*, which purported to analyse borderline personality disorder in a young girl. Brenda has an intensely co-dependent relationship with her younger brother, Billy (Jeremy Sisto), who has been diagnosed with bipolar disorder, and she has shelved many of her life projects in order to be emotionally available to him. Nate's own younger brother, David, finds himself in an initially secret, and perennially turbulent, relationship with a local policeman, Keith Charles (Mathew St. Patrick). Keith oscillates disconcertingly between brittle personae of near-saintly supportiveness and frighteningly persecutory authoritarianism. In his role as a (Black) member of the Los Angeles Police Department (and later as a security guard), he has a tendency to explode violently. Exonerated for his "good shooting" of a young Black man, he is later fired from the LAPD for his brutal beating of a white man. The youngest Fisher sibling, Claire, who is in her final year at high school, attempts to navigate her status as school misfit and family "lost child", whilst finding herself in a series of short-lived relationships with variously unstable or unreliable boyfriends. The mother of the family, Ruth, who has been having an affair with her hairdresser Hiram (Ed Begley Jr.) during the last years of her marriage to Nathaniel, tries to find out who she is outside of her dying identities of wife and mother. And the funeral home's embalmer, Rico Diaz (Freddy Rodriguez), a young Latino man who was taken on by a paternal Nathaniel when he lost his own father – but is resented by David for a whole host of reasons – struggles to achieve the respect within the all-white Fisher family business he feels he deserves. All the while, the corpses being treated at the funeral home refuse to keep quiet. So does the frequently returning ghost of Nathaniel Fisher.

Over the course of the five seasons, we witness a series of developments in the lives of Claire, Ruth, David, Keith, Nate, Rico, and Brenda. Some of these developments are slow-burning and, in televisual terms, extremely subtle; others strike both characters and audience with a dramatic, even cataclysmic force. The series communicates the emotional intensity of all these developments with a mounting psychological and spiritual seriousness that transcends – and, in some ways, tramples on – the knowingness, irony, and cynicism of many of the jaded characters themselves. At times, the sheer enormity of these eruptions of traumatic experience may feel overwhelming, or even poisonous, to viewers; at other times there may be something eerily comforting about the unflinching way in which the series presents the almost sublime dimensions of breakdown and loss. Ruth's series of relationships with emotionally unavailable men takes us more and more deeply into a kind of bottomless despair; when she finally meets and marries the academic geologist George Sibley (James Cromwell), only to discover some months later that he suffers from psychotic depression, something inside her character breaks. Claire goes through an analogously soul-destroying set of narcissistic partners. At last seeming to find a loving partnership with a college friend Russell (Ben Foster), she seems to hit a nadir when Russell sexually betrays her with their toxic and controlling art lecturer Olivier Castro-Stahl (Peter Macdissi). She terminates the pregnancy she and Russell have just co-created, briefly attains some fleeting recognition as a talented artist-photographer, before falling into a worldly, drug-fuelled personality disintegration.

Keith and David struggle and fight their way through every season, entering couples counselling after just a few months of living together, and losing custody of Keith's niece Taylor (Aysia Polk), whom David has tried in vain to rescue from Keith's emotionally neglectful mother and physically dangerous father, following the imprisonment of Keith's drug-addicted sister Karla (Nicki Micheaux). Just as Keith and David seem, in the fourth season, to be establishing some form of relational equilibrium, David is brutally tortured and nearly killed by a young man he flirtatiously picks up on the highway, Jake (Michael Weston), and subsequently struggles with severe post-traumatic breakdown. Rico's wife Vanessa (Justina Machado) falls into a deep depression following the death of her mother, and he endangers their relationship by pursuing an erotic dancer named Sophia (Idalis DeLeon). Nate's relationship with Brenda undergoes a strange set of metamorphoses, as they find themselves going to increasingly ruthless measures to protect their inner core of vulnerability from the gaze of the other. As her ego becomes more and more bruised from emotionally abusive interactions with her brother Billy, father Bernard (Robert Foxworth) and, above all, mother Margaret (Joanna Cassidy), Brenda becomes increasingly addicted to sexual encounters with anonymous people – mostly men, but on one occasion a married man and woman and, on another, a pair of teenage stoner boys. She blames her descent into addiction on her brief friendship with a sex worker shiatsu client named Melissa (Kellie Waymire), explicitly refusing to address the potential role played by her own complex childhood relational trauma in her compulsive behaviour and unshakable sense of emptiness. Meanwhile, Nate is so terrified of revealing his discovery of a potentially fatal brain condition to Brenda that he retreats further and further into secrecy and emotionally withholding behaviour. Visiting an old friend in Seattle, on a trip to collect a body, he has sex with this friend, a woman named Lisa (Lili Taylor), apparently causing her to fall pregnant with a baby girl. The relationship between Brenda and Nate implodes in horrible acrimony when he discovers her secret sexual life. Nate abandons Brenda, survives brain surgery, develops mild pre-cognitive dreaming capacities, and subsequently marries Lisa. Brenda hovers tantalisingly on the periphery, entering 12-Step Recovery for sex addiction, whilst remaining resistant to the core concept of a "higher power". Some kind of ungraspable intrigue between Brenda and Nate persists.

When an increasingly jealous, desperate, and ego-depleted Lisa suddenly disappears, her body surfacing months later, inexplicably drowned, her ghost hovers over the reunited (but still disconnected) Nate and Brenda, who eventually marry, only to descend into explicit, mutual hatred once she becomes pregnant and, for the first time, both emotionally and physically available for regular relating. Nate becomes interested in Quakerism, has sex with George's Quaker daughter Maggie (Tina Holmes), and promptly dies from his brain condition. He and David, asleep in the hospital room next to him, dream the same dream of Nathaniel Sr. during the final minutes of his life. Nate's ghost will haunt Brenda and their newborn baby girl, taunting her for her unhealed trauma and resistance to spiritual surrender; eventually, however, both he and Nathaniel Sr. appear to Brenda in a spirit of apparent benevolence and reconciliation. She continues her training as a cognitive behavioural therapist, cares for Nate's two daughters, and sells her inherited part of Fisher & Diaz (as the funeral home has become) to Keith and a partially recovered David, who have now become adoptive fathers to two young Black boys, Anthony (C.J. Sanders) and Durrell (Kendré Berry). Ruth, separated from but on amicable terms with George, spends increasing amounts of time in the heavenly Topanga Canyon with her friend Bettina (Kathy Bates) and her formerly estranged sister Sarah (Patricia Clarkson). *Six Feet Under* ends with a grief-stricken Claire at last leaving home, driving in a new car (her trademark hearse having been destroyed in the penultimate episode) to start a new life in New York, fragmented visions of the future lives and deaths of Ruth, Keith, David, Brenda, Rico and herself flashing on the screen as she travels her unknown path.

Transformations at the soul level

There's a man on YouTube (Ashley, 2014) who has recorded his unfettered emotional response to the last six and a half minutes of *Six Feet Under*. The camera, placed squarely and unflinchingly on his bearded, white, bespectacled face, captures his gasps, muffled screams and tiny, horrified guffaws; a stream of tears runs unstoppably down his cheeks. Meanwhile, underneath, the comments roll in. A commenter named "A.T." writes: "Every few years I watch the final episode of *Six Feet Under*...those final 6 minutes to reorient myself...to remind myself that life is truly miraculous...to hold tight to it and fight for it. Cherish it. 'You can't take a picture of this... It's already gone'". Another commenter, "Tara Sigidi", says: "My 13-year-old remembers me bawling like a baby while watching...she was 3 and kept saying 'What's wrong Mommy? Why you crying?' I couldn't compose myself to explain why...man, I will never forget the first time I saw the finale". Tara's comment has, at the time of writing, received over a hundred likes and two replies. The first, from "Nathan Giovani", posted three years after the original comment says simply: "Tara Sigidi same!" The second, from "Garrett11111", a year after "Nathan Giovani", says: "Me neither. It had just ended and my roommate came home and I was sitting there sobbing. I had to go up to my room to properly finish crying hard". The comments steadily continue beneath this YouTube post, in as seemingly unending a stream as the tears of the original bearded, weeping poster. Somebody named "figurehead1971" says: "It is testament to the characterisations of this show that we all bawl like babies upon watching it. Any show worth its salt draws the viewer in to have feeling for its characters, but none other than *Six Feet Under* wrenches at your soul if you ask me". Four years later, "figurehead1971" receives a reply, from "My Pet Crow": "See, that's the thing. It's as if SFU changed me at the soul level".

The purpose of this chapter is to try to give words to individual and collective transformations by *Six Feet Under* of human lives "at the soul level", as "My Pet Crow" so poignantly puts it. The hundreds of people reaching out to one another on the internet to share their feelings about not only the last six and a half minutes of *Six Feet Under*, but also about the years they have lived (and continue to live) with the other 63 hours of the series, constitute a community bound by shared obsession. The narrative of *Six Feet Under* itself revels, from start to finish, in the careful exploration of its human characters' seemingly inexplicable, soul-transforming attachments to various haunting objects. Sometimes these objects are ghosts, that is, manifestations of people who have physically died. In many episodes, Rico, David, and Nate, the workers who not only transport, prepare, and embalm the corpses, but also counsel and joust with the surviving friends, family, and community of the deceased, find themselves in frequent supernatural dialogue with the suddenly lively cadavers. Key protagonists – Nathaniel, Lisa, and Nate – also die in the course of the show, reappearing in spectral form to converse with the living. Nearly always, the haunting is presented as an opportunity for both parties, living and dead, to "work through" an unresolved emotional, spiritual, or somehow relational issue together. Often, though, the thing that haunts and helps the struggling human characters in *Six Feet Under* is an eerily potent cultural artefact. The lonely, middle-aged widow Ruth is granted one celestial evening of seeming "togetherness" with her erotically inaccessible, "on-the-spectrum" love-object, Arthur (Rainn Wilson), when they watch the cult science-fiction film *Silent Running*, 1972 together. A group of emotionally inept comic superhero fans who have lost one of their number – he is crushed, Leonard Bast-like, by a bookcase full of his own comics – play out their intense love, hatred, and envy for one another via the transitional object of an especially prized first edition. The siblings Brenda and Billy, who have sustained significant psychological damage through prolonged exposure to their narcissistic father and mother (both of whom, the series repeatedly reminds us, are corrupt psychotherapists, originally female patient and male analyst), find themselves fascinated and contained, for many years, by their shared attachment to a series of children's books, *Nathaniel and Isabel*. This series offers the siblings not only narratives and characters with which to identify, but also serve as the culturally legible cornerstone of their indescribably intense trauma bond with one another. Brenda has had the name "Nathaniel" tattooed onto her back since her youth; Billy, bears the name "Isabel" on his.

The importance of the *Nathaniel and Isabel* series (an invention of the writers of *Six Feet Under*) for Brenda and Billy is introduced early in the first season, but *Six Feet Under* never gives up, throughout all five of its seasons, on an extraordinary commitment to the exploration of how human beings in desperate circumstances turn, as both creators and consumers, to fundamentally haunting forms of cultural production for the sake of their psycho-spiritual survival. It's almost as if the creators of the show were anticipating that, just as their protagonists depend, with utter desperation, upon the guardianship of ghosts, in the same way, some of the fans of the series itself would turn to *it* for a primitive kind of care. The show is obsessed with dangerous authority figures who try to block the protagonists' access to natural and spontaneous creativity: Brenda's intrusive analyst from childhood, Dr Gareth Feinberg (Jed Allan); Claire's grotesquely abusive art lecturer, Olivier Castro-Stahl; Lisa's controlling and infantile employer Carol (Catherine O'Hara); Keith's megalomaniacal pop star boss, Celeste (Michelle Trachtenberg); the list could go on for much longer. There remains, though, a constant, whispered injunction to the harried, harassed, infantilised protagonists – and to the viewer – to remain receptive to a higher, perhaps fantastical authority, one that might be capable of overruling the narcissism of these pathetically worldly commandants.

Hatching a positive plot

There's a moment in Claire Denis's extraordinary 1990 documentary *Le Veilleur* ("The Nightwatchman"), about the filmmaker Jacques Rivette, in which Serge Daney asks Rivette about his experience of solitude in the intermittently withdrawn life that he apparently lives. Daney is intrigued by the way in which Rivette's films seems to explore people who are anything *but* lonely: characters caught up instead in passionately bizarre experiences of relationality, and intense, often mysterious interactions with one another. Something seems to be getting played out, Daney suggests, in which the human and spiritual connections that Rivette finds difficult to realise in "real life" are brought to fruition in the imaginary, filmic dimension. Rivette responds by telling Daney about the letters he receives from all over the world, often years after a given film has been released, in which people tell him of the extraordinary effect a particular movie has had on their lives. One such letter that sticks in Rivette's mind arrives from a young girl in California. Even before reading the letter, Rivette sees a sign, the letter-writer's playful and iconic announcement that the subject of her communication will be his 1974 film *Céline et Julie vont en bateau*: a red handprint on the back of the paper. Rivette is moved to speak of the radical individuality with which each person expresses their movie-attachment; but also of the existence of a virtual international community that emerges around the shared love of a film: "une société secrète très diffuse" ("a highly diffuse, secret society"), organised around "un complot positif" ("a positive plot"). Rivette could be described as the "night watchman" of this secret society, a sporadically non-relational filmmaker, making strange movies about highly relational ghosts, oddballs, and post-traumatic conspirators, who, once the film has been completed, curates the communications of a spectral crew of souls who have been inexplicably drawn to his eerie signals.

Rivette's characterisation (both in these comments and within so many of the narratives of his films themselves) of such obsessive communities as quasi-mystical groups organised around a "positive plot" is one I find resonant for the "secret society" of the fans of *Six Feet Under*. The siblings

Brenda and Billy Chenowith in *Six Feet Under* form a Rivettian "secret society", organised around a "positive plot": the ritualised detoxification of their parent-tainted souls. As is the case in a number of Rivette's films, and as is the case for Brenda and Billy, for the haunted, receptive viewer of *Six Feet Under*, a connected network of ghosts living within an apparently fictitious frame begins to cast a strange glow over the often fragmented network of ghosts living inside the viewer's "lived" life. The viewer finds themselves helplessly "drawn in" more and more. The ghosts inside the fictitious frame talk and talk and talk; they will not keep quiet. Meanwhile, the mesmerised viewer begins to change in unforeseen ways. Their changes, unbeknownst to them, are mirrored in the changes of other haunted viewers who are watching the same ghost-show. This community of viewers – this "secret society" – do not necessarily interact "in the flesh", but instead its members touch each other spectrally: on the ghostly stage of the comments section of YouTube, for example; and in the pages of this chapter.

The *Six Feet Under* research project

My research project involved asking twelve unpaid volunteers, all of whom identified in some way as having struggled with trauma-related issues, to watch (or re-watch) all five seasons of *Six Feet Under* over a period of five months, from September 2018 to February 2019, staying in touch with me on a weekly basis, by phone or by email, to free-associate about their week-to-week emotional experience of the show. I wanted to find out how these people were "using" *Six Feet Under*, in the Winnicottian (1971) sense, consciously or unconsciously, as a psychical object associated with emotional revelation and healing, as opposed to "just" escapism or entertainment. I wanted to find out if the fictional universe of the show could be tangibly demonstrated, through discussion, to be a helpfully therapeutic televisual intervention for viewers suffering from conditions of anxiety, depression, and various kinds of developmental trauma disorder, or even just people who sometimes felt overwhelmed by the conditions of their everyday existence.

In the discussion that follows, paying attention to a diversity of attachment styles, I engage seriously with some of the users of this series' fantastical world. The emotional importance for the participants of particular characters, narrative arcs, settings, and sequences is assessed, together with the impossible-to-ignore paradox of the show's often potentially re-traumatising use of violence and cruelty. Whether or not a genuine psychical de-toxification can be said to occur through interaction with the moving images of *Six Feet Under* is the serious question at the heart of this chapter. I asked the participants to watch two to three episodes per week, preferably not "binge-watching" (cf. Bainbridge, 2019), but instead trying to use each episode a little bit as one might use a therapy session, a Recovery meeting, a religious or spiritual service, a conversation with a close friend, or other some other form of interaction in which one might reasonably hope to feel less distressed or alone. I let them know that I was particularly interested in how their viewing each week helped – or didn't help – in the processing of their own problems, especially problems related to long-standing trauma. I told them that I was interested in points of identification and non-identification (e.g. around class, family, community, race, gender, sexual orientation, spirituality, disability), but also in feelings of joy, sadness, rage, annoyance, exclusion, inclusion, embarrassment, excitement, and any other kind of emotional (as opposed to intellectual) response they might have to the show. I asked if they'd be willing to share any dreams or daydreams the show might have stirred in them. Finally, I made it clear that I wanted to know if they felt indifferent or irritated or disappointed by a particular moment, scene, episode, season, or indeed the entire series, or annoyed that they'd agreed to take part in this project (which they were free to abandon at any point). I wanted to know if they felt as if they'd wasted their 50 minutes on a particular episode; or if, conversely, they felt they'd done something which in some way may have been helpful to them; or whether, perhaps, they felt a combination of these feelings.

In the end, the twelve participants grew to fourteen. There was a reasonable diversity in their demographics: they covered a spectrum of ethnic groups (including Black British and North American, British Asian, White British, and Eastern European, though not "mixed race"); sexual orientations (including lesbian, bisexual, gay male, and heterosexual); genders (including non-binary, cis female, and cis male); classes (including working class, middle class, and mixed class backgrounds, but not upper class). The category of religious/spiritual backgrounds was the most limited, with roughly half of the participants *not* identifying themselves in terms of religious belonging, a third alluding to a *non-specific* spiritual orientation, and the remaining participants identifying with broadly Christian (but not Muslim or Jewish) beliefs. Doctoral candidates and academics were over-represented, comprising just under half the group. It feels important to note, finally, that six participants watched the series, at least in part, as couples (two romantic, one platonic), and their experience of the implications of participation *for their coupledom* is reflected in some of what they have shared. All of the participants who watched the series as part of a couple, either platonic or romantic, noted that their attachment to the viewing experience was impossible to disentangle from their experience of being in relationship with the other person.

In the case of a participant named Bee, watching *Six Feet Under* with her housemate created a deepening sense of intimacy and connection between them: the show started to be felt as a relational container for the friendship:

> Overall, I have really enjoyed watching this this week, and especially enjoyed watching it with someone else, it brings an additional sense of

shared enjoyment, and connection with another person. In this instance, it is someone I share a home with, and it provides a way for us to enjoy spending time together. I also like the fact that in doing so we are helping someone with a research project. It's a WIN for everyone, so far.

A few episodes later, Bee notes that this play in the presence of another is proving so nourishing as a regular object-relating experience, that it has begun to supersede the "real-life" pursuit of a romantic partner:

My housemate and I already planned ahead during the week that we would watch this episode together on Sunday evening. It was a great thing to do, as running a retreat was hard work, and it was good to have a plan of something to do at home that involved relaxing (often I may get home and switch the computer on and just end up spending the evening doing crap like looking at Facebook which is diverting but ultimately not very relaxing somehow). I had been on a date with a man on Saturday but decided to go home early as my housemate and I had planned to watch *Six Feet Under* together. I was joking to my date that, seeing as my housemate can now make me a perfect cup of tea, I really don't need a man at all. I think watching the TV series together has improved our sense of household togetherness. I think, when we finish *Six Feet Under*, we will probably start something else, as it's become a good thing to do together.

Meanwhile, a participant named Donna reflects movingly on anxieties that arise within her as a result of watching the series as part of a couple, with her partner Robin:

Because 6FU is something Robin and I both like, I have been using it to some extent as a bonding exercise with him. I know if we watch it together that we will have shared moments of recognition and laughter and that the show will raise issues that we'll find it interesting to discuss with each other afterwards. The episodes in the latter half of the series did spark some conflict between us, though. This was particularly around the storyline of Billy's mental breakdown. Due to our real-life experiences, Robin and I both had different reactions to it. I felt quite connected to this storyline through Brenda, because her struggle to cope with the guilt of putting herself before rescuing Billy is familiar to me. When I told Robin this, he could absolutely see why that would be, but reiterated that, from his point of view, he didn't think that aspect of the show really spoke to him. I was frustrated because I wanted him to engage with my feelings about it, and his swiftness to reiterate his own experience made me feel like he was disinterested in mine. I'm aware that this may have been unreasonable on my part, because he spends a lot of time engaging with my experience of life and supporting me. But that's how I felt in the moment when we were discussing it.

Bainbridge (2019), analysing the psychodynamics of "binge-watching" television box sets, either alone or as part of a couple or group, notes that

> binge watching ironically also sustains relatedness in an era when loneliness is never far from the headlines. The "Netflix and chill" phenomenon is a playful means of establishing flirtatious, sexualised relationships with romantic partners, and there is an emerging etiquette of couple behaviour around shared viewing of box-sets, such that watching episodes alone is seen as a rebuff to one's significant other, a greedy form of selfishness that communicates a lack of commitment to intimacy. That binge watching can bring people into contact with others engaged in watching the same material, whether this involves contact with people in the same room, or with others in the virtual spaces of social media, must also be acknowledged.
>
> (p. 77)

The participants in my study who watched *Six Feet Under* as part of a couple seemed to note the "relatedness" of their experience almost as much as they registered the content of the series itself and its impact on their individual psyche. Many of the participants, both single and in couples, furthermore reflected positively – and frequently – about the pleasant psychical effect produced in them through knowing that other people, even people they didn't know personally, were simultaneously engaged, for the few months of the study, in the same viewing patterns as them.

Latching on

Reflecting on his re-watching of the pilot episode of *Six Feet Under*, several years after his first experience of the show, Robin told me:

> Since the first time I saw it, I'd been aware that *Six Feet Under* was the best TV show of all. Quite easily so. What I had forgotten, or not previously noticed, was how miraculously complete the world portrayed in the first episode is. I started watching the episode in an extremely bad mood and ended it in a significantly better one. A more relational mood. It felt as though what I was watching was not as complicated and convoluted as the relationships in my own life, but that it captured the spirit of how real life is. The frequent, almost casual outbursts of contempt, embarrassment, bemusement and anger that characterise interpersonal relations. The episode is full of moments that strike a chord, one after another after another. Most of all, watching the first episode

made me feel that little bit less lonely, and more willing to believe in the possibility of communication. And the beneficence of the universe. The show understands how the capacity for joy is inextricably linked to the capacity for sadness – I've not seen that elsewhere. It's conceived by people who actually understand what joy is and what sadness is. *And* it's funny. These are the things that keep me coming back.

Six Feet Under, at its best, seems to be capable of generating images that function for the viewer as a longed-for symbolisation of hitherto inexpressible emotional experience. At very special moments indeed, this experience of being offered a representation of experience one didn't know could be represented would appear to result in a strengthening of the viewer's sense of self and a lessening of the viewer's feelings of existential isolation. Anzieu's (2016) description of the therapeutic evolution of a "film of dreams" within the traumatised psyche starts to feel appropriate:

> The wrapping of anxiety (the first defence, which works through affect) prepares the way for the film of dreams (the second defence, which works through representation). The holes in the Skin-ego, whether produced by one major trauma or an accumulation of micro-traumas [...] are transformed by the work of representation into theatrical locations in which the scenarios of the dream are played out. The holes are thus stopped up with a film of images that are essentially visual [...] Zénobie's dreams helped her weave a psychical skin to replace her weak protective shield [...] I felt as if her dreams were hovering above her and surrounding her with a bower of images. The wrapping of suffering was being replaced by a film of dreams that made her Skin-ego more firm and consistent.
>
> (pp. 242–7)

Rignell (2017) has examined the possibility of our "using" certain films as if we'd regressed to infancy, suggesting that the moving image may lovingly offer itself to the spectator-baby in us who is "on the brink of unbearable anxiety". In a related vein, Bellour (2009) seizes upon the observational work of Stern (1985) to claim a direct analogy between the "hypnotised" film spectator and the desperately relational pre-verbal infant. For my own part, trying to find words for my own peculiar attachments to specific artworks, I've attempted to sketch out (Asibong, 2015b) a post-Bowlby discourse of "disorganised attachment" to explain the strange satisfaction I'd sometimes been afforded by certain representations of broken and fantastically repaired relational bonds. Gravitating towards filmic and televisual symbolisations that seem prepared to acknowledge and represent the mad enormity of specific kinds of (often culturally silenced) emotional rupture, I'd derived an ambivalent comfort from – and formed a "disorganised attachment" to – texts that seem to *do justice* to the violence – and potential reparation – of "unborn" relational ties.

Many of the participants in the *Six Feet Under* research project displayed evidence of a deeply object-related response to the series – and to participation in the project itself – from the very outset. I'd describe some of these responses, in line with some of the studies outlined above, as comparable to the attachments of infants either to transitional objects or symbolic caregivers. However, the "object" that was found and used in each case turned out to vary a great deal from person to person. A psychotherapeutically literate participant named Esther remarked in her notes before viewing an episode in the first season that "all my parts (in the internal family system) are relatively quiet, except Fat Sue ('protector'), who is struggling with overeating. I tried to talk to her, and she is acting less blindly, but still eating". After watching the episode, she observed the following:

> I feel like myself in relation to *Six Feet Under* after watching this episode…the way it rewards the sense of your own complexity as a viewer – more like the sensation of reading a novel, but richer because you can see the people! The language felt smooth and symbolically coherent, and I don't feel disjointed or discombobulated, or in a traumatic flashback, but like an intelligent, emotionally responsive person, among family. (I don't know whether the family are the characters or the writing itself – when I think about it I feel more immersed in the show-world than in the relationships I have with the characters, but I also feel an unbearable love for them when I am away from them (i.e. the moment it ends).

Esther seems to be gathered up in some way by her viewing of the episode. Her addictive "part" (Fat Sue) seems quietened down by Esther's experience of having the whole of her mind engaged by the "symbolically coherent" language of the "show-world". Her language of "immersion" is especially interesting: it's as if the series has become a womb-like container for her for the duration of the episode, allowing her to feel "unbearable love" for the characters once they're no longer there to be related to on-screen.

However, a participant named Barbara, also struggling with an addictive part of her psyche, starts to distrust *Six Feet Under* as a container of any sort at precisely the same point in the first season as Esther has just been writing about. Prior to her viewing of the seventh episode, Barbara comments:

> As always, I'm lying in bed, tired yet eager to watch a few episodes of *Six Feet Under*. But I have to admit that I've been trying to avoid this show lately, simply because of how intense everything feels in my life right now. Work demands so much of my mind and energy and spirit, and then I come home to an awkward living arrangement with my ex.

The solution, predictably, has been weed. But that's not sustainable. What I need right now is balance, and as good as *Six Feet Under* is, it definitely tips my mood over the edge of anxiety.

Barbara feels truly ambivalent about the series, "eager" to engage with it at the end of a long day, yet at the same time wanting to avoid its "intensity". Barbara isn't getting her psychical fragments gathered up by the viewing experience as she'd hoped she might, and it's possible that cannabis may be a more immediately attractive (if not "sustainable") option.

For a participant named Muriel, the simple practice of watching episodes on a regular, carefully "dosed" basis, and taking part in the project in a deeply "responsible" way (providing me with helpful and informative viewing notes every week) seemed to offer a sort of protective cocoon in which to take shelter from some of the stress of their untenable domestic situation. As early as the third episode of the first season, Muriel is starting to experience the viewing experience as a form of self-care:

12.9.18 S1 E3

Before viewing: Have been looking forward to this moment all day. Was first day back at work after my holiday, and I spent the meetings booking my next trip on my phone. Have barricaded myself away with drinks and snacks – viewing SFU has already started to feel like a ritual for myself, protected time and space. I feel like I can't get in the house without having to pretend to be human to someone, and not pretending very well. I am therefore feeling a bit guilty about my barricade.

Two episodes later, Muriel becomes even more explicit in terms of describing what immersion in the series/research project is starting to mean to them:

1:5 Still feeling very tense about this person in my house, feeling the need to barricade myself away from them and their strong negative emotions and what they might need/ask from me. I forget about it when I am out, and when I turn the corner into my street, I tense up, wondering what pain and needs are lying in wait for me at home. I try to get through the house, picking up my snacks and computer to hide away in my room without meeting them. I also like the feeling of closing down any work-related stuff that was open on my computer and just having the video to attend to. (...) I just lost myself in the episode and I don't really know what to report. When I'm watching, I think oh I should remember that for the notes, but then I just let myself get absorbed because the pace and rhythm of emotions is so finely crafted. I don't even pick up my phone or whatever for a whole hour. I have started looking at my evenings as SFU versus ones where I don't get this ritual time for myself. (...) I love that I have SFU to focus on instead of ruminating over how I did today or dealing with messages etc. That can wait for tomorrow. I'm finding this whole process of viewing and making notes, like an odd kind of diary with company, really interesting. It's helping me get a longer view instead of feeling nailed down by each day's emotional textures.

Muriel's comments on their experience of writing this "odd kind of diary" feel reminiscent of Marion Milner's (2011 [1934]) classic self-analysis in the form of journaling, which would be published *A Life of One's Own*. As Muriel proceeds more deeply into the series, they start to reflect as much on the way in which individual characters and situations are starting to affect their sense of being-in-the-world as on the containing function of the viewing process itself:

15.11.18 S2 E11

I find that scenes from SFU flash into my mind during the day disconnected from anything. Today it was Brenda's dad saying to Ruth: "How are you planning to treat your daughter's depression?" That moment of choice, to pathologise or not. My therapist is always trying to get me to not pathologise myself, but where is the place between not pathologising and not recognising what is happening?

16.11.18 S2 E12

Before: I feel like I should slow down watching episodes as I am getting too far ahead. But there's nothing else I want to do than watch the next episode. Today has been quite good, I thought a lot about Claire being told by various people to stop being so resentful of existence. I told myself that while I was at the gym, what's the point of being so moody about everything. [...] I would like to shake myself out of being so grumpy and resentful as default. [...] I don't feel such a crushing need to hide this evening, though still really glad of having my own space.

Three months later, when Muriel is getting close to the end of the fifth and final season, and the end of participation in the research project, they register some alarm that, in itself, feels like a preparation for a kind of imminent death:

20.2.19 S5 E9

Before: last night I wanted to suddenly watch the rest of the season all in one go. Nate dead seems infinitely more interesting than Nate alive. I am worried that I won't be able to empathise with everyone else's grief but looking forward to the aesthetics of how it patterns out in contrasts and comparisons, counterpoints of grief. I am also a bit worried that there are 4 episodes to go and I don't want anything else horrible to happen to anyone that's left. I've had a really intense day in little ways that feel big, and I'm hoping for the intensities of SFU to hold me. It's going to be hard to leave this and not have it as a companionship or reference point after the end of this season.

Interviewing Muriel about their experience a month later, I was struck by a number of features within their description of their "attachment" as they'd experienced it. Firstly, I noticed the way in which they continued to frame their relationship to the series as one of friendship and care, but a friendship and care which at times appeared to have both *collective* and *mildly fantastical* qualities:

> I was treating it as a friend from the start. But I was also very conscious of the fact that I was part of this viewing community, and so I felt like I wasn't alone watching it. I imagined we had the same viewing rhythm. The show itself was an odd kind of company. If I was watching it, that meant that I was having an evening for me: it held me in a way. It connoted freedom and self-time, and so a triumph over external pressures. The structure of the exercise offered structured leisure, which suits me well. The show was like a dream, repackaging my own life by mirroring and distorting it, enabling me to process personal issues without having to recognise that I was doing that. It enabled me to ignore things and maybe acknowledge them at the same time. I kept thinking that the show was sensate and that it could read my mind. I was convinced that the show had been planned and calculated for me to hate Nate in precisely the way I hated him, and that it would then do something to make me realise the error of my ways. But the revelation never happened. I felt cheated when he didn't die in Season 2.

Muriel's final reflection on what the series has meant to them since ending their regular viewing fascinated me: "I haven't missed it at all, barely thought about it", they said. "Yet when I was watching it, I'd think about the characters between episodes and wonder what they were doing". This capacity to lean so intensely on psychical interaction with the show for the duration of its usefulness, only then to seemingly toss it aside once playtime is over, reminded me of Winnicott's (1971) characterisation of the classic dynamic between infant and transitional object: the teddy bear or piece of blanket is (apparently) forgotten about even though, for a time, it has been the portal to a magical universe that really has shaped the emotional development of the child.

This tendency of Muriel's to cuddle the object to the point of disintegration, but for a time-limited period only, seemed even more pronounced for another participant, Hugh. Very soon after the start of his viewing, Hugh realises that he is going to struggle not to "gobble":

> 1:3: I have to confess that I have failed on the no binge-watching today. I watched this episode right after episode 2, because already in the bath and wasn't ready to get out. I'm going to try and not do it again, and not watch it in the bath. I feel relaxed and comfortable with the Fisher family and want to know what happens next.
>
> 1:4: Full confession: I watched this straight after episode two because still (!) in the bath. Still feeling very relaxed.

As his viewing of the show progresses, the ability to consume it voraciously, and in intimate, bodily, naked environments, becomes even more intense: "I entirely broke my promise. I have realised that I really struggle to watch this show in any measured, clean manner. I cannot stick to the rules. Maybe this is the same with all of my shows? 6FU is maybe especially like a Brendasian addiction here. I watch it in the bath mainly, in bed, on the toilet". Another participant in the project, Donna, is, like Hugh, highly conscious of her tendency to gobble, not only this series, but television shows in general:

> I often use TV watching for this reason, as an addictive behaviour. I am aware that part of my attraction to taking part in this research project may be to legitimise this behaviour. However, I'm also hoping that the necessity of reflection before and after each episode may have a transformative effect on the way that I habitually consume television – that I may engage in a way that is more enlivening than deadening, and that fuller engagement will help me to consume less but to get more sustenance from what I do consume. I also need to learn this with food. I have just consumed too much food that is not nutritious. I wonder if there are more areas of my life in which I consume too much of what is tantalising but ultimately deadening, rather than enough of what seems harder to bring into myself but would be positively transformative? Perhaps I do not want the latter process because that would lead to change.

Bainbridge's (2019) analysis of the "box-set mind-set" adopts a psychoanalytic attitude towards the compulsive consumption of television, noting that

> the reassuring glow of television drama provides containment, but it also permits the development of a greedy, yet envious, mode of consumption, allowing viewers to expel the poisonous feelings inside by attacking some characters and performers whilst simultaneously reifying others [...] Television shifts from being a transitional object to a transformational one in this sense. As a transitional phenomenon, Silverstone (1994) argues that television fosters ontological security,

offering reassurance that, as individuals, we will survive in society. However, as we have seen, bingeing signals that notions of ontological cohesion are in disarray, and any sense of security gives way to overwhelming loss and precarity. In this context, binge watching has more in common with Christopher Bollas's (1987) notion of the transformational object. For Bollas, the transformational object is linked to the early relationship with the mother and is intricately bound up with feelings of experiential intensity.

(p. 77)

Were Donna and Hugh using *Six Feet Under* as a transformational maternal object? Was there something about the way they tended to "binge watch" the series that suggested a desperate desire to find an improbable cohesion in the intensity of its putative gaze?

Hugh finds, when I interview him a few months after the end of his viewing participation, that he has seemingly forgotten much of his poignant – at least to me – experience of consuming the series at great speed. "I don't know if I will ever get over this, or ever stop crying from it", he'd written, movingly, of the final episode. A month later, he's forgotten many of the characters' names, referring to "Kevin" instead of Keith, and asking, "Which one was Brenda, again?" At one point, puzzled by the contradictions inherent in his own increasingly apparent shift from passionate attachment to partial oblivion, he wonders aloud if he may unconsciously be punishing the characters for leaving him. I myself was put in mind of the ghost-Nate's laconic remark to Claire in the final moments of the show, as she is preparing to leave the funeral home for a new life in New York: "You can't take a picture of this: it's already gone". Meanwhile, Donna makes use of a somehow mythologised recollection of her viewing of the show with her partner, Robin, in order to create new narratives around their psychical and relational life. Discussing her watching of the finale, Donna recalls (in a post-study interview with me) that the two of them watched it together in her parents' house, connecting, crying and holding hands. This memory is disputed by Robin, however, and there ensues some confusion as to whether it has been combined with another memory of Donna's, when she watched a pop video ("Smalltown Boy" by Bronski Beat) with her mother at her parents' home, and felt a sense of connection with her mother through *that* shared viewing experience. Donna acknowledges that whatever the truth of the time or location of the two viewings, they are linked by an unconscious longing to connect with a loved (m)other through a shared cultural object. Robin then points out, somewhat poignantly, that these two mini-movies (the *Six Feet Under* finale and the video for "Smalltown Boy") have a lot in common: a flight from the family home under traumatic circumstances, set to music, moving disconcertingly between present and future. Two different cultural objects are conflated in Donna's memory, as are two passionate attachments (her partner and her mother); but it's as if the *recollection* of an affect-laden viewing experience is itself being used as a transitional object, to regulate potentially traumatic comings and goings, to ease the pain of separation and loss, through a flexible memory of shared televisual joy and sorrow.

On psychopomps and the potency of non-normative relating

Towards the end of their viewing of the third season, Muriel is enraged to the point of physical discomfort by a number of narrative arcs that seem to pile relational trauma on relational trauma: "I feel angry in my stomach that Claire gets Lisa's baby on top of everything. This episode is making me sick. And anyway, how does Nate know where Brenda lives now? I feel extremely agitated and annoyed. If Brenda takes him back, I may just stop watching". Meanwhile, Esther, after her viewing of the pilot and second episodes, notes a visceral repulsion towards a character, writing: "I hated Ruth all the way through, from her stupid smug gardening accessories, to the slap to David's face, to the weird stroking of Nathaniel in his grave-clothes. I briefly pitied her". Finally, Donna, in the course of the first season, becomes so incensed at the spectacle of Ruth's mothering that she feels moved to take action by reaching out to the character by letter:

Dear Ruth,

Please could you try and be less of a selfish, fucking bitch. (Ughh I don't think fucking bitch is totally fair, but the way that you're often so insensitive to your children and so martyr-ish about your own pain is really **intensely** annoying.) It is quite nice that you didn't give Claire a hard time about the foot, but I'm not sure it's really adequate. And I'm not sure about Claire's counsellor encouraging her to help you. I mean if it's in her power, then that's OK but YOU'RE THE PARENT AND YOU SHOULD BE RESPONSIBLE FOR HER SADNESS NOT THE OTHER WAY AROUND. I know you're not evil and sub-par probably doesn't even begin to describe the parenting you received, but if you could at least attempt to engage with the emotional realities of your children's lives that would be great. I know you're trying to be less cold these days but... really... try harder.

Regards
Participant whatever number I am.

Donna goes on to reflect on the (non)representation of the (doubly) dead father Nathaniel, moving quickly (after an initially intellectual and political analysis of the situation depicted) into a nakedly emotional response to the fictional characters and her experience of their parenting:

> The whole thing makes me sick. I bloody hate Nathaniel. He's such a smug twat. Again, I know that's unfair. But I'm fed up of holding my anger towards my own parents and it's too disruptive to unload it onto them so I'm afraid Ruth and Nathaniel will have to take it, and they're not real (in the sense of being independently conscious outside the TV programme) so it can't hurt them. Because as we all know it's only ungrateful little fucks who upset their "real" parents, who are so fragile and have sacrificed SO MUCH, and as Ruth said, had it so much worse themselves, and are therefore incapable of behaving differently but it's not their fault and what, you, my child, are angry with me, but why, how can you cause me so much pain?! What do you mean I've traumatised you and you were only a child so you had no defences?! Hmmm. I may feel slightly better. I'm not sure. I still feel angry, but I think I might feel slightly less numb.

What shifts a viewer's experience of *Six Feet Under*'s multiple depictions of bad or non-relating from depression or rage to enlivening transformation? At times, the disturbance Muriel expresses after witnessing an instance of real relational malaise in the show does seem productively alive. Their comments after watching an episode from Season One entitled "The New Person", for example, are instructive in terms of the specificity of physical memory it elicits in them:

> Angela [a guest embalmer played by Ileana Douglas] saying how depressing it was [at the funeral home] and like she felt she was walking on eggshells around all of them (she didn't use that phrase) reminds me of my family. I grew up in an environment where saying what you really thought or felt was bound to hurt someone. None of us knew how to deal with anyone else's feelings or how to express our own safely. So that you don't even know what you are really upset about. What I am really anxious about in my body feels like something to do with never being able to make up for all the times I hurt and upset my parents with my inappropriate behaviour. All the times I was wrong. So I can never achieve enough, because nothing I achieve can ever make up for the pain and disgust I caused, they are unmakeupable for, they are bottomless. Maybe that's the cause of the feeling I have in my throat, that feels like someone is pressing on my windpipe, that makes me want to eat all the time because when I'm swallowing the food pushes my throat back against the force of that hand around my neck.

Reflecting on the data I gathered from participants in the project, it seemed to me that viewers felt most free to take shelter in un-self-critical identification with characters only when they could (no matter how naively) start to experience that character as in some way *capable of transcending social and familial classifications*.

The character that appears to lend herself most to this kind of "post-social" identification to my participants is, without a doubt, Claire. In his writing on Jungian approaches to individuals' emotional use of the films they have watched, Hockley (2014) reflects on a particular client, noting her enthusiastic connection with the character played by Sally Hawkins in Mike Leigh's film *Happy-Go-Lucky* (2008). Hockley remarks that, for this patient, "[the film character] Poppy was not an identification figure in a traditional sense, rather she became a source of psychological inspiration – almost like an inner spirit guide or psychopomp" (p. 103). Claire seems frequently to be channelled psychically as precisely this kind of "psychopomp" by the participants in my study. Hugh notes, in passing, that "I am connecting quite a lot with Claire at the moment – I think she is very charismatic and impulsive. Maybe Claire is a little too identifiable somehow?" Meanwhile, Christopher says:

> I like Claire a lot and remember feeling a strong connection to her when I first watched the series. There are these amazing and supportive role models for the confused, innocent young person. In the way I feel that Claire is my therapy in this series. Claire's innocence and impertinence is extremely authentic and still speaks to me.

Esther notes, immediately after her viewing of the second episode, that

> the scene where Claire is talking to Gabe with an openness and humour we haven't yet seen within the family, resonated with me personally – the child's ability to save herself by replacing the inchoate rage and shame that characterise her interactions with the parent with articulate honesty with "outsiders". It felt genuinely therapeutic.

A participant named Anna is unequivocal in her articulation of how deeply the figure of Claire is internalised by her psyche over the course of viewing *Six Feet Under*. When I interviewed Anna after she had watched all five seasons, she was keen to tell me about her multiple dreams:

> All my dreams have been about Claire. In one dream, I was in a burning building. I was trying to rescue myself, but Claire had been in the building, trying to rescue a man I think was my dad. They were killed. I felt guilty for trying to rescue only myself. I later misremembered the dream, thinking that I had saved my dad myself. But checking through my notes, I realised it had actually been Claire, not me. In another dream, I was Claire, and my brother was Nate. He was injured, he was having

a seizure. I was calm and I knew what to do. I called the emergency services. I woke up feeling competent and in control. In another dream, Claire was taking crack. It was nice to have someone else show me experiences which I didn't have to do myself. It felt protective – like having a guide, somehow. I didn't realise the extent of my identification with Claire until these dreams. Consciously, I had found Claire quite irritating, and I had associated her with my not-so-good friend Amy. Claire's lack of place in the family was maybe something I latched on to. I had two older siblings, though I also had a younger sibling, so there was no clearly defined role for me in the family. Claire struggles with this feeling too, yet Claire finds a place for herself in the world. She finds her own voice in a way I haven't yet been able to. She manages to make something of her unpromising family position. I think my dreams of Claire reflect where I am at in my therapy at the moment. Not being able to save my family was very much my previous position. But right now, I feel more confident of my abilities. She really did become a sort of guide for me.

Brenda's character also seems capable of giving viewers a strange sense of being both understood and held, though the way she does this feels far more ambivalent than the "Claire dynamic" of straightforward identification. Muriel notes a perplexing shift in their experience of Brenda over the course of the show. The shift is first recorded in their comments before and after the fifth episode in the second season:

Before. The past few days I've been trying something my therapist suggested which is when I notice that I am "pacing the corridors" – which is the phrase I use to communicate with him about inherited anxiety. He relates this to inherited trauma. The trick he has suggested is simply to observe myself pacing. I am finding this really effective. I think it is also related to Buddhism.
After. Okay, this is weird. Brenda has a Buddha head on her mantel piece and, with it in shot, she says: "The act of observation changes that which is being observed". And the whole episode is about beliefs. But all entwined with identity politics and assimilation vs separatism.

It feels, increasingly, as if Brenda, despite all her initially repellent characteristics of smugness and privilege, has the capacity to retain Muriel's fascination, through her capacity to suffer and change. Writing after their viewing of an episode from Season Three, Muriel says: "The massage with Lisa was the first time in SFU I have respected Brenda". And by the time they are writing about Season Five, Muriel is able to say: "Brenda in this season is so compelling. The contrast between her being different and Nate being the same takes me back to the idea of SFU being a musical composition somehow. With Ruth getting crazier and crazier". For all

Muriel's oft-stated irritation with both Brenda and Nate, their comments over the course of viewing the series suggest to me that the transformations undergone by both characters, especially those transformations which feel un-yoked from social classification, find themselves folding into Muriel's experience both of their own psychotherapy and of their very experience of being in the world:

> The thing that really sticks with me though is what Brenda said about not being able to know – and having to live with that. That fits in an odd way with what came up in therapy today. How knowing and not knowing go together. So, when Nate finds stuff out, he also finds out that he doesn't know things. It felt good to laugh about Nate and the MDMA. I loved the image of him going into the waves. That's what everything feels like for me at the moment, like waves that can't be argued with. It's a good reminder that I can sit on the beach and watch myself in the waves. Maybe I will even look up the *Bhagavad Gita*.

Participants who found that they were becoming significantly attached to the series manifested a tendency to note in their viewing records a single image, or occasionally a short sequence, in which some highly affecting instance of connection between characters is allowed to take place. The types of represented relationality that seem capable of "holding" the viewer are various. The scenes aren't always about characters coming or staying together; sometimes it's in the depiction of particularly honest conflict that the viewer gains the greatest sense of satisfaction. Muriel, writing about the penultimate episode of the second season, says: "That was an absolutely fantastic argument between Nate and Brenda. I loved every second of it. They said exactly the right things. The whole show feels like it is simultaneously in another art form, like it is incidentally a TV show but at the same time, a piece of music or a solar system or an ocean". Muriel moves immediately from reflecting on the fantastic "rightness" of what is said – in a state of immense pain, rage, and grief – between these two characters (both of whom Muriel has hitherto experienced as deeply irritating) to a lyrical appreciation of the show as "a piece of music or a solar system or an ocean". It's as if there is something about feeling *honestly communicated with*, even by irritating characters, that leads this viewer to rapturous, even cosmic feelings of being at peace in the world, as if they are being rocked by a universe that is attuned to their own personal needs. It doesn't matter to Muriel that a scene of discord and conflict is being played out between Brenda and Nate; the point is that watching it is both psychologically and existentially containing because it reveals something that Muriel experiences as fundamentally true. This sense of a representation of relational truth subsequently triggers in the receptive viewer a sense of greater connection to, and holding by, the universe itself.

Hope (2014) notes, in her compelling thesis on "politicising agency through affect", that

> where the artwork or image looks on the viewer from a position of love, the image itself, via its maker, or the identified with actor, may become a proxy for the kind of "look" that we would like to receive from a parent. In cinema or television, the confident pose of an actor, and her open display of emotions, might enable the protagonist to become the ideal person with whom we would most want to interact. The actor may appear to show us the love that we seek in life, albeit that the actor actually directs this "emotion" towards his co-star in the film. This suggests an experience with images that in some way accords with "attachment", one which may underscore the affective "pleasure" of relating to the image. This may be further underscored by the overuse of visual media by an "insecure" self; with this insecurity being said to have a particular relation to capitalist life.
>
> (pp. 95–6)

Robin provides a wonderful illustration of Hope's thesis when he says, of the second episode of the first season:

> The part that really did move me was where Brenda arranges for David and Nate to ride on the same bus that killed Nathaniel. There's something profoundly moving about the sudden outpouring of grief from David, and the way in which this silences Nate's reprimanding of Brenda. The way in which a seemingly "irresponsible" approach is the axe that breaks that frozen internal sea.

In an interestingly chiasmic movement, Robin later recalls being overwhelmingly moved in the second-to-last episode of the last season, when "Brenda really connects with Billy about the experience of growing older and losing friends. I feel the truth of that conversation even more deeply now, ten years after first watching this show. It's what I've spent most of my life complaining about". Robin is also especially touched by David being met by the ghost of Nathaniel in the final episode of Season Four, when Nathaniel exclaims to his traumatised son: "You're alive, for God's sake! What's a little pain compared to that?" Participants reflect again and again on the way in which they feel weirdly moved, touched, or addressed by the show's apparent precision in representing relational coming together, especially when this coming together is fantastical, or even simply unexpected. Almost every participant writes of the powerful effect of the episode named "Familia" in the first season, in which members of the Fisher family hold hands with members of a Latino "gang" after the funeral of one of the "gang" members. Muriel notes, poignantly, of the tenth episode in the fifth season that "Nate had to die so that David could be holding hands with Keith and Ruth at the same time". Meanwhile, Hugh, writing about the famous flash-forward to the future of the fifth season finale writes, with less and less attempt to cover his emotion: "Brenda (with very grey hair) and a middle-aged Claire, talking at the table: I am weeping again".

There's something about these brief testimonies by my participants of being deeply affected by seeing characters talking seriously and sincerely and, above all, *listening* to one another, that once again recalls the work of Hope (2014), whose writing about the ways in which media representations of specific forms of relating can actively intervene in our psychical and socio-political processes is fascinating. I wonder if, when Hugh literally weeps at the fantastically futuristic sight of the grey-haired Brenda and Claire talking seriously with one another in their late middle age, something may perhaps be getting helpfully affirmed for his psyche about the possibility of becoming and staying attached to people over long periods of one's life, even unto old age and death. Although, over the course of the five seasons of *Six Feet Under*, Claire's and Brenda's interactions have been minimal, there's always been the whispered suggestion – perhaps never more poignantly glimpsed than when Brenda spontaneously drives Claire to her abortion in Season Three – that the connection between the two of them, if nurtured over time, could offer a possibility of real, authentic relating. Claire's Cassandra-like vision of the realisation of the two women's potentially very real, mature, adult friendship at the very end of the show offers Hugh, offers all of us, if we are receptive, a radical vision of honed empathy and deepened attachment over time, the kind of vision we especially need if such relational blueprints have been in short supply in early life.

Swaddled in music

Chion (2019) has famously emphasised our need, as media scholars, to pay attention to the aural and acousmatic aspects of our experience of cinema and television every bit as much as we pay homage to the visual. Grant (2015b), meanwhile, writing and video-editing in the context of the audiovisual essay, notes that

> while there appears to be no shortage of image-centric audiovisual essaying in this new field, studies that foreground or listen more closely to film, video and televisual sound are distinctly in the minority. This won't surprise anyone working in sound studies, of course, since this unfortunate under-representation simply mirrors the long-standing ocular-centricity of existing, written film and moving image studies.

In the realm of psychoanalysis, there are also calls – albeit relatively isolated ones – for theorists and clinicians to pay greater attention to the role of sound in the development of the psyche. Reik's (1960) work on "the haunting melody" is a key example of how music can represent and structure unconscious thought in ways that are completely alien to linguistic forms, whilst Anzieu (2016) has written compellingly about the importance of sound as a means of communication between mother and baby or foetus.

Given that my own remembered experience of what felt like some kind of personal transformation under the influence of *Six Feet Under* seemed inextricably linked to the show's use of music during key representations of relationality, I was surprised that relatively few participants in the research project reflected explicitly on sonic equivalents of the visually containing relational moments described above. My memory of the opening bars of Radiohead's song "Lucky" during Claire's strange, musical curation of the Fisher family's bonfire in the third episode of Season Four ("Parallel Play") is, I think, indelible. A participant named Christopher, himself a professional musician, noted: "I found the music at the funeral – *Ave Maria* and later Beethoven – to be triggers for tears. It does remind me strongly of funerals when I was a child". But it was a participant named Marin whose testimony contained the most consistent references to the therapeutic use of music in the series, reporting that most of his overwhelmingly transcendent experiences of *Six Feet Under*, especially when he first watched it being broadcast on UK television for the first time, from 2001 to 2005, came via the show's abundant use of songs as vehicles for the aural exploration of relational connection and disconnection. In his interview with me, Marin speaks of repeated impressions of a musically emotional truth-telling taking place in the show, each instance of which seems to trigger a deeply felt sense of holding and containment.

The first significant musical experience Marin mentions is Ruth's private (though secretly overheard by Claire) rendition of Joni Mitchell's song "Woodstock" in the closing moments of the episode entitled "Back to the Garden" (2:6). Marin describes a sense of immense poignancy as he first listened, along with Claire, his virtual sibling in that televisual moment in 2002, to Ruth's eerily nostalgic singing in the kitchen.

> It was so moving. Like some weird glimpse into a side of Ruth we've never seen before and will never see again. She really did love that kind of music, from the sixties, even though it's Aunt Sarah who is associated with hippies and Woodstock and the whole scene. It's a side of Ruth that's hidden but comes to light through the song. And I love that song anyway.

Listening to Marin's words, I couldn't help but feel there was something in this unexpected musical moment with the "sister" Claire and the "mother" Ruth that was facilitating an incredibly important sense of familial bonding in him. Thanks to the playing of Joni Mitchell's "Woodstock", Marin was being given access to forms of intimacy he simply had not seen – or heard – coming. And they stayed with him. The second important musical experience Marin discusses in relation to his own sense of being known and responded to by *Six Feet Under* is the moment, early in the second season, when Brenda smokes cannabis and clears her bedroom whilst listening and dancing to P.J. Harvey's song "One Time Too Many":

> This was less intense than the "Woodstock" moment with Claire and Ruth. But it was still really important, I think because of how much I already identified with Brenda at that point in the show. And here she was, acting in a way I myself would act, cutting herself off from humans in the same way, but listening to one of my favourite musical artists. I was like…wow, yes, Brenda would love P.J. Harvey. This feels so right.

By the time Marin starts to discuss his response to Nate's desperately sad listening experience of Todd Rundgren's song "I Saw the Light" towards the end of Season Three, at the height of Lisa's disappearance, it is starting to become clear that music in the show is working on him as an intensifier of feelings surrounding inter-psychical connection and, above all, missed connection.

> That moment is amazing. I don't really understand why, I can't explain it in words, I mean, but it's like the only way the show or Nate himself can get in touch with the fact that he actually *did* love Lisa, and now she is gone. It's so sad. Could it have been another song? I guess, but I don't know what. The one they choose, that… "when I saw the light in your eyes"… that is the exact right thing, it's hard to imagine anything else in its place.

In his moving recollection of these three musical moments in *Six Feet Under*, Marin makes clear an almost magical sense of somehow being met just where he needs to be met; of being sung to with the lullabies of his infant-heart's deepest desire; of being rocked and held by the *sounds* of the show.

Of nests, nappies, wombs, and cocoons

As well as feeling psychically held by certain visual and sonic configurations of what may feel like unprecedentedly truthful relationality in *Six Feet Under*, participants also mention the occasional sensation of containment by aspects of the show that feel literally, physically *touching*. Muriel is explicit in articulating their experience, at times, of a viscerally touch-based response to the series:

> I like Keith's bed linen, his bed looks so comfy – earth colours and clean, right at the start of the episode. Everything else outside of Keith's

bed is seething with mess and shit, literally, in the hearse. I'd love to learn how to look out for "Keith's bed" moments and to know that they do happen even though everything around them can be full of raging emotions and complications.

Marks (2000) has done much to popularise discussion and debate within an academic context of the specifically *haptic* (that is, touch-related) potential of certain moving images, writing that "haptic cinema does not invite identification with a figure – a sensory-motor reaction – so much as it encourages a bodily relationship between the viewer and the image" (p. 164). It's almost as if Muriel feels corporeally *wrapped up* (thus anticipating the words of Sia's iconic song in the show's final moments) by Keith's bed, internalising its image for psychical usage in times that might feel too seething, raging, messy, shitty. The series later, interestingly, thematises precisely Muriel's haptic desire to stay enveloped in a warm, clean bed, when in the third episode of Season Four, a bereaved and broken down Nate longs to stay wrapped up in the warm bed of a particularly glacial character he has just had sex with, the wealthy, Thich Nhat Hanh-quoting mother of one of his toddler daughter's friends. The prospect of his imminent eviction from that bed causes him to hallucinate a vision of himself impossibly alone and adrift in an icy steppe.

Hugh focuses, in his post-viewing notes relating to the episode entitled "Back to the Garden", on the specifically sensual, feeling, haptic dimensions of the episode. This is the episode that was so musically resonant for Marin, as we have seen; Hugh, meanwhile, becomes positively lyrical when reflecting on the safely cocooned sensation that Aunt Sarah's dwelling in Topanga Canyon provokes in him. Outlining the contours of a meditation practice in which he imagines a "sacred space" where he can "disappear in order to relax", Hugh states unequivocally that, as a result of watching the show, Sarah's version of Topanga is on its way to *becoming* that "sacred space" for him:

> Topanga in *Six Feet Under* has greatly added to this psychic topography, and has extended the space that was already in my mind – isn't that weird? The bits that specifically come from Topanga and have been added to my mind's place are:
>
> - The mobile hanging from the tree with the butterfly and the fish
> - The table with a bottle of wine and glasses on it that Bettina and Ruth are drinking from
> - The hammock that Bettina and Ruth are lying on
> - The steps up to the house
>
> I love the bit where Ruth and Bettina are drinking wine there in the hammock whilst Sarah goes through withdrawal for her medication addiction, etc. I love when Claire goes there and meets all of Sarah's

artistic friends. I want to inherit Topanga!!! OMG if *Six Feet Under* has taught me anything it is: I want to live in Topanga.

Hugh is moved, in the course of writing up his notes, to paint his impression of Sarah's house in Topanga. He takes a photograph of his painting, sending it to me along with his weekly viewing notes.

When I see Hugh's photograph of his painting of Sarah's world, I too feel touched, physically, by the materiality of the feelings that he has felt and has been compelled to externalise. It's as if there's no way that the Topanga of *Six Feet Under* can be allowed to be left as something merely abstract or theoretical; its warmth must be literally felt, painted, passed on. I feel a sudden desire, never before experienced to this degree, to visit Topanga myself, in the flesh, and I start, shortly after receiving Hugh's picture, to make arrangements with my American niece to do so.

"This is my painting of Sarah O'Connor's house in Topanga. This is a space of immense calm and beauty for me". – "Hugh"

On potentialities (the other heaven)

By the time I began to process even half the participants' viewing notes and interviews, one thing was starting to emerge very clearly for me: those who had taken to the show in an intense manner, who had "latched on" and were hungrily feeding, whose "object-use" of the show could broadly be described as a positive one, were all marked by an increasing tendency, no matter what their stated religious or spiritual beliefs in the opening questionnaire, to relate to *Six Feet Under* in a manner that seemed to take *otherworldliness* very seriously indeed. Muriel reflects explicitly on the level at which they start to imbibe and interact with the situations on screen, stating, part-way through their viewing of the third season: "It has taken me ages to realise *Six Feet Under* is a supernatural opera". Later, they become very specific with regard to their growing awareness of *potentiality* in their experience of the show:

> Those "should have" moments run all through SFU. The moment when Nate was talking in the bar [after his schoolfriend's death in an early episode of Season Five], I can't remember exactly what he said, but I felt my shoulders relaxed and a sigh came out. And when he returns from his first death in Season Two with pre-cognitive abilities, his glimpsing of a parallel existence which might have unfolded – this was so well informed, this rang so true for me.

During our interview after their viewing of the entire show, Muriel became most excited upon their recollection of "the tantalising feminist utopia that doesn't happen" in the episode of Season Five entitled "The Rainbow of Her Reasons". They experience Ruth's disappointed realisation that this utopia was just stoned talk from the night before, that the seismic social change won't actually happen, as profoundly moving, going on to play (in their dialogue with me) with various fantasies of different, medium-sized and "minor" women characters from the show – Bettina, Melissa, and Lisa – meeting and setting up a new fictional universe together in the form of a spinoff series. Meanwhile, Anna's interview with me focused in large part on her powerful response to Nate's and David's shared dream as Nate is dying: "Nate's last dream is so utterly beautiful. It's beyond psychology. That really was Nate entering the afterlife". But the detail of the dream that emerges with the most intensity for Anna is the bizarre dream-depiction of an *alternative* David, now reconfigured as a slacker-style stoner, the opposite of his character as we have come to know it, which, whether in his pre- or post-coming out phase, has been relentlessly controlling, co-dependent, and conservative (with a small "c"). "I *love* this alternative David, I can't get him out of my head", says Anna, before adding, with mild puzzlement: "Why is this so intense for me?"

Throughout all five seasons of *Six Feet Under*, there's an indefatigable commitment on the part of the writers to repeated representations of an imaginal reality of alternative dimensions and multiple selves. The self is absolutely not *fixed* in this series, and the manner in which it can be re-imagined in radically different (yet weirdly believable) form sometimes feels inexplicably moving. The first season flirts comedically – and yet also very movingly – with this trope in its playful, Lewis Carroll-esque representation of Ruth on Ecstasy, when she accidentally takes a pill whilst on a camping trip with her lover Hiram, thinking it's aspirin. This is, of course, the occasion of her first meeting with Nathaniel after his death – most of the other characters have already been talking to him for several episodes now – and it is a deeply communicative one. This is a version of Ruth *as she might have been*, had she not had to stay at home to look after her legless grandmother, had she been able to study "the French feminists", had she not married Nathaniel, had she decided to explore the implications of her "little crush on Jane Fonda". Ruth is so full of alternative selves, and the one glimpsed singing Joni Mitchell quietly to herself in the kitchen is just one of them. This leitmotif of multiple selves, all of them waiting in the cosmic wings to be released or fully realised, is condensed beautifully in "Perfect Circles", the opening episode of the third season, in which Nate, unconscious and hovering in the borderland between life and death following his brain surgery, glimpses visions of the many different lives he might be living in parallel to this one: dead, alive, married to Brenda, married to Lisa, brain-damaged for life, living in a trailer park.

Six Feet Under seems deeply preoccupied, as a collective, creative project, with what I feel to be a fundamentally post-traumatic capacity to imagine both self and others as radically reconfigured, and reconfigurable across time and space. The image of Brenda at Jeffrey Shapiro's funeral in the second season – a funeral which, of course, she never attends – hallucinated momentarily by Nate as a grieving Jewish widow has always fascinated me: Brenda in a different, fuller, spectacular iteration of a partial ethnicity (she is half-Jewish). Nate is fascinated by the unrealised nature of a potentially sincere manifestation of "whole" Jewishness. Of course, Brenda, as the most fragmented character in the show, is the character through whom the wonder of metamorphosis and potentiality is most relentlessly and realistically explored, not least via her trajectory of genius, trauma, falseness, addiction, breakdown, partial recovery, blandness, and eventual experiments with sincerity. My sense of both my own and my participants' enthusiastic response to the show's otherworldly facilitation of imagined selves beyond the bounds of socialised coherence is that it touches something of the godly in us, whether we consider ourselves to be spiritual or religious, or not. Something is opened up that is so deeply transcendent of narcissism, the prison of believing that one is a frozen image, to be known – or defiantly not known – only by the contours of one's own frantically egoic machinations. In *Six Feet Under*, characters seem, at least on occasion, to be capable of so much *more* than this: they are afforded a fantastical, shape-shifting dimension; and there may something potentially liberating when we are truly open to witnessing that.

From both sides now

As this chapter draws to its close, it feels important to register that the participants of the study were by no means uniformly seduced or contained by the potentially therapeutic aspects of *Six Feet Under* that I've up until now chosen to emphasise. Again and again, the element of the show that returned for exasperated critique, in many different participants' viewing notes, was the dimension that might be described as the polar opposite of the kinds of "potentialities" I've been exploring above: its cynical revelry in a certain kind of stuckness. Muriel notes that "I found people's powerlessness to shift dynamics, their stuckness, very uncomfortable. For I too was stuck in patterns". Meanwhile, Sandra was repeatedly disappointed to the point of rage by the characters' failure to transcend what she perceived to be limited and depressing conceptions of themselves. Why doesn't Brenda stay in Recovery? Why don't Keith and David break up? These questions bothered and irked her, and increasingly seemed to make her resent the show at a profound level. Mark too was explicit, post-study, about his wary ambivalence towards the writers' tendency to keep the characters trapped in sometimes intolerable situations:

> The show was often not a safe space for me. It proved itself on a number of occasions to be untrustworthy and I had to keep myself safe from its potential cruelty and perversion. I really needed it sometimes to show me something in the characters that wasn't either just passivity or plain nastiness. There was just so much self-destruction and self-denial and self-delusion, so much hurting people they care about! Seeing that repeatedly became wrenching, especially when there is the tantalising glimpse of a different way of being, and then they don't follow through.

As for Robin, the participant who described *Six Feet Under* as "quite simply the best television show of all time", he also felt irritated and let down by the series on a number of occasions, especially in the final episode:

> Claire's death was so normative. What's the message here? If you do what you were "supposed" to do in life, then you will die at peace? The Sia finale felt like a betrayal of the entire show, the Alan Ball of *American*

Beauty horribly revived. It's like the last episode betrays the spirit of the show in a pathetic attempt to be "iconic". They were trying too hard to be clever and they sold themselves out. And the deaths of all the main characters were also just too much, too sadistic, it's like they were telling people what their life choices would mean. It was too didactic. I hated it.

Furthermore, I had little sense of the participants of gendered, sexual, or ethnic minorities in the study I conducted feeling significantly helped by the show with regard to the internalised representation of their minority identity, even if a number of the participants identifying as white gay men did mention feeling positively engaged with the normalisation of David and Keith's relationship. In some cases, there was conscious recognition by the "minority participant" that the show was very definitely *exploring* sad or problematic situations in relation to stigmatised identities, but this recognition of an exploration did not necessarily equate to any sense of emotional satisfaction. A participant named Sandra is explicit when it comes to this, reacting strongly to an episode from the first season in which the character of David is struggling with his gay identity:

> Definitely identifying with David. I am so angry with God at the moment for making me gay. I feel like my life would be so much easier if I were not attracted to women. I would probably be married with children. I probably never would have moved to London. I'd have a stable job and own a home and be raising a family in my country of origin and not living the life of a poor person in London struggling to find someone to just love me for who I am. Life is shit!

Meanwhile, observing the unspoken class and race-related hierarchies that play out at the funeral home via the Fishers' interactions with Rico, a participant named Shelley notes:

> I feel for Rico being treated different because he is not a member of the family, also because he is Hispanic and feels like a second-class citizen in this white, middle-class family, although he has skills that make him a very valuable commodity. The brothers are in fact prepared to let him go and although he has been given this chance by their dad, he will never get to earn that much money with them or get the opportunities to run his own place. A lot of feeling of cultural differences affect me as I am Indian. It is difficult because underneath I always feel less than. I am not sure how to grow and develop and to feel equal. When I am watching stuff like this, I always come from a place of feeling inferior just because I am not white and the subconscious effect that has on what I feel I deserve and what I can have. I feel this is holding me back a lot. I feel a lot of stuff is holding me back a lot. I am not sure how to get over it.

I shall return more specifically to the problem (and it really is a problem) of "race" in *Six Feet Under* in the fourth and final chapter of this book. For now, though, I will note that participants from both inside and outside social minorities seemed palpably disturbed by characters who felt overly identified with forms of material privilege. This disturbance tended to become most negatively pronounced around the character of Brenda. As Brenda moves more deeply into forms of behaviour that might be characterised as sexual addiction, Sandra's experience of *definitely not being helped* by the representation of this character feels palpably enflamed:

> Before viewing
>
> Still sad, lonely and irritated.
>
> After viewing
>
> Fucking Brenda. I hate liars. I am so irritated by people at the moment, and this episode has not helped that at all. Just confirms for me that people are assholes!

Meanwhile, Shelley notes her own feelings of class and race identity related discomfort as she starts to gather more information about Brenda's class- and whiteness-related privilege:

> Seeing Brenda's family, though, makes me see her in totally another way. The fact that she has loads of money alienates her from me – I thought she was this outsider bohemian type which I guess I can relate to much more. I realize how much money affects me as I am constantly thinking about my own situation and how we do not have much money and my parents are poor and this makes me feel sad. I'm constantly feeling bad about it but maybe there is something I can do and ending up in panic and then in paralysis and confusion and not knowing how I can help.

A participant named Naomi echoes the emerging theme:

> I am continuing to be triggered by Nate and Brenda and the trauma bond they are experiencing – and perhaps the manipulation of Brenda. The scene with the tattoo freaked me out a bit. She feels like a predator to me. I really want the character Nate to walk away from this woman, as I think it's just a distraction for him from his own life. I identify with that attraction to greater drama than my own and that feeling of aliveness that comes with it.

Sandra's annoyance with the series and its characters, meanwhile, seems to build to some kind of boiling – or freezing – point:

> Before. Feeling irritated. Wondering how *Six Feet Under* is going to irritate me even more today.
>
> After. Watching the lies and deceit in this relationship with Brenda and Nate just plays into my whole outlook at the moment that people are trash! I don't want to shut down, but I am shutting down.

Moreover, some of the (white) participants in the study register feelings of discomfort – perhaps even mild shame – over their ambivalent identification with Brenda. During his viewing of the second season, Hugh remarks:

> Brenda's doing that thing where she has sex with loads of people behind Nate's back and justifies it to herself as inspiration for her writing. I find that a bit of a boring and lazy thing for Brenda to do, and how she was so totally unaware of her privilege in using the sex worker kind of like interesting "gritty" fodder to write about. But Brenda totally reminds me of the same gross and boring things about myself sometimes.

Muriel's malaise at the possibility of being identified with either Brenda or Nate, but especially Brenda, goes through a series of metamorphoses as their viewing of the show progresses. Reflecting on the first episode, they remark:

> I also feel a bit embarrassed as I feel like I am a cross between Brenda and Nate and I find them both excruciating. I have had sex with a stranger in an airport toilet and even worse, I do shiatsu just like Brenda. I actually felt like I was stoned from watching the emotional and behavioural patterns – that feeling of being outside myself looking in which comes from smoking weed, kind of paranoid but also with the potential to shift only not quite there. On the train back home tonight, I was thinking about Brenda explaining shiatsu to Ruth, and cringing. Please god can I not be like Brenda.

It would appear, then, that *Six Feet Under* doesn't offer a straightforward form of spectatorial comfort for viewers experiencing their identities as either painfully stigmatised *or* embarrassingly over-privileged, instead provoking them to feel discomfort and even rage at the all-too-believable inequalities they see depicted on screen. This is the other side of the show's capacity to draw the viewer into a realm of limitless potentiality, beyond the structures and prisons of socialised selfhood. It would seem that the show needs us to be content to walk the line between the incessant representation of shackles and their merely *occasional* transcendence.

On the capacity to love an imperfect object

My exploration of the participants' generous, multi-layered responses to the show, suggest to me that, in the final analysis, we may be being asked, especially in the show's finale, to let go of any stifling, frozen reverence we wished to preserve at the altar of *Six Feet Under*. It's as if my initial impulse back in 2005 – and, if truth be told, in the fifteen years since then – to embalm my love for *Six Feet Under* like some sort of dead mummy may have been waiting for a project such as this one in order to transform itself into a more balanced appreciation of what the show was and wasn't able to do for me. *Six Feet Under* delivers some enormous disappointments. The punches it pulls around race, racialisation, and racism (of which much more in the next chapter), together with its refusal to go "all the way" in its exploration of emotional abuse and estrangement within the family – the dishonest recuperation of Margaret Chenowith for the purposes of pure comedy – remain my own particular bugbears. The participant named Anna links her own mild experiences of "betrayal" by the show to the character of Ted in the fifth season: his stupid mixtape; the impertinence of Sia; Claire's implied loss of authenticity by being prepared to have a relationship with a Republican.

The final episode is, of course, entitled "Everything Ends"; and I think that this declaration is meant to be taken very seriously indeed. Just as the aliveness and apparent wisdom of Aunt Sarah have the capacity to disappoint us appallingly – her awful reversals of judgment and opinion are experienced by Claire in particular as unbearably galling – so too does *Six Feet Under*. And yet, on the whole, my sense of the participants who loved the show, who felt cared for by it, was that they were willing to forgive this adopted love-object for its occasional failings, even when those failings felt quite mad. Robin is lucid on this point: "The show is a beloved object for me. But it's one which I don't need to be perfect. It doesn't matter that it fucked up the last reel. The feeling of betrayal there isn't like it would be for something short and one-off like a film. This series provided sustenance for so long". And Marin's sober summing-up of what this series meant for him when he first turned to it for care, back in 2001, during a time of unutterable trauma, is very moving indeed:

> I can see the flaws and betrayals of this show now, I really can. Some of them are really glaring. But it's hard to explain…this show was like a kind of *partner* to me at a time when my life was completely broken and terrifying. In a really weird way, I feel nostalgia for a time of such suffering and vulnerability, because it makes me really feel my loyalty towards a television show that could actually meet my desperate needs in this way. I can't see myself ever relating to a show like that again, not only because it's unlikely there will be a show as good as that one, but

also because I won't ever be in a position like that again. I don't need it to happen again. But, in a strange way, I'm glad it did.

Listening to Marin, I found myself wondering if the position he'd reached perhaps was the perfect expression of what orthodox Kleinians might call a mature and "depressive" (1946) recovery of his lost good object. His final appraisal seemed so clear; and it didn't seem to require Marin to lie to himself or to anyone else about what had or hadn't taken place. Unlike the intolerable forms of neglect or violation sometimes perpetrated on infants and children by real-world caregivers and their wider environments, the failures, deaths, and half-deaths "perpetrated" on its loyal viewers by *Six Feet Under* could truly, happily be accepted, integrated, and loved by them, along with its multiple manifestations of aliveness and care. The exquisite challenge of "whole object relating" seemed, at least for the time being, to be solved.

Chapter 4

In this here place, we flesh

Racialised vulnerability and collective dreaming: film groups in the time of #BlackLivesMatter

The company of wolves

On the day Marvin Gaye died, 1 April 1984, I was six and a half years old. I already knew and loved Marvin's songs, thanks to my father, who played his records loudly on a regular basis. It was my father who smilingly told me the news: "Marvin Gaye is dead". When I asked him how such a thing had happened – surely Marvin was too young to die? – he let out a strange giggle and said: "He disrespected his father". My father had already long occupied a place in my mind as an agent of the worst kinds of terror, but there was something about that moment, mediated through the just-departed figure of dear, lovely Marvin, that stands out in my memory with the nightmarish clarity of a scene from Kafka's (1912) *Judgment*. My father's macabre endorsement of Marvin's father's act of filicide crystallises the predicament I found myself in when it came to the challenge of accessing a place of safety within the strangely violent culture I inhabited. Already brutally minoritised as a Black/"mixed-race" boy in the all-white enclave of Birkenhead, in that moment (and in most moments before and after) I experienced my father – the only Black parent available – as an unimaginably persecutory figure, offering no protection whatsoever from the violence of racism, of organised white terrorism. Instead, my father appeared to revel in the murderous destruction of a "wayward" Black son by his authoritarian Black father, a Black son with whom, I later realised, I felt an enormous identification. I felt a similar sort of eerie identification with my father's murdered brother, whom I had never met, who had apparently been "sacrificed" in Lagos, in the 1950s, aged twelve, when my father was eight. My father would talk about my dead uncle in the same censorious tones he was now using for Marvin, devoid of any compassion for the slaughtered child, fixated only on the fact that his brother had disobeyed their parents that night by going out when he should have stayed home.

There's a memorable scene in Charles Laughton's film, *The Night of the Hunter*, in which the grandmotherly protectress of the two little orphans, played by former silent movie star Lillian Gish, intensifies her levels of protectiveness by chasing the psychopathic "big bad wolf" figure, played by Robert Mitchum, away from her safe house, pointing a rifle at him as he flees. Such scenes as these conjure up indelible images of the wronged children's belated – but lifesaving – opportunity to be truly watched over, Gish's sentinel-saviour going quite some way to repair the damage done by the weak, dead, love-addicted mother (Shelley Winters), who now lies, definitively unable to mother anyone or anything, at the bottom of a lake. Such scenes as these are surely the reason a self-described *ciné-fils* like Serge Daney found himself, as a young boy, cleaving to Gish's otherworldly presence; the reason too why a filmmaker like Arnaud Desplechin includes images of Gish in his documentary *L'Aimée* (2007), using her to embody a lost figure of maternal love speaking to her abandoned child from another world. But when I first saw *The Night of the Hunter* as a younger teenager, I found myself uncomfortably divided. I drank in these images of the strong, kindly, grandmaternal Gish, pointing her gun at that iconic source of archetypal danger, embodied by Mitchum, but, for me, Gish couldn't be separated from her earlier, equally iconic role in D.W. Griffith's *The Birth of a Nation* (1915). In that film, Gish's purity and goodness had been famously associated with a specifically white identity, so much so that the embodiment of evil against which she was pitted was represented as Black. Black men (grotesquely portrayed by whites in "blackface") were her enemy then: rapists and monsters to be destroyed by none other than the Ku Klux Klan.

As a child, I found myself moving nervously away from the unfortunately racialised, "big bad wolf" figure of my father and briefly, in true fairy tale style, towards the figure of my (white) maternal grandmother, who lived a hundred miles away in Yorkshire and was, seemingly (though not in fact), my father's mortal enemy. But there was a part of my young, Black/"mixed-race" boy self, who could not *un-know* what he knew about my grandmother and what she stood for, at least partially, in the white terrorist culture I was growing up in. I couldn't unproblematically internalise this white-haired old lady as someone actually willing to watch over me; no more than I could ever hope for the same kind of love, care, acceptance, and protection she extended to my white cousins. Her contemptuous, racist remarks towards my sisters and me spoiled our (nevertheless persistent) hopes of turning to her home as a refuge from our parents. Neither she, nor my father, nor Marvin Gaye, nor Lillian Gish afforded me anything resembling a psychical shelter or protective membrane in childhood; on the contrary, they fired weirdly intrusive, violating bullets of *excessive presence* into my developing mind, eroding still further whatever might be left of my identity once the dangerous environment outside the house had finished with me. As for my ghostly mother, in masochistic thrall to both of them, she was, in Fisher's (2016) formulation, eerie rather than weird, her emotional *hyper-absence* resembling nothing so much as that of Shelley Winters in *The Night of the Hunter*, dead-yet-uncannily-moving, at the bottom of a secret and faraway lake.

In the autoethnographic chapter of this book, I explored my early turn to eerily moving images for the experience of containment I so desperately sought. This final chapter attempts, as the earlier chapter could not, to face the limitations of this kind of move when, in addition to developing within an unsafe home environment, one also finds oneself racialised in the society in which one lives as "Black". Something usually gets spoiled in the psycho-digestive tract of the Black spectator who tries to feed from the table of white culture amid omnipresent racism. Even when the image-food s/he tries to take in to remedy the starvation of traumatic abandonment and neglect is not actually poisoned, as in the case of Lillian Gish, the film-orphan racialised as Black, "mixed", or otherwise not white, will often find themselves gnawing at scraps. It feels important to me to build on and extend André Green's (1986) idea of a "dead mother complex" – that is, a psychical state in which no living imago of nourishing maternal containment can be successfully introjected by the eerily abandoned infant – in order that it may include a psychosocial dimension and, in particular, a racialised one. What happens to the psyches of children who are orphaned not only by the (non) facilitating environment of their parents, family, and family home, but also by the pathologically neglectful (non) container of a hostile dominant national culture? Ought we not to speak of a "dead mother complex" not only in the haunted children of deadly and deadening caregivers, but also, on a mass scale, in the racialised "children" of a deadly and deadening white terrorist system that refuses *ever*

to let them feel that they are really at home? How do we go about understanding the complex ways in which private-parental neglect *connects* to collective-systemic neglect, often channelled through individual members of the family, who perform their destructive "caregiving" in simultaneously universal and racialised ways? If the ordinary, non-racialised survivor of familial trauma can find his or her way towards certain kinds of moving image that may offer an "alive" path beyond a chronic state of dereliction, how might we need to adapt this act of cultural inventiveness in order to accommodate the needs of the doubly-orphaned, racialised viewer? Charlotte Beradt (1985), writing specifically about the racialised particularities of dreaming under the Third Reich, expresses brilliantly what may be at stake for us here:

> Their dreams – although just as much motivated by anxiety and horror as the dreams of others – nevertheless constitute a separate category, just as the Jews themselves were a separate category under the Nazi regime. For from the very beginning, they were the focus of direct, not indirect, terrorization. For this reason, I have decided to deal with the dreams of Jews in a separate, final chapter.
>
> (p. 130)

(Not) dreaming of Keith

Watching *Six Feet Under* for the first time in the autumn of 2005, I remember feeling worried, halfway through the third season, that some kind of "Marvin moment" might be creeping up on me, when Keith (Mathew St Patrick) confronts his quietly terrifying father over his abuse of him and his sister Karla (Nicki Micheaux) in childhood. The filicidal moment doesn't arise, of course: Keith survives the confrontation with his father, and goes on, after much wrangling, to adopt two sons and build a family with his partner David (Michael C. Hall). He's eventually murdered brutally, however, in a shooting, decades later, in the famous closing sequence of the show's finale. It's as if there is no place to hide for Keith: if he isn't despatched by his monstrous Black dad, then he must be killed by the act of daring to move through the white world as a Black man in America. What's even more disturbing about Keith, of course, is that he himself is an agent of anti-Black, racialised terror: he's an officer of the LAPD. And yet it's never clear whether this murderous role he ends up embracing on behalf of the state is even acknowledged as such within the context of the series. The viewer is left instead in a state of insecurity and doubt. Or rather, the *Black* viewer is left in a space of insecurity and doubt. Are we supposed to see a grotesque irony in Keith's choice of career? Or are we instead meant to admire his identification with the Law?

Of all the lines spoken between the characters, living and dead, over the 63 episodes of *Six Feet Under*, there is one in particular that enters my ears as a toxin, a lie, a "leperous distilment" (Shakespeare, 2006, p. 216), as Hamlet's ghost-father puts it, at variance with any conceivable sense of being watched over or taken care of by the series. The line, ironically enough – but perhaps this is no irony whatsoever – explicitly concerns the voiced experience of one of the white protagonists of feeling looked after. After a significant separation in the third season, David and Keith come together again after church to discuss the possibility of a reconciliation. Explaining to Keith some of the context of his initial attraction to him, David blurts out: "I loved that you were a cop. It made me feel *safe*". Hearing that line of David's again in the spring of 2020, when I was revising this research project for publication as a book, a time when the systematically racialised and murderous regime of American and European policing was being challenged through public protests on a scale unprecedented in my lifetime, I couldn't help but feel even more disappointed by my favourite series than usual. How grotesque, I thought, that the white-skinned David gets to feel "safe" in the arms of his partner – the Black policeman Keith (although he complains for most of the first three seasons that Keith's anger makes him feel scared) – even as Keith colludes on a daily basis with a white terrorist system of "law enforcement" to maim and murder his African-American brothers and sisters, at one point actually facilitating the imprisonment of his actual sister Karla. The writers of *Six Feet Under* may have been aware of the racialised irony of this particular caregiving situation (and there are tiny hints, from time to time throughout the show, that some of them were), but the privilege and unconscious horror of David's loving remark is left unexplored, and the viewer, especially the Black viewer, is left stewing in a state of mixed-up, gaslit neglect. I'm tempted to describe this kind of cultural experience as a confusion of tongues (cf. Ferenczi, 1949) in the context of *racialised* potential space (cf. Winnicott, 1971). Reaching out for a transitional object to soothe or look after him or her whilst in a state of distress, the viewer racialised as Black instead finds that they may be playing with a toy that was not only not made for them, not only might prove dangerous for them to touch, but that also whispers to them in the language of their abuser.

The *Six Feet Under* episode entitled "Nobody Sleeps" (3:4), features a surprise birthday party for Ruth (Frances Conroy), in which Nate (Peter Krause) shares a recent dream with his mother and the other guests, who include his wife Lisa (Lili Taylor), brother David, and David's partner Keith. Like much of Nate's psychical material following his brain surgery at the end of the second season, the dream, as narrated, appears to be mildly pre-cognitive in tone, having apparently anticipated some form of the foot massage (performed by his wife, Lisa, on his mother,

Ruth) he now watches in fascination. During his narration of the dream, Nate specifies that whilst Ruth, Lisa, David, their younger sister Claire (Lauren Ambrose, absent from the actual party), and their dead father Nathaniel (Richard Jenkins) are all present in the dream, Keith – who has featured, in some form, as David's partner, love-object or significant other from the first episode of the first season, and will continue to do so until and beyond the final episode of the final season, that is, beyond death – was definitely *not* present in his dream. Nate's voluntarily offered detail is somehow jarring: the brief shot of a perplexed and hurt Keith is followed by an equally brief image of David's blank and impenetrable embarrassment. Nate, vaguely aware of the discomfort that his incapacity to dream of Keith has caused, carries on regardless with his description of the kinsfolk who *do* feature in his unconscious – the related dream will shortly feature his baby daughter Maya squirming, Lewis Carroll-esque, like a pig – muttering, before he does so, the cryptic non-apology to no one in particular: *no offence*.

There's something fascinating about the way in which *Six Feet Under*, like Nate himself, murmurs, almost under its breath, its own inability – or unwillingness – to "dream" its ethnic minority characters' existences with the same kind of aliveness with which it depicts its white characters' inner worlds and transpersonal spirits. That aliveness, as the previous chapter has tried to demonstrate, holds the capacity to offer, to certain viewers, revitalising energies which, at times, seem nothing short of miraculous. But those viewers must apparently accept, if they are to continue "playing" with the series as a psychical object that might, in some way, be "caring" for them, that the dreaming taking place through the show, and through them, is, by and large, a white dreaming. I asked Sandra, a (Black) participant in my *Six Feet Under* research project, what she thought of the show's representation of "race" and racism, filtered as it might be, at least potentially, through the depicted experiences of Keith, his sister Karla, his niece Taylor (Aysia Polk), and his and David's foster children Anthony (C.J. Sanders)and Durrell (Kendré Berry). "Nothing", she replied, scarcely missing a beat. "I wasn't expecting anything; and I didn't *get* anything". The responses of two other participants, Anna and Mark, both white, and watching the series together, in Northern Ireland, as a couple, were equally disturbing. Anna expressed a sense of unease at the way in which both David as a character and the show as a narrative seem to lose all emotional curiosity about Keith as the series develops. "Keith stops having any dimensions to him", she said. "He just becomes David's partner".

Sandra's and Anna's different but equally sobering reactions regarding the question of race in the show seemed to me both entirely justified and – suddenly, secretly – dangerous, causing my judgment to waver and split. I found myself frantically trying to defend the show from racism in my own mind. Was it altogether fair, I whimpered internally, to judge the writers of a wonderful television series so harshly? *They were only doing their best!* It felt almost as if some loyally neglected child-fragment of myself was suddenly bristling and silently twittering, all because of the critical insight of these two participants. The whole maddening process reminded me of the way my mind began to stutter whenever I tried to integrate the flashes of ordinary parenting offered by my mother into a putatively "fair" appraisal of my violent and dangerous childhood. In much the same way, any balanced assessment of my much-loved (and equally white) televisual "mother", *Six Feet Under*, felt, at least in this new context of a possible charge of racism, somehow beyond my ken. On and on went the confused and defensive inner voice, trying to respond (without talking) to Anna's remark about Keith. What about the integration of the adopted Black boys, Anthony and Durrell, into the Fisher dynasty? What about the utopian, multi-ethnic metamorphosis of Fisher & Sons/Fisher & Diaz/Fisher & Sons in the show's future-glimpsing final sequence? Were these not generous gifts indeed for a poor, orphaned viewer such as myself?

The truth is, I think, that both Sandra and Anna are right: none of *Six Feet Under*'s liberal "generosity" can overcome Nate's, the show's, or the viewer's *inability to dream of Keith*, to stay with Keith's dreams, to treat Keith as a full and *bona fide* human being. Mark, Anna's partner, noted how even minor white characters, introduced as late as the fourth season, seem to be effortlessly granted subjectivities, and articulation of those subjectivities, that are at once more moving and more psychologically nuanced than Keith's. When Ruth, in Season Five, describes the problematic "layers around George's heart", for example, George's (James Cromwell) post-traumatic schizoid seclusion *comes to life*, exclaims Mark, in a way Keith's own behavioural and relational issues never do, not even in the hey-day of his family storylines during the second and third seasons. Even George's daughter Maggie (Tina Holmes) is given emotional life of a kind never afforded Keith, when, towards the end of the fifth season, we catch a glimpse of her unbridled, justified, infantile rage towards her father. I finally asked Mark and Anna if, given everything they were now pointing out, they felt the writing of the show could be characterised as racist. Their hesitation, heavy with awkwardness – at least, as I experienced it in my own body – lasted more than a few seconds. At last, Anna spoke:

> I guess it is racist. [Pause.] It *is* racist! In the sense that they are denying the only significant Black character the humanity and the depth that they do the white characters. I think I held back from answering your question because I was trying to .... All the characters move between 2D and 3D representation. But Keith is the only one who gets definitively put *back* in the 2D box. He is made to go backwards. And then he is shot dead in the coda. It really upset me that they did that. It felt cruel. And then you're supposed to see his death as a tragedy for *David*!

The first time I watched the show I really latched onto the character progression of Keith. But then this second time around ... I feel ... it's as if you're supposed to not feel intimacy with Keith.

Where things get even more confusing is that the chief writers of *Six Feet Under*, all of whom appear to be white, are clearly very much aware of not only their own racialised limitations as writers, but also of Keith's capacity to be represented – and not represented – in a problematic, ignorant, or even racist, way. They seem to go back and forth between racially aware (self-) critique and lazy, disappointing, racialised neglect. In her DVD commentary of the twelfth episode of the second season, Jill Soloway makes repeated – and often jarring – reference to her own "super-whiteness" and the ways in which this led her to make apparent errors of judgment in her representation of non-white characters. (Interestingly, her self-critique, which causes her to fall into the trap of assuming that there are in fact authentically African-American ways of bringing up children, on which she can be educated by talking to a single African-American person, seems at least as problematic as her original state of white ignorance.) Early in the first season, Claire's memorable conversation with Keith, as the two of them hunt for a disembodied foot in a field at night-time, demonstrates Claire's (relative) sensitivity to Keith's potential predicament as a Black gay man who is all too susceptible to being ensnared in the racialised sexual fantasies of white men. But, as Guy Mark Foster (2006) notes, simply pointing out Keith's potential to be pornographically objectified as a "big, black sex cop" does not preclude the show's capacity to participate in precisely the same kinds of objectification and erasure.

Claire tends to be the one character in the show who dares to speak of racism. Revolted by a hidden mammy moneybox discovered in a kitchen cupboard in the fourth season or pointing out the gendered and racialised division of kitchen labour at another birthday party at the Fisher household (again in Season Four), Claire "calls shit out" before calling shit out even became a "thing". However, not unlike Soloway, her interventions tend to feel simultaneously overstated and under-effective. Claire's friendship, dating, art, and professional worlds remain dazzlingly white; meanwhile Keith's Blackness – and, more importantly, his humanity – is kept firmly restrained by the guilty, mumbling screenwriters. They're happy to represent, in a comedic mode, how out-of-place Keith feels at an all-white party of performatively camp, white gay men. His failure to "identify himself" as the C-list Hollywood actor Jeanne Tripplehorn in a ridiculous game of "Leading Ladies" – like all the other party guests, he has the name of a mystery celebrity pinned to his back – is amusingly presented as his supreme badge of cultural shame. In a rare glimpse into Keith's inner world, we see him hallucinating the other party guests as grotesque, white school bullies who shriek his "clue", the forgotten (or never known) film title (*Waterworld*), again and again. But it's up to the viewer to guess whether his later reluctance to allow David a speaking role in a conflict at Keith's own parents' house may or may not be linked to his earlier, (perhaps) racialised marginalisation at David's choral buddy's party.

In short, when it comes to the possibility of *Six Feet Under* as a vehicle for exploring in a specifically racialised context the kinds of psychical starvation and complex trauma with which this book has been concerned, the viewer is offered only crumbs of Black aliveness. These crumbs are certainly tantalising; and they raise a lot of questions. In what sense are Keith and his addict sister Karla survivors of racialised trauma? How do issues of racialised shame and inequality get played out in Keith's and David's relationship? And, perhaps the most chilling question of all: to what extent does Keith, or anyone else, understand that the violent death that waits for him in the show's – for some viewers unforgivably flippant – coda is inextricably linked to his perennially precarious status as a Black man in America? It all remains frustratingly under-explored. And the ghosts have nothing to say about any of it. Viewers of *Six Feet Under* who find themselves in a condition of racialised trauma must not count on either the show or its ghosts to "watch over" them when it comes to this particular aspect of their suffering. There may appear *flashes* of excitingly progressive writing, not least given the era in which production took place. As Munt (2006) points out, "there is [...] a determined anti-colonial strategy evident in the script – especially in the overt way that the unconscious racism of Nate and David is exposed, for example – that goes some way to sustaining the radical, or counter-discursive ideology of the show" (pp. 265–6). But the show's capacity to dream freely of race, racism, and racialised trauma remains stuck. The deep, psychical, physical, and structural realities of racialised living and dying feel unbearable, invisible and unexplored, seemingly beyond the emotional limits of the show, its writers, and its characters. All three seem vaguely aware of the regrettable borders erected by their excruciating whiteness, but they carry on maintaining these walls regardless, merely muttering: "No offence!" And there is none taken.

A few drops of spectral milk

It is documented that, throughout the Hollywood era, certain movies, ostensibly having nothing to do with the Black experience, seemingly "spoke" to Black – often, surprisingly, poor Black – audiences. Heffernan (2002) excavates fascinating material regarding the distribution of George A. Romero's zombie film, *Night of the Living Dead* (1968), to urban audiences, and its often extremely positive reception by Black American spectators. Meanwhile, more recently, contemporary Black filmmaker Marc L.

Abbott (Beckerman, 2020), in an interview devoted to the history and resurgence of horror film and television amongst Black audiences, remarks:

> As kids, when we would sneak in and see these movies, we would see an African American on screen and all of us were like, "OK, set your watch, let's see how long he lasts". [...] Some years ago, I read somewhere that African Americans make up a very large portion of the people who go to see horror films. Even Stephen King said he went to a Black neighborhood to see *Carrie* to see what our reaction was going to be. People were screaming and yelling at the screen.

Coming across these kinds of anecdotes for the first time, I was fascinated and comforted by the notion that I wasn't the only person racialised as Black who'd felt drawn to and identified with the inexplicably fantastical sufferings of the telekinetic outcast Carrie, or even, perhaps, the feline Serbian immigrant Irena. As Beckerman (2020) notes: "The idea of being subjugated, silenced, turned into a puppet, is the special horror of people who have – historically – been robbed of self-determination". It seems that many Black people have been doing our best, for a long time, to find our way towards fundamentally bizarre objects in film-culture that we may psychically internalise and, perhaps, reconfigure, as nourishing figures – simultaneously eerie and moving – that we've hoped or intuited, despite everything, might somehow watch over us from the cinematic heaven of their sacrificial abjection.

Tellingly, many of the films towards which we have historically gravitated have tended not to be straightforwardly celebrated by the mainstream critical culture of the time in which they emerged, and have often been somewhat overlooked, accused of poor taste and/or pretentiousness, or deemed in some way to be culturally unreadable. Jancovich (2012) notes that "critics in the 1940s presented the [Val] Lewton films [such as *Cat People*, *The Curse of the Cat People* and *I Walked with a Zombie*] as existing in a no man's-land between the cheap thrills of 'lowbrow' horror entertainments and more respectable, quality women's horror film" (p. 35); the *New York Times,* Jancovich tells us repeatedly, was especially inimical to Lewton. At the same time as enjoying these multiple, thrilling, racialised-not-racialised identifications with horror film characters and scenarios, I've sometimes wondered if we weren't a little like the Black ghetto procession of mourners at the end of the wonderful "urban legends" movie, *Candyman* (1992) – itself a brilliant reflection on the unspoken connections between Blackness and free-floating, "universal" horror-trauma – pouring out of our humble dwellings in the "projects" to pay our respects at the film-funerals of fallen, white (yet somehow, unspeakably, blackened) horror-queens, thanking them, as we might, in the Haitian culture of *vodun*, thank a postmodern, hybrid god or *lwa* such as Ezili, for their oblique, sacrificial connection to our collective, racialised suffering. It has seemed to me, especially in the last decade of my film-watching, that a truly adequate film "rescue operation" for people like us might require finding our way towards *new* eerily moving images, no longer clinging, necessarily, to the pale and ghostly figures of Sissy Spacek, Simone Simon, or Virginia Madsen (who plays the hapless PhD-student-turned-folk-heroine Helen in *Candyman*). But where are we meant to find truly reinvigorated forms of psychosocial rescue?

The cultural theorist bell hooks has explored the various means by which viewers racialised as Black have continued to feed themselves through mainstream moving images, against all the odds. hooks' (1992) concept of "the oppositional gaze" is a crucial one, allowing us to make sense of the psychical acrobatics performed, often unconsciously, by Black film fans who must negotiate the images they take in inventively, refusing certain significations and ideological content which may prove harmful to them, whilst at the same time introjecting those elements of representation that are genuinely pleasurable:

> Spaces of agency exist for black people, wherein we can both interrogate the gaze of the Other but also look back, and at one another, naming what we see. The "gaze" has been and is a site of resistance for colonized people globally. Subordinates in relations of power learn experientially that there is a critical gaze, one that "looks" to document, one that is oppositional. In resistance struggle, the power of the dominated to assert agency by claiming and cultivating "awareness" politicizes "looking" relations – one learns to look a certain way in order to resist.
> (p. 116)

Bobo's (1988) classic reading of the multiple gendered and racialised readings of Steven Spielberg's (1985) film adaptation of Alice Walker's (1982) novel, *The Color Purple*, explores the various strategies available to viewers who may need to create alternative introjections of problematic filmic representations in order to experience a pleasurable feed. Bobo evokes the "schizophrenic reaction" of Black viewers, quoting a man speaking on the *Donahue* show who states simply that "you're torn in two" watching *The Color Purple*, as you find yourself having to navigate the obnoxious knowledge of appalling racist stereotypes of Black men and the nourishing satisfaction of seeing Black women depicted on screen in generous close-ups the like of which you've never seen before.

Being "torn in two" is never a straightforward process, of course, and sometimes our consumption of problematic images can have nothing oppositional about it. At worst, the Black viewing of white cinema can lead the hapless spectator into what we might now call, post-*Get Out* (2017), a cinematic "sunken place". hooks recalls the wretched character of Miss Pauline in Toni Morrison's first novel, *The Bluest Eye* (1999

[1970]), when the latter narrates her profoundly cinematic memory of only ever being happy when at the movie theatre, gobbling up images of Clark Gable and Jean Harlow in all their pseudo-perfect, resplendent whiteness. Miss Pauline's recounted experience as a starving Black film viewer in desperate need of soul-food, but instead losing a tooth as she bites at poisonous candy, is truly painful to read. My own sense of many of the moving images from Hollywood I took in as a hungry adolescent is that they constituted a form of what Eigen (1999) has called "toxic nourishment". My feeding process was always messy and disorganised. Whilst it's undeniable that, at some important level, I *was* being poisoned, my need for images of quasi-parental – and later quasi-angelic – containment was such that I was willing to run the risk of splitting my system in order that *one* (seemingly "post-racial") part of me might be fed, even as the *other* (racialised and vulnerable) parts withered to a state of even more pronounced orphandom and enfeeblement. I took care to screen out those recurring, relentless aspects of the movies of my "New Hollywood" heroes and heroines that were undeniably – often bizarrely – racist or which, at best, simply eradicated Black experience. The aggressively snow-white worlds of David Lynch, Brian de Palma, Robert Altman, and Woody Allen just had to be sucked or snorted up; it would do me no good to question the intentions of my new cine-guardians; there came a time, it seemed to me, when beggars really could not afford to be choosers. I'd already learned the drill a decade earlier, in any case, when I'd decided it was worth submitting to Enid Blyton's obsessively racialised hatred – she couldn't mean *me*, surely? – in order to get high on the indescribable wings of her various secret islands, wishing chairs and faraway trees. Like Black film viewers for generations before me, I made do with what was on psycho-cultural offer; and I did my best to turn those frequently toxic scraps into a decent meal. In what remains of this chapter, I try to explore what it might mean to move from foraging for scraps to demanding (and finding) actual food.

In the spring of 2020, the strange, metamorphosing period of pandemic, lockdown, and what felt, in the wake of George Floyd's murder by police officers in Minneapolis, like the beginning of another racialised revolution in the United Kingdom and the United States, I had one more in a series of bizarrely vivid dreams that seemed to speak to me about my most intractable complexes through the language of movies and television:

> I am talking animatedly (and with more than a little reverence) to a fifty- or sixty-something Katharine Hepburn about how excited I am to be accompanying her to an anniversary screening of *Guess Who's Coming to Dinner?* (1967). Hepburn is both polite and friendly, and there are no bad vibes whatsoever. However, she is also incredibly distracted and doesn't seem to be really listening to me, or even remotely

interested in my childlike enthusiasm. I realise, with a heavy heart, that she is still obsessed with the absence of the dead Spencer Tracy and is unable to concentrate on me or anything else.

There was something powerful about this dream for me at that particular time, as it seemed to present, in the most indisputable terms possible, my need to face up to the impossibility, once and for all, of getting fed by a certain imago of phantasmatic white parenting, incarnated in the figure of the "liberal" Katharine Hepburn. The dream seemed to scream, in glorious Technicolor, Green's (1986) memorable line in about the impossibility of ever making real emotional contact with the "dead mother", in either her external or internal versions, as, despite going through some of the performative motions of caregiving, her "heart is not in it" (p. 151). Green never racialises his vision of the "dead mother complex", of course, but, for me, Katharine Hepburn in my dream is reminiscent not only of my own inaccessible (white) mother, but also of the white, *almost*-mother figures (played by Claudette Colbert and Lana Turner), so clung to and shrieked at by the desperately hungry Peola (Fredi Washington) and Sarah Jane (Susan Kohner) in the two different film versions of *Imitation of Life* (1934 and 1959). These white mothers hover, tantalisingly, on the brink of availability; but there's always something distracting them from being actually present. (In the two *Imitation of Life* films, of course, they are not even the actual mothers of the frantic Black daughters.) Meanwhile, the racialised child, doubly orphaned, feels herself growing less and less real, "un-homed" not only in her own body and conception of herself, but also in the wider environment of a relentlessly racialised and racialising society.

hooks (1992), writing about her own viewing experience of Peola as a young Black girl, frames the situation poignantly:

> She was tragic because there was no place in the cinema for her, no loving pictures. She too was absent image. It was better, then, that we were absent, for when we were there it was humiliating, strange, sad. We cried all night for you, for the cinema that had no place for you. And like you, we stopped thinking it would one day be different.
>
> (p. 122)

Strangely enough, in *Six Feet Under*, Keith does, at one point, draw an unexpected comparison between himself and Sarah Jane in *Imitation of Life*. Curiously, though, his comparison has nothing whatsoever to do with racialised invisibility, but is instead made as a comment about internalised homophobia. This move by the writers of the show feels counter-intuitive, unsettling – are they even aware of the fact that they are, once again, involving Keith in a double, perhaps triple erasure of his own specifically racialised experience? At this point, though – and it seems to me that my dream of Katharine Hepburn serves as an almost cosmic indicator of this – the moment may have arrived to stop caring about what "they" are (or aren't) thinking, what "they" are (or aren't) capable of thinking. It may be time, instead, to focus on a less "scraps"-based form of feeding, something closer to active spectatorship, to creative, collective imagination.

Dreaming of aliveness while Black

This chapter charts some of the current explorations of film-dreamers racialised as Black, living under historical, contemporary, and emerging forms of systemic white terrorism. If this book has hitherto been content to deploy the concept of psychical decolonisation in a relatively apolitical manner, examining the various ways in which the (adult) child, whose mind and body have been thrown under the bus (or into a "sunken place") by his or her caregivers might, with a little luck, discover alternative forms of care in the eerily moving images of film and other media, I want to turn now to a more explicitly politicised version of the same cultural odyssey. In a society in which a violently racialised minority of the members is abandoned, neglected, and violated, both physically and emotionally, throughout their lives, long beyond the period of childhood, and even into old age – if they even make it that far, the odds being stacked against this – what does it mean for this minority to be "watched over" by the moving images produced by that same culture? It seems to me that in order to answer this question and to actively pursue its implications, we need to be willing to racialise our own discussion of trauma, of caregiving, of transcendence, of time-travel, and of dreams, all the while lamenting the omnipresent and violent forms of racialisation that oblige us to make this necessary adjustment to theories of spectatorship that ought to be able to be applied to everyone.

I want to write from the fullness of my experience as a racialised person living in neo-fascist times. Multiple and overlapping zones of psychical impingement must be *joined up and thought about* if we are to produce theories and practices of emotional recovery adequate to the intersections of psyches formed simultaneously within non-facilitating families *and* non-facilitating societies. It's from this intersection that I want to share glimpses of a (mainly Black) community of viewers for whom new possibilities of selfhood are being shaped through active participation in watching, dreaming, and communing through film. Green's (1986) psychoanalytic formulation of the "dead mother complex" posits the existence of a child-psyche that grows simultaneously listless and frantic in the shadow of disavowed maternal neglect. Meanwhile, in a very different philosophical register, Agamben's (1998) biopolitical theory of the hapless outcast, the *homo sacer*, stripped of citizenship and condemned to the active *non-care* of the state, moves towards the portrait of an analogously zombified figure, beyond both hope and despair, as the natural outcome of a process of environmental abandonment. Green and Agamben are unable to meet each other on clinical, philosophical, or political ground, failing to recognise that they are describing comparable processes of violent dereliction, wherein defenceless or infantilised figures are rendered homeless, motherless, and stateless by the structures that are supposed to be watching over them but which, for complicated reasons to do with their own narcissistic psychopathology, are unwilling to do so.

Neither Agamben nor Green has ever (to my knowledge) engaged with the psychical and physical harm that has for centuries been perpetrated against those of us who are racialised as Black. But theories from race-conscious philosophers have begun to emerge over the last three decades that begin to grapple with the idea of a mass deadening – at both a corporeal and an emotional level – of Black Life by white minds and systems presenting themselves as facilitating environments. We know that people racialised as Black within contemporary European and American – and we could add Australian, Asian, and Middle Eastern – societies often find themselves attacked, maimed, and killed, via brutal and dehumanising processes of literally deadly racialisation. Whilst much has been written about the hyper-vulnerability of "Black bodies" to physical violence, relatively little has been written about the vulnerability of the "Black psyche" to racialised projections, mainly emanating from white minds, which would seek, consciously or unconsciously, to rob it of its very sense of aliveness. Fanon (2008), Davids (2011), and Lowe (2014) have all demonstrated by means of psychoanalytic theory how white racist practices and projections at the interpersonal level can contribute to the destruction of a capacity for thinking in both the white racist and in the human "object" s/he would seek to racialise. As thinking is eroded, and the living links between minds find themselves under attack, something emotionally vital dies, and a phenomenon we might term psychical murder by racialisation starts to set in. We can build a bridge between two theoretical concepts of vulnerable forms of life – the infantile and the racialised – that are dependent on the recognition and nurturance of their facilitating environments for their survival, and which find themselves progressively deadened when they are prevented from internalising good, living, reflective imagoes of protection, willing to acknowledge and affirm them as loveable and real. Holland (2000) theorises the disturbing repetition in Black-authored literature and film of the idea that we are already at least partially deceased, our proximity to the ghoulish figures of ghosts and zombies sometimes so intense that we appear indistinguishable from them. And Butler (1993) investigates a spectral dimension of non-speech and non-life at the heart of Larsen's novella, *Passing* (1929), in which (apparently unspeakable) manifestations of Blackness (or mixed-ness) and homosexuality (or bisexuality) become subsumed into murderous (or suicidal) urges within the protagonists Clare and Irene.

But Black culture under white enslavement and colonial rule has *always* known about the eerie erosion, or attempted erosion, of Black aliveness through the structures and systems of racialised projection. From the syncretistic cultural formation of vodun in the plantocratic Americas in the eighteenth century, to the "marvellous realism" (predating the "magical realism" of Gabriel García Márquez and other Latin American novelists of *el boom*) of mid-twentieth-century Haitian writer Jacques Stephen Alexis, artists and sorcerers racialised as Black have demonstrated an unshakable conviction that we are in some way bewitched, rendered in some way unreal, by the murderous minds of a white-identified desire to deaden and enslave. Toni Morrison's (1988) novel, *Beloved*, is, of course, a profound meditation on the insertion of a complex of "undeadness" (embodied by the ghost-ghoul character of Beloved herself) at the heart of the post-plantation Black family, a family for which there can be no "post" in the sense of "post-traumatic", since the trauma of racialisation is lived out again and again, every moment of every day, in the unrepentantly genocidal United States. And Octavia Butler (1979) demonstrates just as relentless a preoccupation with the fantastical eeriness at the heart of the Black experience in America, her novel *Kindred* experimenting with time travel in order to reveal the embedding of a collective antebellum plantation psyche within the everyday reality of 1970s American life. The portmanteau horror movie, *Tales from the Hood* (1995), revolves around a literally funereal set of Black characters in various stages of fantastical disintegration, whilst Spike Lee's underrated film, *Bamboozled* (2001), a decade later, invokes the uncanniness of racist puppets, dolls, and automata to insist on a collective hollowing out of Black consciousness, as both bodies and souls are replaced by the mainstream white media with the humiliating masks and bestial iconography of brittle, post-human, un-life.

We find ourselves living through a veritable cultural renaissance of "afrosurrealism" (cf. Baraka, 1974); our film and television screens are filled with more mainstream magical or pseudo-magical representations of racialised dreams and complexes than ever before. This is the age of acclaimed television shows such as Donald Glover's *Atlanta* (2016–present) and the much-discussed HBO series, *Lovecraft Country* (2020–present). As I write this in 2020, I am looking forward, like many other people obsessed with the intersection of film, horror, and representations of Blackness, to the cinematic release of a Black-directed remake of the 1992 film, *Candyman*, to be scripted by Jordan Peele, Win Rosenfeld, and Nia DaCosta. What does it mean, I wonder, for a Black person in the United Kingdom, the United States, or anywhere else, to be excitedly awaiting, during a global pandemic, and during a terrifyingly widespread reassertion of white terrorism across Europe and the Americas, *a new version of Candyman*? Does our desire for the cinematic reincarnation of this movie – and the ghoulish icon at its heart – merely suggest an infantile limitation in our capacity to face political realities too ferocious to process, or is an altogether more serious desire making itself felt?

"Love your hearts!"

There's a memorable flashback sequence in Jonathan Demme's much-ignored film adaptation (1998) of Toni Morrison's (1988) novel, *Beloved*, in which we're allowed to witness brief images of the post-plantation community of formerly enslaved people gathering under the leadership of the old woman Baby Suggs (Beah Richards). The original words of Baby Suggs, as written by Morrison, are, in themselves, tremendously moving, as she famously exhorts the traumatised Black children, women, and men over whom she watches to take note of their dehumanisation by white terrorism and to "love your hearts!" accordingly. Such active self-love is the only recourse possible when one has been so obscenely reduced to the status of meat; the only recourse, that is, if one is to survive, to thrive, and, ultimately, to transcend the murderous structures from which one has miraculously escaped. And the flashback images of Baby Suggs, preaching to her "children" at the Clearing are, in Demme's film, for me, eerily moving at a visceral level.

The living character of Sethe (Oprah Winfrey) is able to make contact with her memory of her (long dead) mother-in-law Baby Suggs and her miraculously enlivening sermons in the Clearing through seemingly direct time-travel, staring into Baby Suggs' eyes and smiling, via a shot-reverse shot, receiving a smile and a wave of loving recognition from Baby Suggs, across time, in return. There is, in other words, a connection between the past and the future that's rendered fantastically literal and visible through the language of film. Sethe is enlivened in her present-day (1870s) struggles with racialised, post-traumatic terror, through her ability to access, both in her mind and on the screen, the moving images of an 1850s-era Baby Suggs and her sermons of protection.

What I want to explore in the remainder of this chapter is the possibility that, for those of us still living in the shadow of racialised terror and trauma, we need to be able to access our own eerily moving images of Baby Suggs and her sermon in the Clearing. Following the lead of certain strands of contemporary African American Jungian analytical writing, such as the account of transgenerational maternal loss offered by Fanny Brewster (2018), or Samuel Kimbles' (2014) discussion of intergenerational transmissions of racialised trauma, I ask my questions in the relatively pragmatic terms of a film curator, psychotherapist, and political activist. What if we were able to come together in our collective orphandom, in order to experience being watched over by something "unspeakable", something making its way to us simultaneously from both the past and the future? This isn't meant to be either a mystical or a wilfully opaque formulation. I'm making the serious suggestion that the sequence of Baby Suggs' sermon in the Clearing in *Beloved* be used as a paradigm for what it might mean to survive and thrive through the culture of moving images when one finds oneself and one's community framed, in a seemingly ongoing manner, as dead, dying, and deadened minds and bodies. What sorts of emotional and political processes of *reversed* deadening and active enlivening might take place among Black audiences, watching together, and being watched over together, by the same eerily moving images? How might those processes become even more integrated within the recovering psyche-soma when racialised audiences are furthermore enabled to talk together, even to "pray" together, about what they are experiencing together?

Different modes of environmental deadening and dereliction meet at the psychical crossroads inhabited by the mournful figure of an orphaned viewer racialised as Black. This figure is often strangely connected to his or her own sense of eerily introjected ghostliness, and dimly senses that the only way in which this sense of ghostliness might be overcome, or transformed, in the service of enlivening change, may be to actively witness the integration of his or her twin conditions on a fantastically alive screen of eerily moving images. The orphaned viewer racialised as Black realises that this active witnessing should probably, for maximum effectiveness, take place in a consciously alive and politicised community film-space. I take the questions and intuitions of this doubly orphaned spectator very seriously indeed. How might eerily moving images intervene in their felt sense of themselves as not only zombified by the environment into which they have been born, but also selected, via relentless systems of racialisation, for premature death? What might a recovered good object look like in these kinds of eerily moving film-dreams? Could certain forms of cultural testimony of racialised deadening and deadness paradoxically transmit something eternally alive, something that resists and transcends genocidal structures, instead watching over, protecting, and fortifying the beleaguered, racialised psyche that still suffers? Where is the something to watch over us in this terrible Fourth Reich of dreams through which we find ourselves currently stumbling?

Alone again or

In the early spring of 2014, I found myself watching Ryan Coogler's film *Fruitvale Station* on the plane to New York. I was on my own. The film recounts the last day in the life of Oscar Grant, a 22-year old African-American man, who (totally unarmed) was shot in the back by a white police officer Johannes Mehserle on the Bay Area Rapid Transit (BART) platform of Fruitvale Station, whilst being held down in a prone position by another white officer, Anthony Pirone, who knelt on his neck, in the early hours of New Year's Day 2009. Oscar died a few hours later, at a hospital in Oakland. Coogler's film re-creates in moving images Oscar's last day on Earth, 31 December 2008. We follow Oscar, played in the film by Michael B. Jordan, over the course of 24 hours, as he works through very different relational and attachment-based issues with his partner Sophina (Melonie Diaz), his mother Wanda (Octavia Spencer) and his young daughter Tatiana (Ariana Neal). *Fruitvale Station* makes thinkable, through an alternately "realist" and lyrical kind of film-dream, the everyday dread that's consciously or unconsciously carried in those of us who are racialised as Black under white state terrorism, in the place where a nurturing internal representation of a protective homeland or good enough "facilitating environment" might be.

In some ways, *Fruitvale Station* could be described as a hyper-modern "dying man's flashback picture", in the tradition of *Sunset Boulevard* (1950), that substitutes Michael B. Jordan's Oscar Grant for William Holden's "ordinary (white) Joe", an Oakland subway platform for Gloria Swanson's Hollywood swimming pool, and a dozen mobile phone film cameras – a gaggle of aghast subway traveller onlookers capturing the dying Oscar's final moments as "evidence" – for Wilder's crew of ghoulish paparazzi cameras. The film is as much concerned with Oscar's emotional sense of aliveness (and deadness) – senses that are refracted through his personal relationships, his internal objects and his introjected impressions of safe and unsafe (though always racialised) spaces – as it is with the biopolitical structures that allow him to live and die in the material realm. One of the great strengths of *Fruitvale Station* is that it weaves together these different experiences of being alive, and of having one's aliveness spoilt, showing how they necessarily intersect in the life – even one day in the life – of a person racialised as Black. Oscar's relationship with his mother Wanda is central to our understanding of how he moves through the world, Wanda's loudly-stated best intentions for her son, whether he's in prison or preparing to travel through the Bay Area on New Year's Eve, ultimately conflicting with her sense of herself as a protective figure who can actually keep her son safe. The protection of Oscar, the facilitation of his aliveness, is beyond his mother's – any mother's – control, the film repeatedly shows us; for there are larger forces at work.

We watch in all-too-familiar discomfort as Oscar's rage at his never-decreasing vulnerability and exposure to the violence of racist institutions starts to harden and solidify into something that looks like psychical deadness. As he yells at the disappearing back of his mother during her abortive visit to him in prison (represented in the film as a brief flashback to the previous year), or morphs into a seething, menacing shadow, whispering the ghost of a threat at the boss who's let him go, we see how non-negotiable is the knife edge on which he dances through a life always

ready to tip into either carnage or zombification. The film's most poignant moments are those that capture the desperately moving potential within his life for a passage into something that's more consistently, energetically alive. When he plays, runs, and cares for his daughter Tatiana – even as she desperately worries about, cares for him, knowing, somehow, that his is a life constantly under the shadow of death – Coogler's camera reveals energies that are positively fantastical in their capacity to mirror, link, hold, and contain.

Via Oscar's flickering, alive-dead psyche, *Fruitvale Station* shows us a consciousness that's constantly aware of itself as having to exist within an ontologically unstable space, that's constantly being pulled over towards death, even as it attempts to generate and sustain life. This pull is not indicative of some Freudian or Kleinian "death instinct", innately emerging from within Oscar himself – the very suggestion that such a dynamic might be inborn feels almost obscene in the context of any discussion sensitive to the reality of systemically organised projections – but rather of what it means to inhabit a life that's constantly under threat owing to the deathly, envious attacks of the white structures around him. Oscar appears to be able to communicate both with the deadening aspects of his destiny (a communication that reaches its apotheosis in his encounter with a dying dog, roughly halfway through the film) but also, importantly, with all in his present that is passionately, movingly alive. The film itself could almost be said to function as a quasi-angelic presence, watching over the final day of this man whose existence is so painfully fragile, were it not, of course, for the brutal reality of its inability to rescue either him or those of us who, watching the movie in terror, know not only what Oscar's fate will be, but also what our own could be, within a violently racist environment that makes of us not the survivors of past (e.g. childhood) trauma, but the victims, day after day, of repeatedly traumatising attacks.

Fruitvale Station travels back in time not to falsely pluck Oscar out of the way of murder – as Tarantino claims to do for Sharon Tate and her hapless friends in *Once Upon a Time in Hollywood* (2019) – but instead to show us, again and again, the impossibility of his rescue, even by time-travelling cinema. The ones who the film seeks to rescue are us viewers who, like Oscar, are most likely to find our necks under the knee of a death-driven agent of a genocidal state. But how could such a rescue be performed by a film like this? All I knew, travelling on that plane from London to New York, that day in March 2014, was that this was too much to take on my own. The film, especially its last twenty minutes, during which we watch, helpless, as Oscar enters into what we know will be his final hours alive, generated a response of such unprecedented emotional intensity in me that I later found it hard to be sure exactly what had happened. I remember sobbing in my seat; covering my eyes; shouting; groaning. I was, for once, oblivious to whatever white stares might be fixed upon me. For the film was showing me the culmination of those stares, the place we end up when those stares are allowed to enact their projections in bodily form. Accordingly, the stares themselves felt, in that moment, far less necessary to worry about than they normally did. It was as if the look of the film – for it truly looked back at me in love, concern, and anger – was suddenly bigger than both myself and the racialising "real world" space through which I was moving at thousands of miles an hour.

Hard upon my return to London, I decided that I had to try to understand what psychical use I may have been making of the film as I took in its electrifying representations of Oscar's sparks of aliveness and final, tragic deadness. I also wanted to know what would happen if I watched the film with people like me, people who found themselves in a similar predicament of ceaseless and non-consensual racialisation. What can film viewers racialised as Black, viewers who know they could meet a similar end to Oscar's any day of the week, *do* with a film such as *Fruitvale Station*? To what collectively life-saving ends might such a film be turned? Was it ludicrous even to ask such a question? A part of me, especially the one that felt awestruck by the pragmatic endeavours – court support, stop-and-search workshops, direct action – of my anti-authoritarian activist comrades, felt that perhaps it was. And yet a number of emerging theories and practices of group-thinking and collective action were beginning to capture my imagination, and I started to wonder if there was any way in which the mass viewing of movies could be yoked to such endeavours.

The "Thinking Space" project at London's Tavistock Clinic, initiated by the psychotherapist Frank Lowe, some of whose speakers later came together in book form (Lowe, 2014), deployed clinical concepts from object-relations psychoanalysis, especially Bion's (1962) "container" model, in order to explore how "thinking" may be generated around topics such as race, racism, and racialisation, topics that so often lead the groups attempting to discuss them into borderline psychotic states of what Bion (1962) called "-K", that dreadful lack of capacity to think or know about emotional experience, either one's own or somebody else's. Alongside Lowe's concept of group-based illumination and enlivening, through the sharing of unconscious material, I was becoming aware of, and occasionally participating in, a "queer social dreaming matrix" (cf. price 2017), a collective which met once a month in central London, not only to discuss the dreams of the individuals in attendance, but also, more crucially, to seek to make visible, through group conversation, the unconscious threads of psychical connection that might be binding us all together *through* those dreams. Finally, Raluca Soreanu's (2018) research into the creative potentialities of the Brazilian uprising of 2013 captured my imagination, drawing as it did on Ferenczi's (1995) theories of post-traumatic splitting, not to further develop an individual theory of psychical development, but instead, boldly, to suggest that in the coming together of multiple fragmented and traumatised psyches, truly revolutionary, collective, symbol-, thought-, and action-producing energies might be synthesised "in the squares and in the streets":

> Yet there are collectives that are capable of producing symbolic analogies: by putting together a mesh of things – matter, words, chants, rhythms, geometrical forms, occupations of physical space, movement, memories of different temporalities – the working-through of traumatic residues becomes possible. The collective mourns in a new way. The collective mourns new content. "The morning after" still bears a consistent mark. From the precise mesh of things which characterises each moment in the life of a collective, some symbols are born and endure.
>
> (pp. 19–20)

In 2015, with the support of my comrades in the London Campaign Against Police and State Violence (LCAPSV), a collective in New Cross (South London) named The Field, and a little later, my former colleagues at the Birkbeck Institute of the Moving Image (BIMI), I set up the Fruitvale Film Club.

Hanich (2014) states persuasively that

> collectively watching a film with quiet attention should be regarded as a joint action. When silently watching a film together in a cinema (or elsewhere), viewers are not engaged in individual actions that run parallel to each other: watching a film with others often implies a shared activity based on a collective intention in which the viewers jointly attend to a single object – the film.
>
> (p. 338)

I didn't need much convincing of this. What I wanted to know was how Black and other minority ethnic viewers might be able to work internally, externally, and, above all, *together* with various filmic imaginings of post-traumatic aliveness, deadness, and potential resurrection within the context of white state terrorism. Could the psychical and emotional work taking place in film groups watching films such as *Fruitvale Station* together, especially when members of the audience included the friends and/or family of people racialised as Black, and harmed or murdered by state violence, amount to something that might be felt and thought about in such a way that political and emotional action could take place in a truly "alive" way? Could a set of startling, thoughtful and enlivening – yet death-acknowledging – moving images function for our film groups as a regenerative facilitating environment? How might these film groups be used with the purpose of not only helping their members to heal, but also enlivening them in such a way that change can take place on both an individual and collective level?

Prior to the official start of the Fruitvale Film Club, LCAPSV and I had, in October 2014, screened *Fruitvale Station* at the Haringey Independent

Cinema, for a special discussion of racialised state violence, in the company of director Ken Fero (creator of such films as *Injustice* (2001)) and the mother (Myrna Simpson) and son (Graeme Burke) of Joy Gardner, a local Black woman who'd died at the hands of police officers during an immigration raid in her home in Crouch End, London, in 1993. This screening was like nothing I'd previously experienced, in the context of either film-watching or activism. Myrna and Graeme related to the assembled group, as clearly as they could manage, some of the impact on their lives of losing their daughter and mother respectively in such a violent manner. Joy, of course, wasn't present to explain the impact of her own death on her life. And then we watched *Fruitvale Station* together. It was obvious to the group, just as it is obvious to me as I write this, that Joy Gardner is *not* the same person as Oscar Grant. The differences between their stories are multiple; and the gendered and local specificities of the ways in which they were killed are important to remember. But the projection of Oscar's last day on Earth, in the form of Coogler's film, brought to that evening's gathering an emotional and representational intensity that would, in my view, never have been manageable had we *only* listened to the testimony of Myrna and Graeme. Something which those police officers in Crouch End had seemingly asphyxiated when they gagged Joy with thirteen feet of adhesive tape that summer night in 1993 came back to life in the audible sobs of dozens of people watching *Fruitvale Station* together: gasping, crying, making links they would never before have made.

We didn't talk formally again as a group once the lights went up, although some of us did continue to reflect together in the pub across the road on what had just happened. But, for me, there was no turning back from the discovery I'd just made: the only way to deepen our emotional *and* political solidarity as a group under constant threat of abuse and even murder from the state in these increasingly dangerous times was to continue to engage with what was happening to us at the level of both testimony *and* narrative; words *and* images; dreaming *and* action. Once officially born, the Fruitvale Film Club met, on average, once a month, from October 2015 to January 2019. We began the group in New Cross, before re-locating in 2017 to Bloomsbury. Both the first and last coming together of this film collective featured screenings of *Fruitvale Station*. The final screening, at Birkbeck Cinema, was a double bill of *Fruitvale Station* and Ryan Coogler's more popular film *Black Panther* (2018), just a few days after the tenth anniversary of Oscar Grant's death. Over the course of the three and a half years of screenings and post-film group discussions, the Fruitvale Film Club functioned as a space in which participants could watch together moving images of (usually racialised) neglect, abuse, deadness, death, and – crucially – possibilities of aliveness, protection, and resurrection, before moving into a dynamic conversation about what these moving images had done, and were still doing, to our minds and bodies. We often found that our feelings developed and changed in the course of our collective conversations. As we stayed with a particular moment from a film, turning it over in our group-mind, pushing or pulling it from deadness to aliveness through our discussion, we found that it was capable of shifting, and we found that the movies themselves seemed to take on new meanings. Often we were able to share experiences from our lives which the viewing of the films had shaken into consciousness, re-evaluating such experiences both in the light of the film's depiction of something comparable or similar, and in the light of discovering that others in the audience had had comparable or similar experiences.

The films we watched and discussed together in the Fruitvale Film Club were varied, but they usually contained situations and scenarios of race and class-inflected vulnerability, combined with a willingness to imagine, often in quasi-magical form, spaces, and experiences of transcendence that we needed, in order to feel that the world we inhabited *was* actually habitable. The films included Horace Ové's *Pressure* (1976); Mathieu Kassowitz's *La Haine* (1995); Alessio Cremonini's *On My Skin* (2018); Joseph Losey's *M. Klein* (1976); Jonathan Demme's *Beloved* (1998); Ava du Vernay's *13th* (2016); Raoul Peck's *I Am Not Your Negro* (2016); Franco Rosso's *Babylon* (1980); and Menelik Shabazz's *Burning an Illusion* (1981). We also watched more seemingly light-hearted films such as John Singleton's road movie, *Poetic Justice* (1993); Bernard Rose's horror film, *Candyman* (1992); and a television documentary about the psychiatric imprisonment of a young Black British man diagnosed with "schizophrenia", *Whose Mind is it Anyway? John's Story*, featuring the renowned anti-racist activist psychiatrist Dr Suman Fernando, who also attended and participated in that day's Fruitvale Film Club as well as most of the subsequent ones. By the time I'd attended and facilitated just a few of the Fruitvale Film Clubs, my sense of the duty and destiny of "alive" Black cinema and "alive" Black film curation in the dangerous age in which we were (and still are) living began to crystallise. It seemed to me that, no matter how different the films themselves were, what the audiences and groups in attendance appeared to crave – and desperately, gratefully appreciated when it was delivered – was both the cinematic representation of the omnipresence of racialised forms of violence and death, and, crucially, at the same time, the creation of a filmic container capable of somehow mourning, surviving, and surpassing that deathly, racialised violence.

We needed help with emerging from fear and despair, and we realised that our emergence felt more and more real when we could talk together about the often fantastically strange representations that were cinematically available to us. During the remarkable post-film discussion we had in January 2019 of *Black Panther* – a film which deserves a separate book-length study of the nurturing, positive impact it has had on the mental health and internal self-representations of so many of the Black audiences who flocked to see it in cinemas in 2018 – the group seemed to come collectively to a bizarre and unbearably poignant conception of the relationship between that film and Coogler's *Fruitvale Station*, also starring Michael B. Jordan, which had been screened immediately before it. Was *Black Panther* not, we wondered together, in some incredible way, an outlandish, cinematic dream of Oscar Grant, as he lay dying on the platform of Fruitvale Station? There was something about our surreal group-formulation of a death-defying relationship, across time and space, between the two films, that felt so *right* at the time we discussed it. It hasn't left me yet.

Arising from the sunken place?

As this chapter moves towards its end, I want to share aspects of a screening and post-film discussion at the Fruitvale Film Club of Jordan Peele's horror film, *Get Out* (2017), which took place at Birkbeck Cinema in 2018. As is well known, *Get Out* was a ground-breaking cinematic phenomenon as soon as it was released, the story of a young African-American man, Chris (Daniel Kaluuya), who goes to stay for the weekend with the apparently well-meaning, liberal family of his white girlfriend Rose (Allison Williams), only to discover, to his horror, halfway through the film, that Rose and her family, the Armitages, have lured him – as they have lured several of Rose's previous Black boyfriends (and apparently one Black girlfriend) before him – into a death-trap of the soul. The Armitages' intention is to kill off Chris's mental and emotional functioning, leaving his "powerful", "athletic", Black body alive, ready to host the mind of some white friend or family member who may be ill, infirm, or close to death. The rescued white relative will live on psychically in Chris's body, whilst Chris himself, in all his consciousness and aliveness will simply *sink*, as Rose's psychotherapist mother Missy (Catherine Keener) chillingly phrases it, when putting him under for the first time. Although the Armitages, thanks to a combination of the mother's "psychotherapeutic" practice and the father's (Bradley Whitford) brain surgery skills, have successfully engineered many of these body-swap operations in the past, resulting in the creations of their Black housekeeper Georgina (Betty Gabriel), their Black handyman Walter (Marcus Henderson), and the mysteriously false party guest Logan (Lakeith Stanfield), in Chris's case, for reasons to do with his own post-traumatic resourcefulness and the loving concern of his best friend Rod (Lil Rel Howery), they fail.

The first time I saw *Get Out*, in a predominantly white cinema in central London on a weekday evening, it provoked me, not unlike my first, solitary viewing of *Twin Peaks: Fire Walk with Me* back in 1993, into a somewhat defensive state of emotional shutdown. It felt like too much to take in, somehow; and in any case, the Odeon on Tottenham Court Road wasn't the right environment to ingest this kind of meal. It wasn't until later, when I was able to see the film in "Blacker" surroundings, and, later still, when it was screened at the Fruitvale Film Club, that I started to relax enough to allow Peele's film to nourish me. Much has already been written about not only the cinematic but also the cultural and political significance of *Get Out* since its premiere at the Sundance Film Festival in January 2017, a month that saw the presidential inauguration of Donald Trump, an open racist and defender of white terrorist organisations, during whose presidency racialised polarisation and anti-Black violence have arguably been intensified to a more disturbing degree in the United States than at any time since the Civil Rights era (cf. Ricard, 2018, Ortiz, 2019). Two recurring topics of conversation emerged in the days and weeks following the film's general release, far more compelling than the various, sometimes smug explications across social media of its "clever" racialised symbolism. The first was Peele's racialisation of the obscene betrayal motif that had been explored from a gendered perspective in earlier films such as *Rosemary's Baby* (1968) and *The Stepford Wives* (1975). The second was the sheer uproariousness of cinema audiences – especially Black audiences – responding to the film.

To me, it seemed that the two observations, especially when thought about as potentially linked, might provide the key to understanding more precisely why *Get Out* might be functioning with such an extraordinarily cathartic intensity for many people in 2017 who were racialised as Black. Might it not be that the post-traumatic "sunken place" now so routinely referred to in blog posts, press articles, and online discussions of the film was becoming a tremendously helpful representation of a psychical phenomenon familiar to almost everyone who is racialised as Black, but for whom very few containing formulations actually existed within the general cultural arena? Beckerman (2020) makes the point well:

> "A real Jekyll and Hyde", we say, when our amiable friend turns into a mean drunk. "He's gaslighting me", we say, when someone tries to make us doubt our own reality – like the scheming husband in *Gaslight* (1944). Then there's "the sunken place". It's the place where we are made powerless, voiceless – like the African-American hero (Daniel Kaluuya) in *Get Out*. It, too, is a useful shorthand. It describes something familiar that never had a name before. From the moment it dropped, in Jordan Peele's groundbreaking 2017 horror film, it became a part of everyday conversation.

In its fantastical cinematic revelation of a nightmarish "sunken place", a psychical state of blankness and evacuation into which Black people descend when we are forced – in order not to be killed outright by the white structures and systems that wield such enormous power over our lives – to deaden a large part of our consciousness, Peele's film makes palpable and articulable a phenomenon that a Black psychiatrist and activist like Fanon (1952) could theorise but, perhaps, not bring *fully to life* in his nevertheless paradigm-shifting philosophical writings. Peele shows us something about the racialisation of the psychical splitting and "soul-death" that occurs in both white *and* Black people when we find ourselves playing out dehumanised roles in an inhuman script that is fundamentally underpinned by narcissistic drives bereft of a Symingtonian (1993) "lifegiver". And the resulting representation made Black audiences howl with recognition.

The "sunken place" phenomenon isn't only linked to racism or racialisation, of course. In both Neil Gaiman's (2002) novel *Coraline* and in its film adaptation (2009), the button-eyed "other mother" and her narcissistic capacity to blank out representation, affect, and meaning in both herself and others provides a helpful corollary to Chris's zone of deadness. In this adult-child dynamic, one that could most likely be taking place within *any* ethnic context, the neglected and manipulated little Coraline wanders to the edge of a no-place literally devoid of words, images, and feelings. It's as if the "other mother" has sprinkled this part of the narrative with invisibilising powder, wiping out any potential for the painting of a picture that might later be used in the service of thinking. Donnet and Green (1973), with no racialised intent whatsoever, call the mental state that results from this kind of situation *la psychose blanche*: "white-blank psychosis". Levine, Reed, and Scarfone (2013) assert that Green, having "named Ferenczi as the forerunner of [his] clinical theory, advocated adoption of a theory based on the idea of a psychotic kernel, insisted on countertransference as the major channel for understanding what the patient lives but cannot express" (p. 11). They go on to claim that

> this use of the analyst's psychic capacities for representation and expression [...] is the imaginative and intuitive work required of the analyst in a universe devoid of presences, but where it is impossible to constitute absences – that is, the work required of the analyst when treating those unable to represent the object in its absence. To the extent that this work is intuitive rather than empirical, it might be said to fly in the face of the classical requirement to listen to derivatives and carefully interpret resistances.
>
> (p. 15)

"White-blank psychosis" can only be countered, agree the panel of psychoanalysts, by a bold representation of that which the patient cannot bring themselves to feel or even to suggest. Whilst they may not mean (or even be moved to conceive of) the necessity of such a conjuring into words and images of a non-felt state of *racialised* deadness, with his bizarre filmic creation, *Get Out*, Jordan Peele offers the Black viewer-patient, that zombified (non) survivor of descent into the "sunken place" – s/he who has, to quote James Baldwin (1963), neither "lived...nor...died...through any of their terrible events", but has, instead, "simply been stunned by the hammer" (p. 129) – the very real possibility of seeing, feeling, and living their unseen, unfelt, unlived trance of blankness, perhaps for the first time.

The psycho-cultural implications of such an awakening for a partially deceased Black audience are enormous. The film itself contains two electrifying "jolts", in which we witness zombified Black people – first Georgina, then Logan – momentarily awakened from their trance of denial. Both characters are defined by an eerie refusal to acknowledge to Chris or to themselves either their shared condition of Blackness with him or the equally shared reality of racist and racialised experience amongst white people. These denials – especially Georgina's now famous "Oh, no, no, no, no, no, no, no! That's not been my experience at *all*!" – are among the moments that seem to provoke most loudly expressed mirth and horror in the (predominantly Black) screenings I've curated. But then, out of the robotic trance, comes the flash of an awakening: Georgina's suddenly, inexplicably streaming tears; Logan's suddenly, inexplicably streaming (bloody) nose. With each unexpected flow of a bodily fluid from previously lifeless and stony Black characters' faces, the audiences I've witnessed become, in their turn, excited and alive. And the streams running down not only the minor characters' faces, but also down the face – framed here, in Mrs Armitage's consulting room, as the simultaneous therapy patient and film spectator of his own trauma – of our hero, Chris, end up becoming *Get Out*'s most iconic, most widely circulated, most eerily moving image.

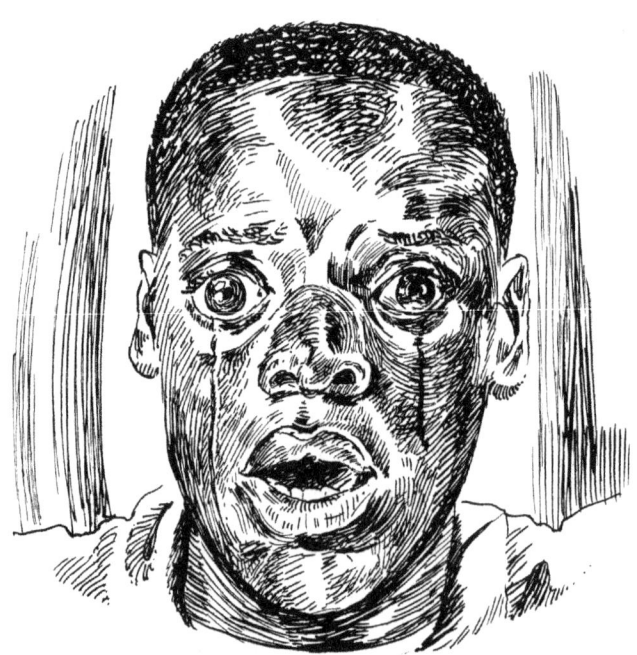

Chris's flow of Black tears on screen offers the viewer, to paraphrase Žižek (2001) – another psychoanalytic theorist I recruit for my discussion despite, or perhaps because of, his seeming disinterest in the wellbeing of Black people – the helpful and containing fright of beholding something they know to be *real*. For me, the constructive horror we read on the face of Daniel Kaluuya's Chris in his most terrified and eye-opened moments are analogous to the contorted, silent screams of Sheryl Lee's Laura Palmer in *Twin Peaks: Fire Walk with Me* (1992) as, terror-struck but lucid, she comes to know her father Leland for what he is. In *Get Out*, the secret "father-daughter plot" of incest, rape, and murder is widened to take in a *secret, racialised, incestuous, genocidal, (inter)national family plot of enslavement and soul murder*. And yet, rather than being re-traumatised by seeing something so sickening unfold on the screen, we feel, instead, somehow held by these representations. For some of us, we have the sensation of being held so powerfully by the film that we emerge from the cinema feeling stronger and saner than we have ever felt before. How can we explain this?

Some of us did not die

We screened *Get Out* at the Fruitvale Film Club in Birkbeck Cinema on the afternoon of Saturday, 3 March 2018. The discussion after the movie took place among about 35 people who stayed and agreed to let me record their comments for this study, although the audience size during the film had been around twice that number. In what follows, I try to pick out what I felt to be the five major movements of our group discussion, quoting unidentified members of the conversation directly and, where appropriate, commenting on some of the implications of the process I feel may have been developing amongst us in the wake of our collective experience of the film.

White flight?

The first part of the discussion focused, with some emotional intensity, on the irritation felt by many of the participants upon the departure shortly before the group process of many (but by no means all) of the white audience members who had been present to watch the (free) film. One man spoke with undisguised annoyance: "I notice that all of a certain demographic have left the cinema. They came for the comedy and horror, but they don't want to stay for the discussion". His observation was backed up by a woman, whose own comment had an added degree of ambivalent poignancy:

> This film really sends a message to white people and at the same time it enters a kind of mainstream. This gives me so much hope. But where

a real sadness and worry start to creep in is where I start to think that the people the message is being sent to don't seem willing to take that message on. The white people in the audience have left!

Another woman directly addressed the white people who *had* remained present for the discussion, saying: "You reflect my hope, you really do! But you also reflect my reality. The hope is that white people will actually learn something about themselves from watching this film. But then I step into the world, and I realise that reality hasn't changed – people are still touching my hair!" A second man was moved to oppose the patronising discourses and behaviours of white people who hadn't been present at either the screening or the discussion, but who, he felt, violated the integrity of the film more generally: "I've seen the film several times. And it feels very personal when white people attack the film. Don't do that to me! This film is a win for us. Don't pick holes in it in front of me. Don't use it as a whip. Don't analyse it as a genre mash-up, a Black version of *The Stepford Wives* or whatever. You belittle it".

A third woman commented on the fact that she wouldn't be able to discuss this film with white colleagues at work; it would simply be too embarrassing. And a third man shared an anecdote about the film's facilitation of an unusual objectification of white audience members: "I went to see the film in Wood Green with a group of Black friends, including a friend who has a white boyfriend. And everyone in the cinema was staring at the white guy afterwards!" This last story about the white boyfriend who had been stared at provoked a number of unrestrained laughs in this audience, and I sensed the emergence of a welcome but somehow transgressive *strangeness* being shared in the room. Was this the strangeness of being allowed, perhaps for the first time, to observe *white people* being made uncomfortable by the images being projected on an ordinary cinema screen? Could this film be providing certain viewers racialised as Black with something resembling a therapeutic and non-violent outlet for their ordinary, post-traumatic aggression? As the Black (and/or "mixed-race") facilitator of the discussion – and also, at that time, an academic employee of the university in whose space the screening was taking place – I noted a desperate urge rising in me (physically felt as anxiety in my chest) to somehow reassure the remaining white participants, to let them know that they weren't being attacked, either by the Black participants, or by me, or by the film. But I said nothing. And gradually, without my needing to do anything or intervene in any way, the expressions of "anti-white" irritation gave way to reflections by several more participants on just how intensely *helpful* it had been to have this experience of a film that spoke to Black people in a way we were simply not used to being spoken to in the cinema. One man shared a personal sense of identification, before sharing his gratitude at being able to see and reflect on the movie in this kind of environment: "I have *lived* this film! It was a weekend away with my white partner's family. And her mother was a psychologist! Unless you're in a forum like this, you will *never* hear these stories". And a woman shared her enthusiasm about seeing the film here, with a predominantly Black audience, before going on to share her memory of a similar experience in West Africa:

> I saw *Black Panther* in Ghana. And to see the film in that context ... it was so joyous! Both these films feel like a win. In horror, we are *always* the first ones to die because of something stupid that we do. But in this film, we didn't have to yell at the screen. We are able to cheer, to feel a sense of real victory. It does something, just ... *something*. I can start to do things differently.

This idea of being enabled by these kinds of film experiences to "start to do things differently" feels crucial. It seems to me that something is being articulated by this participant about actual metamorphosis; a shift in the longstanding psychical patterns and assumptions ingrained through years of social trauma and cultural starvation.

Cracking up

The second major movement of the post-film group discussion centred on the appropriateness – or not – of laughter in response to the film's representations of racialised violence, violation, trauma, and neglect. Some of the different comments that emerged regarding this question included the following:

> I was laughing, but not because I was trying to escape from the pain. It was an inside joke. It was a way of processing.

> He's so vulnerable because of his missing mother. It's uncomfortable to laugh at the things which one recognises but that one can't put into language.

> Every single detail in this film has a function. There's so much going on here that's non-verbal. He is using our collective experience to communicate something else. The iconic image of a Black man over the white woman's dead body, everyone knows what that means. It means he will be lynched. But the comic relief of the friend who comes to rescue him punctures this nightmare of a certain lynching. It takes us to the other side of the image.

These three remarks by different – all racialised-as-Black – members of the film discussion group are structurally similar, in that each foregrounds the question of pain, before going on to say that there is something about the laughter provoked by the movie that facilitates not an avoidance, but rather a processing of that pain. I'm reminded of Bollas's (2011) discussion of the potentially therapeutic function of laughter. Departing from the Freudian axiom according to which jokes are a defence against vulnerability, Bollas takes the discussion of laughter to a different level altogether.

> The mother metamorphoses from her ordinary facial self into a clown; she breaks herself up in order to break up baby. They crack up together. Has she an uncanny sense, then, not only of mirroring alternate states of quiescence and disturbance but of transforming this potential for psychic disaster into pleasure? Does she take into herself, right before the baby's eyes, that internal madness which shakes up baby – as it were, absorbing and transforming the element of shock and disturbance? Does she do what comics and humorists have been doing all these centuries, taking up into their bodies and souls these disturbing aspects of life? If so, then the provocative and disturbing mother who cracks up baby is a vivid and moving expression of the marriage of unconscious and circumstantial material. Her surprising, unpredictable attacks of jocularity seem accidental; but if her timing and spacing are good enough, she senses when the clowning is all right for baby, joining subject and existence in an exciting way.
>
> (pp. 146–7)

It's instructive to note that the two forms of pain that are specified by the latter two *Get Out* participants, are the recurring tropes, first, of the loss of a mother's protection, and, second, of the very real possibility of being murdered within a racist and racialised environment. These are the two forms of trauma that permeate the various chapters of this book. Might a viewer who's been affected by the trauma of even these two terrible situations be effectively contained by a parental film-object that arrives in the form of the Bollassian clown-mother? Perhaps, in the context of a *safely mirthful community*, the "movie-as-clown-mother" really is capable of offering an effective form of post-traumatic holding.

Gaslight

The third movement of our post-film discussion, as I perceived it, was *Get Out*'s striking depiction of "gaslighting", taking place in the form of Rose's systematic attempts to mislead Chris into doubting his own sanity. One man stated the situation, as he felt it, very baldly indeed: "This is a move about racial misplaced trust. Racial misplaced trust is such a hard thing to talk about. I don't mind which culture I date, but misplaced trust is…something I can't deal with". Meanwhile, a woman added: "'I don't know what you're talking about': this is the recurring refrain of the film". There began to emerge from the group discussion, a quite remarkable series of points regarding both the filmic representation of trust, the filmic representation of betrayal, and the racialisation of those filmic representations. Participants commented movingly on how they were psychically affected by the revelation that Rose has been part of the plot to enslave and deaden Chris all along. Many reported feeling physically sick during the "twist", as Rose dangles the car keys at Chris in front of her approving family. Others described sudden flashes, horribly intrusive thoughts – what if their own (white) partner was to betray them in some comparable way? What if – and this was the "killer" – they already *had* been betrayed in some comparable way, but had chosen not to articulate, or even to bring into linguistic thought-representations, the betrayal as such?

I'd never been privy to public discussions such as these, especially not in mixed company. The remaining white members of the group stayed for the most part silent during this sometimes painfully awkward section of the afternoon. Eventually, a (white) person made the following statement:

> I think it's fine to take from the film the message that you shouldn't trust white people. Because it's true. I don't trust any man, or any straight person, and that is fine. It's totally legitimate for people to say that you don't trust white people. You can still love some white people, but trust is not something you *have* to give people. This puts the most pressure on the most marginalised people.

My own sense after this person had spoken was one of immense relief; not only that such a bold statement had been made, but that it had been made by a white person. There was something so paradoxical, and yet so emotionally right, about the way in which this (white) person's willingness to refuse the exhortation to simply trust – an exhortation that is pushed by so many orthodox psychoanalysts in the name of the patient showing a willingness to leave her traumatised state of mind in the past – actually ended up generating an almost palpable feeling of (intercultural) trust in the room. For a film that's mostly viewed as paranoia-inducing, it seemed to me that our discussion of it was starting to create precisely the opposite state of mind.

Happy endings (and the sunken place again)

As the conversation began to move towards its close, the question of how the film itself had ended began to form the basis of the group's fourth major movement. Three different participants offered their view:

> The ending is still ambiguous. Where are they going to go?
>
> A bleak ending would have been too traumatic for the audience.
>
> The ending is brilliant. And it revealed to me how much of a "sunken place" I myself am in. When his friend comes out of the car, I realised

that I must go through life in a state of defeat. Because it is still such a surprise, every time, that he can be allowed to survive.

The woman who made the last point seemed close to tears, as she admitted her astonishment at the representation of survival even being an option. But there didn't seem to be any appetite whatsoever, not from anyone in the audience, for an ending (such as the alternative denouement filmed by Peele) in which Chris would actually die. And this collective refusal to endorse Chris's onscreen killing, no matter how many men, women, and children racialised as Black we know are being killed on a daily basis, seemed, to me, to form the backbone of the group's fifth and final movement, namely, the sense in which the film enables an optimistic exit from and transcendence of the viewer's "sunken place".

As one man put it, very clearly indeed: "I felt that the film was telling me that if I try really, really hard I *can* wake up. I *can* get out. It is so helpful to see things put into words and scenes that you *live* but haven't ever put into scenes and concepts". A woman, again making reference to the film's title and its injunction to *leave*, said:

> When I realised that Logan was telling Chris to "get out", I assumed it was said in hostility. But no...it was like there was this transformation of meaning as you realise he's actually trying to help him understand, this feeling of oh there is something actually positive going on, some weird, good energy coming from some other dimension. But I had just assumed the opposite.

This is, I think, the reality of the film's healing connection to a dream – a glimmer – of awakened consciousness. Not experienced by the audience member as a betrayal or a sell-out, instead this kind of reversal of negative expectation is actually necessary for us to believe in the possibility of something new. This is another exhortation to trust, but the exhortation is coming instead from a source that has acknowledged the reality of our trauma in the first place. This is very different indeed from being told to be "positive" by a person or a structure that has never believed why you were "negative" in the first place. One man frames the situation helpfully, returning us again to this recurrent question of trust: "This film's message for me is very simple: his friend is there for him; and his friend helps him. There's something incontrovertible about this. It transcends everything else, everything so fucked-up that has come before it...and, as a message, we have no other choice but to trust it".

For me, the quasi-angelic manner in which Rod – initially presented as a buffoon, someone there for comic relief only – manifests his love, loyalty, and friendship towards Chris is akin to the solidarity Donna shows, or tries to show, towards her friend Laura in *Twin Peaks: Fire Walk with*

Me, long before (and long after) Laura arrives screaming at her house, begging to know the answer to her desperate question, "Donna: are you my best friend?" Hannah Eaton (2015) addresses a significantly trauma-related question, regarding the potential limitations of Donna's loving kindness, in her incredible graphic short story "In Laura's House". In Eaton's story, Donna is temporarily able to see what Laura sees – the visions, the Red Room, the horse, B.O.B., the Man from Another Place – only when she illicitly steals a pair of Laura's sunglasses. It would seem that these glasses fantastically bestow upon the wearer an insight into what it means to live a relationally traumatised reality, to move through the world with the eyes and the body of one who has experienced an attempted erosion of the soul. But while Donna's insight is momentary and provisional, Rod's solidarity with Chris is based on a shared experience of (specifically racialised) trauma that cannot be switched on and off with the donning and removal of a pair of magical glasses.

Of all the insights I gained during the period in which I curated the Fruitvale Film Club, one that has stayed with me – and on which I would like to build in future projects – is the necessity of keeping hold of a pair of trauma-glasses. The mutual empathy and solidarity that can be created in the context of a trauma-conscious film group is nothing short of remarkable. During the post-screening discussion of *Get Out*, in particular, I was struck by the sincerity of the few white group members who did stay and who did speak. One woman spoke of her reluctant realisation that she was able to identify with some of the strategies of "white fragility" and racialised manipulativeness depicted in the film. Another white woman spoke of her surprising – to her – capacity, whilst watching the film, for a kind of transgendered and transracial identification with Chris-as-Black-man, noting a bodily sense of excitement and urgency in her own spectatorial desire that he kill those white people who would seek to kill him. This was a film group in which not only were the eerily moving images we watched together capable of psychically intervening to help us in our sense of traumatised vulnerability in the world, but also the physical, social, and political connections we started to make during and after the screenings themselves began to be a source of real transformation. The film group started to operate, in other words, as the facilitator of real alliances, an emotionally living crucible, in which potential Rod-saviours and fantastically bespectacled Donnas could be forged, not out of purely intellectual or ideological fervour, but in a genuinely trauma-feeling frame of mind.

Learning from experience

There are many iconic images in *Get Out*, but for me, perhaps unsurprisingly, when all is said and done, the film spins madly and lucidly around that brief vision of Chris as a young boy, watching television alone in his bedroom, as his mother lies dying. Mrs Armitage, the psychotherapist, will, of course, use that remembered image *against* Chris, hypnotically suggesting to him that it's in this act of selfishness and passivity in front of the television screen that he's not only betrayed his mother, but also delivered himself over to a lifetime of paralysed inertia – an inertia upon which she herself intends imminently to capitalise. And yet isn't that memory of young Chris, alone-but-not-quite in his childhood state of neglect, precisely the thing upon which his psychical survival ultimately depends? Strapped, years later, to an armchair, forced to watch hypnotic, pre-recorded video-material, in which the Armitages tell him what he must indubitably become for them – an enslaved zombie – Chris manages to block his ears with the cotton he has gathered and picked from the arms of his chair. Something revolutionary is revealed in this act of Chris's determination to *learn* from an earlier experience of passive television-watching. The helplessness of his childhood viewing habits cannot simply be forgotten, no more than his mother's horrific death can be fully repressed. The two situations are, as Mrs Armitage so expertly unearths in her abusive hypnotherapy session with him, inextricably linked. Instead of denying them, as he has for the whole of his adult life until now, Chris must find new ways to work through both his mother's death and his own simultaneous internalisation of moving images, all the while resisting the temptation to disavow the fundamentally traumatic nature of *both* these formative relationships.

References

Abraham, N. and Torok, M. (1994). *The Shell and the Kernel*. Chicago, IL: University of Chicago Press.
A.C.A (2006). *Adult Children of Alcoholic/Dysfunctional Families*. Torrance, CA: Adult Children of Alcoholics World Service Organization.
Adams, M. V. (2004). *The Fantasy Principle: Psychoanalysis of the Imagination*. Hove: Routledge.
Agamben, G. (1998). *Homo Sacer: Sovereign Power and Bare Life*. Stanford, CA: Stanford University Press.
Akass, K. and McCabe, J. (Ed.) (2005). *Reading Six Feet Under: TV to Die For*. London: I.B. Tauris.
Andersen, H. C. (2009 [1844]). *The Snow Queen*. London: Andersen Press.
Anderson, T. (2008). *24, Lost, and Six Feet Under: Post-traumatic Television in the Post-9/11 Era*. MA Thesis, University of North Texas. Available at https://digital.library.unt.edu/ark:/67531/metadc6137/ Accessed 5 September 2020.
Anzieu, D. (2016). *The Skin-Ego*. London: Karnac.
Arendt, H. (1958). *The Human Condition*. Chicago, IL: University of Chicago Press.
Ashley, B. (2014), *Six Feet Under Series Finale Reaction*. Available at https://www.youtube.com/watch?v=20hf5e8Upoc. Accessed 5 September 2020.
Asibong, A. (2015a). Terreur ou thérapie? Arnaud Desplechin et les métamorphoses de la lettre brûlante. In: M. Irvine, G. de Viveiros, and K. Schwerdtner (Eds.), *Risques et regrets: Les dangers de l'écriture épistolaire* (pp. 187–208). Quebec: Nota Bene.
Asibong, A. (2015b). "Then look!" Unborn attachments and the half-moving image. *Studies in Gender and Sexuality*, 16 (2), 87–102.
Bacle, A. (2016). How *Six Feet Under* helped me grieve after my brother's death. *Entertainment Weekly*, 3 June. Available at https://ew.com/tv/2016/06/03/six-feet-under-anniversary-grief/. Accessed 5 September 2020.
Bainbridge, C. (2014). "Cinematic screaming" or "All about my mother": Lars von Trier's cinematic extremism as therapeutic encounter. In: C. Bainbridge and C. Yates(Eds.), *Media and the Inner World: Psycho-cultural Approaches to Emotion, Media and Popular Culture* (pp. 53–68). London: Palgrave Macmillan.
Bainbridge, C. (2019). Box-set mind-set: psycho-cultural approaches to binge watching, gender, and digital experience. *Free Associations*, 75, 65–83.
Bainbridge, C. and Yates, C. (Eds.) (2014). *Media and the Inner World: Psycho-cultural Approaches to Emotion, Media and Popular Culture*. London: Palgrave Macmillan.

Baldwin, J. (1963). *Another Country*. London: Michael Joseph.
Baldwin, J. (1976). *The Devil Finds Work*. New York: The Dial Press.
Baraka, A. (1974). Henry Dumas: Afro-surreal expressionist. *Black American Literature Forum*, 22 (2), 164–166.
Bechdel, A. (2006). *Fun Home: A Family Tragicomic*. London: Jonathan Cape.
Beckerman, J. (2020). "Get Out," "Lovecraft Country", "Us": Black writers, filmmakers are transforming horror. *North Jersey News and Information*, 6 August. Available at: https://eu.northjersey.com/story/entertainment/2020/08/06/black-horror-movie-writers-filmmakers-turn-genre-its-head/5540171002/. Accessed 5 September 2020.
Bellour, R. (2009). *Le corps du cinéma*. Paris: P.O.L.
Beradt, C. (1985). *The Third Reich of Dreams: The Nightmares of a Nation, 1933–1939*. Wellingborough: Aquarian Press.
Bergman, I. (1989). *The Magic Lantern: An Autobiography*. Harmondsworth: Penguin.
Bersani, L. and Dutoit, U. (2004). *Forms of Being: Cinema, Aesthetics, Subjectivity*. London: BFI.
Bettelheim, B. (1991). *The Uses of Enchantment: The Meaning and Importance of Fairy Tales*. Harmondsworth: Penguin.
Bion, W. (1959). Attacks on linking. *International Journal of Psycho-Analysis*, 40, 308–315.
Bion, W. (1962). *Learning from Experience*. London: Tavistock.
Bion, W. (2005). *The Italian Seminars*. London: Karnac.
Bobo, J. (1988). Black women's responses to *The Color Purple*. *Jump Cut: A Review of Contemporary Media*, 33: 43–51. Available at: https://www.ejumpcut.org/archive/onlinessays/JC33folder/ClPurpleBobo.html. Accessed 5 September 2020.
Bollas, C. (1987). *The Shadow of the Object: Psychoanalysis of the Unthought Known*. London: Free Association.
Bollas, C. (1999). Dead mother, dead child. In: G. Kohon (Ed.), *The Dead Mother: The Work of André Green* (pp. 87–108). Hove: Routledge.
Bollas, C. (2011). Cracking up. In: C. Bollas (Ed.), *The Bollas Reader* (pp. 135–154). Hove: Routledge.
Bowlby, J. (2015). *The Making and Breaking of Affectional Bonds*. Hove: Routledge.
Brenman, E. (2006). *Recovery of the Lost Good Object*. Hove: Routledge.
Brewster, F. (2018). *Archetypal Grief: Slavery's Legacy of Intergenerational Child Loss*. Hove: Routledge.
Brickman, B. (2008). The portrait of an artist as a young fan: consumption and queer inspiration in *Six feet under*. In: L. E. Stein and S. M. Ross (Eds.), *Teen Television: Essays on Programming and Fandom*. Jefferson: McFarland and Company.
Brown, L. J. (2005). The cognitive effects of trauma: reversal of alpha function and the formation of a beta screen. *Psychoanalytic Quarterly*, 74 (2), 397–420.
Brown, L. J. (2012). Bion's discovery of alpha function: thinking under fire on the battlefield and in the consulting room. *International Journal of Psychoanalysis*, 93 (5), 1191–1214.
Bury, R. (2008). Praise you like I should: cyberfans and *Six Feet Under*. In: M. Leverette, B. L. Ott, and C. L. Buckley (Eds.), *It's Not TV: Watching HBO in the Post-Television Era* (pp. 190–208). Hove: Routledge.
Butler, J. (1993). *Bodies That Matter: On the Discursive Limits of Sex*. Hove: Routledge.
Butler, O. (1979). *Kindred*. New York: Doubleday.

Cartwright, D. (2010). *Containing States of Mind: Exploring Bion's "Container" Model in Psychoanalytic Psychotherapy*. Hove: Routledge.

Cervantes, M. (2003). *Don Quixote*. London: Penguin Classics.

Chapman, L. (2016). Father, don't you see I'm burning? In: *Touching the Real* blog. Available at: https://therapeia.org.uk/ttr/2016/10/31/father-dont-you-see-im-burning/#:~:text=This%20is%20the%20dream%20of,days%20and%20nights%20on%20end.&text=The%20dream%20was%20preferred%20to,child%20as%20once%20more%20alive. Accessed 5 September 2020.

Chion, M. (2006). *David Lynch*. London: BFI.

Chion, M. (2019). *Audio-Vision: Sound on Screen*. New York: Columbia University Press.

Clifford, L. (1882). The new mother. *In Weird Fiction Review*, November 2011. Available at: https://weirdfictionreview.com/2011/11/creepy-classic-lucy-cliffords-the-new-mother/. Accessed 5 September 2020.

Coetzee, J. M. (1999). *Disgrace*. London: Secker & Warburg.

Creme, P. (1994). *The Playing Spectator: A Study on the Applicability of the Theories of D.W. Winnicott to Contemporary Concepts of the Viewer's Relationship to Film*. PhD Thesis: University of Kent.

Creme, P. (2013). The playing spectator. In: A. Kuhn (Ed.), *Little Madnesses: Winnicott, Transitional Phenomena and Cultural Experience* (pp. 39–52). London: I.B. Tauris.

Daney, S. (1999). *Itinéraire d'un ciné-fils*. Paris: Jean-Michel Place.

Daney, S. (2007). *Postcards from the Cinema*. Oxford: Berg.

Davids, F. (2011). *Internal Racism: A Psychoanalytic Approach to Race and Difference*. London: Palgrave Macmillan.

Donnet, J.-L. and Green, A. (1973). *L'Enfant de ça: psychanalyse d'un entretien: la psychose blanche*. Paris: Minuit.

Eadie, B. (2020). Baits of falsehood: the role of fiction in documentary or from untheorised practice to unpractised theory. In: A. Piotrowska (Ed.), *Creative Practice Research in the Age of Neoliberal Hopelessness* (pp. 164–182). Edinburgh: Edinburgh University Press.

Eaton, H. (2015). In Laura's house. *Studies in Gender and Sexuality*, *16* (4), 308–310.

Eigen, M. (2004). *Psychic Deadness*. London: Karnac.

Eigen, M. (1999). *Toxic Nourishment*. London: Karnac.

Eshel, O. (2017). Into the depths of a "black hole" and deadness. In A. Reiner (Ed.), *Of Things Invisible to Mortal Sight: Celebrating the Work of James S. Grotstein* (pp. 19–42). London: Karnac.

Fairbairn, W. R. D. (1952). *Psychoanalytic Studies of the Personality*. Hove: Routledge.

Fanon, F. (2008). *Black Skin White Masks*. London: Pluto Press.

Farress, M. (2018). Transmissions of aliveness and deadness in *The Hours*. *Studies in Gender and Sexuality*, *19* (2), 157–169.

Ferenczi, S. (1949 [1933]). Confusion of the tongues between the adults and the child (the language of tenderness and of passion). *International Journal of Psycho-Analysis*, *30*, 225–230.

Ferenczi, S. (1995). *The Clinical Diary of Sándor Ferenczi*. Cambridge: Harvard University Press.

Ferholt, B. (2007). A multiperspectival approach to the process of representing imagination in work with children: Glimpsing the future to study a playworld. Available here: http://lchc.ucsd.edu/Projects/bethPAPER2.pdf. Accessed 5 September 2020.

Ferholt, B. (2009). *The Development of Cognition, Emotion, Imagination and Creativity as Made Visible through Adult-Child Joint Play: Perezhivanie through Playworlds*. PhD Thesis, University of California at San Diego.

Fillol, S. (2016). *Historias de la desaparición: el cine desde los fuera de campo de Franz Kafka, Jacques Tourneur y David Lynch*. Madrid: Shangrila.

Firestone, R. W. (1987). *The Fantasy Bond: Structure of Psychological Defences*. Los Angeles, CA: Glendon.

Flaubert, G. (2003). *Madame Bovary*. London: Penguin Classics.

Fisher, M. (2014). *Ghosts of My Life: Writings on Depression, Hauntology and Lost Futures*. London: Zero.

Fisher, M. (2016). *The Weird and the Eerie*. London: Repeater Books.

Fonagy, P., Steele, M., Steele, H., Leigh, T., Kennedy, R., Mattoon, G., and Target, M. (1995). Attachment, the reflective self, and borderline states. In: S. Goldberg, R. Muir, and J. Kerr (Eds.), *Attachment Theory: Social, Developmental and Clinical Perspectives*. Hillsdale, NJ and London: Analytic Press

Foster, G. M. (2006). Desire and the "big black sex cop": race and the politics of sexual intimacy in HBO's *Six Feet Under*. In: J. R. Keller and L. Stratyner (Eds.), *The New Queer Aesthetic on Television: Essays on Recent Programming* (pp. 99–112). Jefferson: McFarland and Company.

Fraiberg, S., Adelson, E., and Shapiro, V. (1975). Ghosts in the nursery: a psychoanalytic approach to the problems of impaired infant-mother relationships. *Journal of American Academy of Child Psychiatry, 14* (3), 387–421.

Freud, S. (1900). *The Interpretation of Dreams* (*Second Part*). (The Standard Edition, 5). London: Hogarth.

Freud, S. (1909). *Family Romances*. (The Standard Edition, 9). London: Hogarth.

Freud, S. (1919). *The Uncanny*. (The Standard Edition, 17). London: Hogarth.

Freud, S. (1920). *Beyond the Pleasure Principle*. (The Standard Edition, 18). London: Hogarth.

Freud, S. (1937). *Constructions in Analysis*. (The Standard Edition, 23). London: Hogarth.

GAA03. (2016). *Julie Bowden ACOA Co Dependence*. Available at: https://www.youtube.com/watch?v=n9ZAGR5e-2k. Accessed on 5 September 2020.

Gaiman, N. (2002). *Coraline*. London: Bloomsbury.

Gallwey, P. (1991). Social maladjustment. In: J. Holmes (Ed.), *Textbook of Psychotherapy in Psychiatric Practice*. London: Churchill Livingstone.

Grant, C. 2015a. Interplay: (re)finding and (re)framing cinematic experience, film space, and the child's world. Available at: http://www.lolajournal.com/6/interplay.html?fbclid=IwAR0qOSuZX3o5awj3_-HvyWlB0F1i60D8gg9U7j27iOHPc8X2n-Ww0cCIrE64. Accessed 5 September 2020.

Grant, C. 2015b. Turning up the volume? The emergent focus on film sound, music and listening in audiovisual essays. *The Cine-Files: A Scholarly Journal of Cinema Studies, 8*. Available at: http://www.thecine-files.com/turning-up-the-volume/. Accessed 5 September 2020.

Grant, C. (2020). Website. Available at: screenstudies.video. Accessed 5 September 2020.

Grant, C. and Keathley, C. (2014). The use of an illusion: childhood cinephilia, object relations, and videographic film studies. Available at: https://cinea.be/the-use-an-illusion-childhood-cinephilia-object-relations-and-videographic-film-studies/?fbclid=IwAR1HCurdeH-FGR5PRdAk-4sxuer_lJ7iAabXUwhtbpTHLBglGJhgzusxjvI. Accessed 5 September 2020.

Grant, D. (2011). Saved by pop culture: how "Six Feet Under" killed my depression. *Salon*, 8 April. Available at: https://www.salon.com/2011/04/08/saved_by_pop_culture_six_feet_under/. Accessed 5 September 2020.
Green, A. (1986). *On Private Madness*. London: Karnac.
Grotstein, J. (2000). *Who Is the Dreamer? Who Dreams the Dream? A Study of Psychic Presences*. Hillsdale: The Analytic Press.
Guntrip, H. (1968). *Schizoid Phenomena, Object Relations and the Self*. London: Karnac.
Hallward, P. (2001). *Absolutely Postcolonial: Writing Between the Singular and the Specific*. Manchester: Manchester University Press.
Hanich, J. (2014). Watching a film with others: towards a theory of collective spectatorship. *Screen*, *55* (3), 338–359.
Heffernan, K. (2002). Inner-city exhibition and the genre film: distributing "Night of the Living Dead" (1968). *Cinema Journal*, *41* (3), 59–77.
Hills, M. (2013). Media users: an introduction. In: A. Kuhn (Ed.), *Little Madnesses: Winnicott, Transitional Phenomena and Cultural Experience* (pp. 79–88). London: I.B. Tauris.
Hockley, L. (2014). *Somatic Cinema: The Relationship Between Body and Screen: A Jungian Perspective*. Hove: Routledge.
Hoffmann, E. T. A. (2011). *The Serapion Brethren*. San Francisco: Bottom of the Hill.
Holland, S. P. (2000). *Raising the Dead: Readings of Death and (Black) Subjectivity*. Durham: Duke University Press.
hooks, b. (1991). Theory as liberatory practice. *Yale Journal of Law and Feminism*, *4* (1), 1–12.
hooks, b. (1992). *Black Looks: Race and Representation*. London: Turnaround.
hooks, b. (1994). *Teaching to Transgress: Education as the Practice of Freedom*. Hove: Routledge.
Hope, C. (2014). *Politicising Agency through Affect*. PhD Thesis: University of Leeds.
Jancovich, M. (2012). Relocating Lewton: cultural distinctions, critical reception, and the Val Lewton horror films. *Journal of Film and Video*, *64* (3), 21–37.
Jung, C. G. (1963). *Memories, Dreams, Reflections*. New York: Pantheon.
Jung, C. G. (2016 [1913]), *The Theory of Psychoanalysis: Collected Works*. London: Forgotten Books.
Kafka, F. (1912). The Judgment. In: F. Kafka (Ed.), *Metamorphosis and Other Stories* (pp. 29–42). London: Penguin Modern Classics.
Kafka, F. (1990), Letter to Oskar Pollak, 27 January 1904. In: *Letters to Friends, Family and Editors* (pp. 15–16). New York: Schocken.
Kalsched, D. (2013). *Trauma and the Soul: A Psycho-Spiritual Approach to Human Development and Its Interruption*. Hove: Routledge.
Kimbles, S. (2014). *Phantom Narratives: The Unseen Contributions of Culture to Psyche*. Lanham: Rowman and Littlefield.
Kinder, M. (1993). *Playing With Power in Movies, Television, and Video Games: From Muppet Babies to Teenage Mutant Ninja Turtles*. Berkeley: University of California Press.
King, P. and Steiner, R. (1992). *The Freud-Klein Controversies, 1941–45*. Hove: Routledge.
Klein, M. (1946). Notes on some schizoid mechanisms. *The International Journal of Psychoanalysis*, *27*, 99–110.

Kohon, G. (Ed.) (1999). *The Dead Mother: The Work of André Green*. Hove: Routledge.
Knox, J. (2003). *Archetype, Attachment, Analysis: Jungian Psychology and the Emergent Mind*. Hove and New York: Brunner-Routledge.
Kuhn, A. (1994). *Women's Pictures: Feminism and Cinema*. London: Verso.
Kuhn, A. (2002). *An Everyday Magic: Cinema and Cultural Memory*. London: I.B. Tauris.
Kuhn, A. (Ed.) (2013). *Little Madnesses: Winnicott, Transitional Phenomena and Cultural Experience*. London: I. B. Tauris.
Lacan, J. (1979). *The Four Fundamental Concepts of Psycho-Analysis*. London: Penguin.
Laine, T. (2011). *Feeling Cinema: Emotional Dynamics in Film Studies*. London: Bloomsbury.
Laing, R. D. (2010). *The Divided Self*. London: Penguin Classics.
LaMothe, R. (2005). *Becoming Alive: Psychoanalysis and Vitality*. Hove: Routledge.
Laplanche, J. (1987). *Nouveaux fondements pour la psychanalyse*. Paris: PUF.
Larsen, N. (2003 [1929]). *Passing*. London: Penguin Classics.
Levine, H., Reed, G., and Scarfone, D. (2013). *Unrepresented States and the Construction of Meaning: Clinical and Theoretical Contributions*. Hove: Routledge.
Lewis, C. S. (2009 [1950]). *The Lion, the Witch and the Wardrobe*. London: HarperCollins.
Lowe, F. (Ed.) (2014). *Thinking Space: Promoting Thinking About Race, Culture and Diversity in Psychotherapy and Beyond*. Hove: Routledge.
Lubecker, N. (2015). *The Feel-Bad Film*. Edinburgh: Edinburgh University Press.
ЛУбНиН, К. (2013). *Different people, different ways*. Available at: https://www.youtube.com/watch?v=UA49uQ40JS4. Accessed 5 September 2020.
Lussier, A. (1999). The dead mother: variations on a theme. In: G. Kohon (Ed.), *The Dead Mother: The Work of André Green* (pp. 149–162). Hove: Routledge.
Marks, L. (2000). *The Skin of the Film: Intercultural Cinema, Embodiment and the Senses*. Durham: Duke University Press.
Milner, M. (2011). *A Life of One's Own*. Hove: Routledge.
Morrison, T. (1999 [1970]). *The Bluest Eye*. New York: Vintage.
Morrison, T. (2007 [1988]). *Beloved*. New York: Vintage.
Munt, S. (2006). A queer undertaking: anxiety and reparation in the HBO television drama series *Six Feet Under*. *Feminist Media Studies*, 6 (3), 263–279.
Nemerov, A. (2005). *Icons of Grief: Val Lewton's Home Front Pictures*. Berkeley: University of California.
Ness, P. (2015). *A Monster Calls*. London: Walker Books.
Ogden, T. (1991). *Projective Identification and Psychotherapeutic Technique*. Northvale: Jason Aronson.
Ogden, T. (2010). On three forms of thinking: magical thinking, dream thinking, and transformative thinking. *Psychoanalytic Quarterly*, 79 (2), 317–347.
Ogden, T. (2014). Fear of breakdown and the unlived life. *International Journal of Psychoanalysis*, 95 (2), 205–223.
Ogden, T. (2017). On talking-as-dreaming. In: A. Reiner (Ed.), *Of Things Invisible to Mortal Sight: Celebrating the Work of James S. Grotstein* (pp. 97–114). London: Karnac, 2017.
Ortiz, J. (2019). Poll: americans say trump has made race relations worse. *USA Today*, 15 December. Available at: https://eu.usatoday.com/story/news/nation/2019/04/09/survey-race-relations-u-s-bad-and-trump-has-made-them-worse/3418375002/. Accessed 5 September 2020.

Perez, H. (2008). Two or three spectacular mulatas and the queer pleasures of over-identification. *Camera Obscura: Feminism, Culture and Media Studies*, 23 (*1* (67), 113–143.
Pistiner de Cortiñas, L. (2017). Alpha function and mental growth: the aesthetic dimension of the mind. In: A. Reiner (Ed.), *Of Things Invisible to Mortal Sight: Celebrating the Work of James S. Grotstein* (pp. 233–250). London: Karnac.
Plantinga, C. (2009). *Moving Viewers: American Film and the Spectator's Experience*. Berkeley: University of California Press.
Polledri, P. (2012). *Envy Is Not Innate: A New Model of Thinking*. London: Karnac.
Potocki, J. (1996). *The Manuscript Found in Saragossa*. London: Penguin Classics.
price, k. (2017). Queer social dreaming matrix. *Studies in Gender and Sexuality*, *18* (1), 86–87.
price, k. (2020). *The Bureau of Dreams*. (Forthcoming.)
Priestley, J. B. (2001). *An Inspector Calls and Other Plays*. London: Penguin Modern Classics.
Probert, H. (2019). Sex and sexuality in the shadow of death: reflections on the first two seasons of *Six Feet Under*. *Studies in Gender and Sexuality*, *20* (1), 68–71.
Proust, M. (1996). *In Search of Lost Time Vol 1: Swann's Way*. New York: Vintage.
Refabert, P. (2014). *From Freud to Kafka: The Paradoxical Foundation of the Life and Death Instinct*. Hove: Routledge.
Reik, T. (1960). *The Haunting Melody: Psychoanalytic Experiences in Life and Music*. New York: Grove Press.
Reiner, A. (2017). Ferenczi's "astra" and Bion's "O": a clinical perspective. In: A. Reiner (Ed.), *Of Things Invisible to Mortal Sight: Celebrating the Work of James S. Grotstein* (pp. 131–148). London: Karnac.
Reiner, A. (Ed.) (2017). *Of Things Invisible to Mortal Sight: Celebrating the Work of James S. Grotstein*. London: Karnac.
Rey, H. (1997). *Universals of Psychoanalysis in the Treatment of Psychotic and Borderline States*. London: Free Association.
Ricard, S. (2018). The Trump phenomenon and the racialization of American politics. *Revue Lisa E-Journal*, *16* (2). Available here: https://journals.openedition.org/lisa/9832?lang=en. Accessed on 5 September 2020.
Rice, B. (2000). *Pobby and Dingan*. New York: Vintage.
Rignell, J. 2016. *Making, Looking, Doing: An Exploration, from a Winnicottian Perspective, of the Spectatorial Activity Generated through Encounters with the Later Films of Michael Haneke*. PhD Thesis: University of London.
Rignell, J. (2017). The body of the film: the evocation of Winnicott's original facilitating environment in Michael Haneke's *Amour* (2012). *Free Associations*, *71*, 89–105.
Rodowick, D. N. (1997). *Gilles Deleuze's Time Machine*. Durham: Duke University Press.
Roussillon, R. (2011). *Primitive Agony and Symbolisation*. Hove: Routledge.
Rushdie, S. (1992). *The Wizard of Oz*. London: BFI.
Santos, W. (2015). *Nick Drake, Place to Be*. Available at: https://www.youtube.com/watch?v=obOWSCmzEAY. Accessed on 5 September 2020.
Schiappa, E., Gregg, P. B., and Hewes, D. E. (2004). Can a television series change attitudes about death? A study of college students and *Six Feet Under*. *Death Studies*, *28* (5), 459–474.
Segal, A. (2016). *Endings, Art and the Space for Mourning in HBO's Six Feet Under*. MA Thesis, Birkbeck, University of London.

Sekoff, J. (1999). The undead: necromancy and the inner world. In: G. Kohon (Ed.), *The Dead Mother: The Work of André Green* (pp. 109–127). Hove: Routledge.
Sergeant, A. (2016). *The Fantastic in Hollywood Fantasy Cinema*. PhD Thesis: University of London.
Shakespeare, W. (2006). *Hamlet*. London: Bloomsbury.
Shaviro, S. (1993). *The Cinematic Body*. Minneapolis: University of Minnesota Press.
Shengold, L. (1993). *The Boy Will Come to Nothing! Freud's Ego Ideal and Freud as Ego-Ideal*. New Haven: Yale University Press.
Shoshana, A. and Teman, E. (2006). Coming out of the coffin: life-self and death-self in *Six feet under*. *Symbolic Interaction*, 29 (4), 557–575.
Soreanu, R. (2018). *Working-Through Collective Wounds: Trauma, Denial, Recognition in the Brazilian Uprising*. London: Palgrave Macmillan.
Sprengnether, M. (2002). *Crying at the Movies*. Minneapolis: Graywolf Press.
Stacey, J. (1993). *Star Gazing*. Hove: Routledge.
Stallings, C. (2020). *Laura's Ghost: Women Speak About Twin Peaks*. Columbus: Fayetteville Mafia Press.
Stern, D. (1985). *The Interpersonal World of the Infant: A View from Psychoanalysis and Developmental Psychology*. Hove: Routledge.
Stern, D. (2010). *Forms of Vitality: Exploring Dynamic Experience in Psychology, the Arts, Psychotherapy, and Development*. Oxford: Oxford University Press.
Suttie, I. (1988 [1935]). *The Origins of Love and Hate*. London: Free Associations.
Swash, R. (2014). My favourite TV show, *Six Feet Under*. *The Guardian*, 25 March. Available here: https://www.theguardian.com/tv-and-radio/tvandradioblog/2014/mar/25/my-favourite-tv-six-feet-under. Accessed on 5 September 2020.
Szykierski, D. (2010). The traumatic roots of containment: the evolution of Bion's metapsychology. *Psychoanalytic Quarterly*, 79 (4), 935–968.
Symington, N. (1993). *Narcissism: A New Theory*. London: Karnac.
Telotte, J. P. (1985). *Dreams of Darkness: Fantasy and the Films of Val Lewton*. Chicago: University of Illinois Press.
Thompson, J. (1993). Cat personae: Lewton, sequelhood, superimposition. In: D. Petrie (Ed.), *Cinema and the Realms of Enchantment* (pp. 85–97). London: BFI.
Todorov, T. (1973). *The Fantastic: A Structural Approach to a Literary Genre*. Cleveland, OH: Case Western Reserve University Press.
Turkle, S. (2013). *Alone Together: Why We Expect More from Technology and Less from Each Other*. New York: Basic Books.
Van der Kolk, B. (2014). *The Body Keeps the Score: Mind, Brain and Body in the Transformation of Trauma*. Harmondsworth: Penguin.
Vasilyuk, F. (1984). *The Psychology of Experiencing: The Resolution of Life's Critical Situations*. New York: Harvester Wheatsheaf.
Walker, A. (1982). *The Color Purple*. New York: Harcourt Brace Jovanovich.
Walker, J. (2005). *Trauma Cinema: Documenting Incest and the Holocaust*. Berkeley, CA: University of California Press.
Walker, P. (2014). *Complex PTSD: From Surviving to Thriving*. CreateSpace Independent Publishing Platform.
Walters, S. (2011). Everyday life, everyday death: race, gender, and third-wave cultural activism on *Six Feet Under*'s online fansite. *Feminist Media Studies*, 11 (3), 363–378.
Watkins, M. (1986). *Invisible Guests: The Development of Imaginal Dialogues*. Hillsdale: The Analytic Press.

Wilson, E. (2003). *Cinema's Missing Children*. London: Wallflower.
Winnicott, D. W. (1960). Ego distortion in terms of true and false self. In: D. W. Winnicott (Ed.), *The Maturational Processes and the Facilitating Environment: Studies in the Theory of Emotional Development* (pp. 140–152). Abingdon: Routledge.
Winnicott, D. W. (1971). *Playing and Reality*. London: Tavistock.
Winnicott, D. W. (1974). Fear of breakdown. *International Review of Psycho-Analysis*, *1* (1–2), 103–107.
Woolf, V. (2016). *Mrs Dalloway*. New York: Vintage Classics.
Wright, K. (2000). To make experience sing. In: L. Caldwell (Ed.), *Art, Creativity, Living* (pp. 75–96). London: Karnac.
Wright, K. (2009). *Mirroring and Attunement: Self-Realization in Psychoanalysis and Art*. Hove: Routledge.
Žižek, S. (2001). *The Fright of Real Tears: Krzystof Kieslowski Between Theory and Post-Theory*. London: BFI.

Filmography

L'Aimée. (2007). Directed by Arnaud Desplechin.
Aliens. (1986). Directed by James Cameron.
The Babadook. (2014). Directed by Jennifer Kent.
Babylon. (1980). Directed by Franco Rosso.
Back to the Future. (1985). Directed by Robert Zemeckis.
Bamboozled. (2001). Directed by Spike Lee.
Bedlam. (1946). Directed by Mark Robson.
Being There. (1979). Directed by Hal Ashby.
Beloved. (1998). Directed by Jonathan Demme.
The Birth of a Nation. (1915). Directed by D. W. Griffith.
Black Panther. (2018). Directed by Ryan Coogler.
Blade Runner. (1982). Directed by Ridley Scott.
The Brood (1979). Directed by David Cronenberg.
Bunny Lake is Missing. (1965). Directed by Otto Preminger.
Burning an Illusion. (1981). Directed by Menelik Shabazz.
Candyman. (1992). Directed by Bernard Rose.
Candyman. (2021). Directed by Nia DaCosta.
Carrie. (1976). Directed by Brian de Palma.
Cat People. (1942). Directed by Jacques Tourneur.
The Curse of the Cat People. (1944). Directed by Robert Wise.
Céline and Julie Go Boating. (1974). Directed by Jacques Rivette.
A Christmas Tale. (2007). Directed by Arnaud Desplechin.
Coal Miner's Daughter. (1980). Directed by Michael Apted.
The Collector. (1965). Directed by William Wyler.
The Color Purple. (1985). Directed by Steven Spielberg.
Coraline. (2009). Directed by Henry Selick.
Dance, Fools, Dance. (1931). Directed by Harry Beaumont.
Dead of Night. (1945). Directed by Alberto Cavalcanti, Charles Crichton, Basil Dearden, and Robert Hamer.
Dressed to Kill. (1980). Directed by Brian de Palma.
The Electric Horseman. (1979). Directed by Sydney Pollack.

Eraserhead. (1977). Directed by David Lynch.
The Exorcist. (1973). Directed by William Friedkin.
Fruitvale Station. (2013). Directed by Ryan Coogler.
Get Out. (2017). Directed by Jordan Peele.
The Ghost and Mrs Muir. (1947). Directed by Joseph Mankiewicz.
The Ghost Ship. (1943). Directed by Mark Robson.
Guess Who's Coming to Dinner? (1967). Directed by Stanley Kramer.
La Haine. (1995). Directed by Mathieu Kassowitz.
Happy-Go-Lucky. (2008). Directed by Mike Leigh.
Harvey. (1950). Directed by Henry Koster.
The Haunting. (1963). Directed by Robert Wise.
Here Comes Mr Jordan. (1941). Directed by Alexander Hall.
Hilary and Jackie. (1998). Directed by Anand Tucker.
The Horse Whisperer. (1998). Directed by Robert Redford.
The Hours. (2002). Directed by Stephen Daldry.
I Am Not Your Negro. (2016). Directed by Raoul Peck.
Imitation of Life. (1934). Directed by John Stahl.
Imitation of Life. (1959). Directed by Douglas Sirk.
Injustice. (2001). Directed by Ken Fero.
The Innocents. (1961). Directed by Jack Clayton.
Irreversible. (2002). Directed by Gaspar Noé.
It's A Wonderful Life. (1946). Directed by Frank Capra.
I Walked with a Zombie. (1943). Directed by Jacques Tourneur.
Jack and the Beanstalk. (1967). Directed by Gene Kelly.
Jane Fonda in Five Acts. (2018). Directed by Susan Lacy.
La Jetée. (1962). Directed by Chris Marker.
Johnny Guitar. (1956). Directed by Nicholas Ray.
Kings and Queen. (2004). Directed by Arnaud Desplechin.
Lola. (1961). Directed by Jacques Demy.
Looking for Mr Goodbar. (1977). Directed by Richard Brooks.
M. Klein. (1976). Directed by Joseph Losey.
Manhattan. (1979). Directed by Woody Allen.
A Matter of Life and Death. (1946). Directed by Michael Powell and Emeric Pressburger.
A Monster Calls. (2016). Directed by J. A. Bayona.
Moonlight. (2016). Directed by Barry Jenkins.
Mysterious Skin. (2004). Directed by Gregg Araki.
Mulholland Drive. (2001). Directed by David Lynch.
The Night of the Hunter. (1955). Directed by Charles Laughton.
Night of the Living Dead. (1968). Directed by George A. Romero.
On Golden Pond. (1981). Directed by Mark Rydell.
On My Skin. (2018). Directed by Alessio Cremonini.
Once Upon A Time in Hollywood. (2019). Directed by Quentin Tarantino.
Pan's Labyrinth. (2006). Directed by Guillermo del Toro.
Peggy Sue got Married. (1986). Directed by Francis Ford Coppola.
Persona. (1966). Directed by Ingmar Bergman.
Play It Again, Sam. (1972). Directed by Herbert Ross.
Poetic Justice. (1993). Directed by John Singleton.
Poltergeist. (1982). Directed by Tobe Hooper.

Possession. (1981). Directed by Andrzej Zulawski.
Pressure. (1976). Directed by Horace Ové.
Psycho. (1960). Directed by Alfred Hitchcock.
Raising Arizona. (1987) Directed by Ethan and Joel Coen.
Rocketman. (2019). Directed by Dexter Fletcher.
Rosemary's Baby. (1968). Directed by Roman Polanski.
Séance on a Wet Afternoon. (1964). Directed by Bryan Forbes.
The Seventh Victim. (1943). Directed by Mark Robson.
The Shining. (1980). Directed by Stanley Kubrick.
Shoot the Moon. (1982). Directed by Alan Parker.
Silent Running. (1972). Directed by Douglas Trumbull.
Solaris. (1972). Directed by Andrei Tarkovsky.
The Stepford Wives. (1975). Directed by Bryan Forbes.
La Strada. (1954). Directed by Federico Fellini.
Sunset Boulevard. (1950). Directed by Billy Wilder.
Tales from the Hood. (1995). Directed by Rusty Cundieff.
Taxi Driver. (1976). Directed by Martin Scorsese.
The Terminator. (1984). Directed by James Cameron.
13th. (2016). Directed by Ava du Vernay.
The Time of the Wolf. (2003). Directed by Michael Haneke.
Twin Peaks: Fire Walk with Me. (1992). Directed by David Lynch.
The Umbrellas of Cherbourg. (1964). Directed by Jacques Demy.
Le Veilleur. (1990). Directed by Claire Denis.
Waterworld. (1995). Directed by Kevin Reynolds.
Whatever Happened to Baby Jane? (1962). Directed by Robert Aldrich.
The Wicker Man. (1973). Directed by Robin Hardy.
The Wizard of Oz. (1939). Directed by Victor Fleming.

Television series

Atlanta. (2016–). FX.
Game of Thrones. (2011–9). HBO.
The Haunting of Hill House. (2018). Netflix.
Lovecraft Country. (2020–). HBO.
POSE. (2018–). Netflix.
Six Feet Under. (2001–5). HBO.
The Sopranos. (1999–2007). HBO.
Twin Peaks. (1990–1). ABC.
Twin Peaks. 2017. Showtime.

Index

Adams, Michael Vannoy 22
Agamben, Giorgio 139–140
L'Aimee (film) 24, 127
Alexis, Jacques Stephen 141
Aliens (film) 35, 36, 39
Allen, Woody 13, 137
Altman, Robert 137
American Beauty (film) 120–121
Andersen, Hans Christian 12, 15
Andersson, Bibi 30
Anzieu, Didier 78, 100, 114
Atlanta (television series) 141

The Babadook (film) 25
Back to the Future (film) 37
Badalamenti, Angelo 80, 81
Bainbridge, Caroline 15, 16, 44, 96, 99
Baldwin, James 10, 11, 153
Ball, Alan 83, 120–121
Bamboozled (film) 141
Bateson, Gregory 38
The Beatles 49
Bechdel, Alison 59
Bedlam (film) 76
Beethoven, Ludwig van 114
Being There (film) 67–71
Bellour, Raymond 100
Beloved (novel) 141
Beloved (film) 142–143, 150
Beradt, Charlotte 129
Bergman, Ingmar 29, 30, 31
Bettelheim, Bruno 50
Bhagavad Gita (scripture) 111
Big Bird 16, 67, 68, 70, 71
Bion, Wilfred 49, 58, 85; alpha function 50; container model 51–52; -K 147
Birkbeck Institute of the Moving Image (BIMI) 148

The Birth of a Nation (film) 127
Black Lives Matter (BLM) 8, 126
Black Panther (film) 149, 150–151
The Bluest Eye (novel) 136–137
Blyton, Enid 137
Bogart, Humphrey 13
Bollas, Christopher 48, 49, 80, 158
Bowden, Julie 35, 36, 39
Bowlby, John 50, 100
Brenman, Eric 22
Brewster, Fanny 143
Bronski Beat (pop group) 106
The Brood (film) 66
Bunny Lake Is Missing (film) 4
Bury, Rhiannon 89
Butler, Judith 140–141
Butler, Octavia 141

Candyman (film) 135, 136, 141–142, 150
Carrie (film) 66, 135
Carroll, Lewis 21, 119
Cartwright, Duncan 52–53, 55
Cassidy, Joanna 85
Cat People (film), 74, 75, 135
Celine and Julie go Boating (film) 6, 95
Chapman, Leslie 3
Chion, Michel 113
Clifford, Lucy 12, 14, 15
The Coen Brothers, 56–57
Coetzee, J.M. 56, 86
The Collector (film) 52
The Color Purple (film) 136
Coogler, Ryan 144, 146, 149
Coraline (novel) 12, 153
COVID-19, 6–8
Crawford, Joan 10, 11
Crosby, Bing 75

Cruise, Julee 80
The Curse of The Cat People (film) 45, 58, 74–78, 82, 135

Davids, M. Fakhry 140
Dance, Fools, Dance (film) 10
Daney, Serge 9, 23, 24, 95, 127
Dead of Night (film) 72–73
dead mother complex *see* Green, André
Deleuze, Gilles 41
De Palma, Brian 49, 66, 137
Desplechin, Arnaud 24, 127
Doctor Who (television series) 38
Don Quixote (novel) 11
Drake, Nick 38
Dressed to Kill (film) 49

Eadie, Bruce 70, 71
Eaton, Hannah 161
Eigen, Michael 51, 85, 137
The Electric Horseman (film) 34
Elgar, Edward 54
Eraserhead (film) 1, 2
Eshel, Ofer 62, 63, 65
The Exorcist (film) 60

Fairbairn, Ronald 33, 60, 61, 62
Fanon, Frantz 140, 152
Farress, Maria 41
Ferenczi, Sandor 4, 33, 42, 63 66, 71, 78, 81, 130, 147, 153
Ferholt, Beth 38, 72, 73
Fernando, Suman 150
Fero, Ken 149
film blanc 37
Firestone, Robert 11
Fisher, Mark 43, 83; the eerie 26–27, 127
Floyd, George 137
Fonagy, Peter 20
Fonda, Jane 119
Foster, Guy Mark 133
Freud, Sigmund 3, 4, 15, 22, 82; *Constructions in Analysis* 70; death instinct 146; ego ideal 13; family romances 11, 13; *fort-da* 17; the uncanny 26; wish-fulfilment 3
Fruitvale Film Club 148–161
Fruitvale Station (film) 144–147

Gable, Clark 10, 137
Gaiman, Neil 12, 15

García Márquez, Gabriel 141
Gardner, Joy 149
Gaye, Marvin 126, 127
Get Out (film) 136, 151–162
The Ghost and Mrs Muir (film) 21
Gish, Lillian 23–24, 126–128
Glass, Phillip 40
Grant, Catherine 9, 43, 113
Grant, Drew 89
Grant, Oscar 144, 145, 146
Green, André 28, 48, 62–63, 128, 129, 138, 139–140, 153
Griffiths, Rachel 53, 58, 84
Grotstein, James 21, 36
Guess Who's Coming to Dinner? (film) 137–138
Guntrip, Harry 60, 61, 62

Hallward, Peter 44
Hamilton, Margaret 19
Hamlet (play) 38, 70, 130
Haneke, Michael 44
Happy-Go-Lucky (film) 109
haptic cinema *see* Marks, Laura U.
Harris, Julie 6
Harvey (film) 21
Harvey, P.J. 115
The Haunting (film) 6
The Haunting of Hill House (television series) 2
Hawkins, Sally 109
Hepburn, Katharine 137–138, 139
Here Comes Mr Jordan (film) 37
Hilary and Jackie (film) 53, 54, 55, 69
Hillman, James 22
Hills, Matt 15
Hockley, Luke 35, 109
Hoffman, E.T.A. 71
Holland, Sharon Patricia 140
hooks, bell 44, 136, 138
Hope, Claire 112, 113
The Horse Whisperer (film) 34
The Hours (film) 40, 41

I Am Not Your Negro (film) 11, 150
I Walked with a Zombie (film) 76, 135
Imitation of Life (films) 42, 138
The Innocents (film) 6
An Inspector Calls (play) 17
Irreversible (film) 37
It's a Wonderful Life (film) 37

Jack and The Beanstalk (film) 17
Jackson, Michael 16, 49
Janet, Pierre 27, 28
Japan (pop group) 43
La Jetée (film) 38
John, Elton 36
Jones, Grace 58
Jordan, Michael B. 144, 151
Jung, Carl 20–21, 22, 47, 109

Kafka, Franz 28, 126
kairos 66
Kalsched, Donald 33, 34, 35, 49, 66
Kaluuya, Daniel 153–154
Keathley, Christian 9
Kelly, Gene 17
Kerr, Deborah 6
Kimbles, Samuel 143
Kinder, Marsha 16
Kindred (novel) 141
Klein, Melanie 22, 32, 82, 85, 125, 146
Knox, Jean 20, 21
Ku Klux Klan 128
Kuhn, Annette 8, 42, 43

Lacan, Jacques 3
Laine, Tarja 43
Laing, R.D. 31, 32
LaMothe, Ryan 45
Lange, Jessica 58
Laplanche, Jean 68, 69
Larsen, Nella 140–141
Lee, Sheryl 80, 81, 155
Lee, Spike 141
Lewis, C.S. 12, 15
Lewton, Val 74, 75, 76
The Lion, The Witch and The Wardrobe (novel) 12, 73
Lola (film) 72
London Campaign Against Police and State Violence (LCAPSV) 148
Looking for Mr Goodbar (film) 49, 79
Lovecraft Country (television series) 141
Lowe, Frank 140, 147
Lubecker, Nikolaj 43
Lynch, David 1, 76, 78, 137

Madame Bovary (novel) 11
Madsen, Virginia 136
Manhattan (film) 13
Marks, Laura U. 116
Masina, Giulietta 32

A Matter of Life and Death (film) 37
Milner, Marion 103
Miss Piggy 17
Mitchell, Joni 114, 115, 119
Mitty, Walter 13
A Monster Calls (play) 1, 86
Moonlight (film) 40
Morrison Toni, 136, 137, 141, 142, 143
Mrs Dalloway (novel) 40–41
Mulholland Drive (film) 76
Munt, Sally 88, 134
Mysterious Skin (film) 58

Nemerov, Alexander 74, 75
The New Hollywood 49, 137
"The New Mother" (short story) 12, 14
Nesbit, Edith 21
Ness, Patrick 17
Netflix 7
Nhat Hanh, Thich 116
The Night of the Hunter (film) 23, 24, 126, 127
Night of the Living Dead (film) 134

Ogden, Thomas 18, 20, 55–58, 86
Once Upon A Time in Hollywood (film) 37, 146

Parker, Alan 19
Pan's Labyrinth (film) 25
Peck, Raoul 11, 150
Peele, Jordan 151, 152, 153
Peggy Sue Got Married (film) 37
Perez, Hiram 42
perezhivanie 72–73
Persona (film) 29, 30
Pinocchio 50
Pistiner de Cortiñas, Lia 52, 55
Plantinga, Carl 43
Play It Again, Sam (film) 13
Pobby and Dingan (novel) 41
Polledri, Patricia 77
Poltergeist (film) 29
POSE (television series) 2
Possession (film) 21
Potocki, Jan 71
price, kitt 37
Priestley, J.B. 17, 37
Probert, Hywel 88
Proust, Marcel 69, 70
Psycho (film) 4

Quakerism 92

Radiohead (pop group) 114
Raising Arizona (film) 56, 57
Redford, Robert 34, 35, 39
Reik, Theodor 114
Reiner, Annie 64, 65
Rey, Henri 28
Rice, Ben 41
Rignell, John 44, 100
Rivette, Jacques 6, 41, 95, 96
Rocketman (film) 36, 37
Rodowick, David 41
Roussillon, René 5
Rundgren, Todd 115
Rushdie, Salman 19

Sainte-Marie, Buffy 67, 68, 69, 70, 71
Séance on a Wet Afternoon (film) 4
Segal, Amber 89, 90
Sekoff, Jed 32
Sergeant, Alexander 19
Sesame Street (television series) 67, 68, 69
The Seventh Victim (film) 76
Shaviro, Steven 41
Shengold, Leonard 13, 15
The Shining (film) 26, 49
Shoot the Moon (film) 19
Silent Running (film) 84
Sir Lancelot (singer) 76
Six Feet Under (television series) 2, 46, 58, 83–125, 129–134, 138–139
Simon, Simone 76–77, 136
"The Snow Queen" (fairy tale) 12
Solaris (film) 26, 83
Soloway, Jill 133
Soreanu, Raluca 147
Spacek, Sissy 59, 66, 136
Sprengnether, Madelon 42–43
Stacey, Jackie 42
Stevens, Cat 41
Stern, Daniel 40, 54–55, 66

La Strada (film) 32
Sunset Boulevard (film) 144
Suttie, Ian 42
Swash, Rosie 89
Symington, Neville 153

Tales from the Hood (film) 141
Tate, Sharon 146
Taxi Driver (film) 49
Taylor, Lili 84
The Terminator (film) 37
Time and the Conways (play) 37
Todorov, Tzvetan 26
Tripplehorn, Jeanne 133
Trump, Donald 152
Turkle, Sherry 14
Twin Peaks: Fire Walk with Me (film) 45, 78–82, 151, 155, 160–161

Ullmann, Liv 30, 81
The Umbrellas of Cherbourg (film) 71–72

Van der Kolk, Bessel 27, 28, 51
Van Gogh, Vincent 38
Von Trier, Lars 16

Walker, Janet 43
Walker, Pete 14, 15
Watkins, Mary 23
Whatever Happened to Baby Jane? (film) 4
The Wicker Man (film) 4
Wilson, Emma 4
Winnicott, Donald 8, 15, 16, 19, 35, 39, 41, 44, 60–62, 85, 96, 104, 130
Winters, Shelley 24, 127, 128
The Wizard of Oz (film) 18, 19, 20, 23, 39, 48
Wright, Kenneth 41, 44

Yates, Candida 44

Žižek, Slavoj 155

For Product Safety Concerns and Information please contact our EU representative GPSR@taylorandfrancis.com
Taylor & Francis Verlag GmbH, Kaufingerstraße 24, 80331 München, Germany

www.ingramcontent.com/pod-product-compliance
Lightning Source LLC
Chambersburg PA
CBHW052133010526
44113CB00035B/2142